SOCIETY
ON THE
RUN

SOCIETY ON THE RUN

A European
View of Life
in America
Werner Peters

M.E. Sharpe
Armonk, New York
London, England

This English translation was made possible by a generous grant from InterNationes, Bonn, Germany.

Originally published as *The Existential Runner: Über die Demokratie in Amerika*, © 1992 Werner Peters and Edition Isele Eggingen

---

Library of Congress Cataloging-in-Publication Data

Peters, Werner, 1941–
[Existential runner. English] Society on the run : a European view of life in America / Werner Peters ; translated by the author with the assistance of Bettina Hinze and Jerome N. Eller.
p.   cm.
Translation of : The existential runner.
Includes bibliographical references.
ISBN 1-56324-585-X (hardcover : alk. paper).—ISBN 1-56324-586-8 (paper : alk. paper)
1. United States—Social conditions—1980– . 2. Democracy—United States.   I. Title.
HN59.2.P4813   1996
306′.0973—dc20   95–25770
CIP

BM (c)   10   9   8   7   6   5   4   3   2   1
BM (p)   10   9   8   7   6   5   4   3   2   1

Contents

List of Illustrations

Are You Running with Me Jesus?

Eugene J. McCarthy

Are you running with me Jesus,
Asks the Reverend Malcolm Boyd.

May I ask the same?

I'm not matching my stride
With Billy Graham's by the Clyde.
I'm not going for distance
With the Senator's persistence.
I'm not trying to win a race
Even at George Romney's pace.

I'm an existential runner,
Indifferent to space.
I'm running here in place.

Wall to wall unending,
The treadmill carpet flows.
Baseboard to baseboard unchanging,

From the looms of Mohawk.
As I run against the clock,
Are you running with me Jesus,
Or not?

"people are running . . . " *Parade Magazine*
Billy Graham wherever he is,
George Romney every day
Senator Proxmire to the Capitol and home again.

Preface

to

the

German

Edition

This book is about America, about democracy, and about movement being the essence of democracy. The book also represents my personal dialogue with America.

I belong to the first generation of Germans who grew up after World War II under American influence. But since we were ingrained with old-European values, we remained very sensitive to the Americanization of the German and European society. I was influenced in a special way by America because I spent some years there during a turning point in American-European relations at the end of the sixties.

At first I developed my very own anti-Americanism through a *Kulturschock* (culture shock), which I experienced upon my arrival in this country at a time when there were still huge differences between American and European societies. But I went through my personal "Americanization" by getting to know the "American way of life" in the country itself and by accepting it as the dominating cultural force of the outgoing twentieth century. Since those days, I have occupied myself with America and have observed the irresistible advance of American culture that is changing the face not only of Europe, but also of the whole world.

Since the end of the war, America has become the destiny of Germans and Europeans. In the beginning, its political and military supremacy and its economic dominance over our part of the world were obvious. Then came the gradual encroachment of American culture, lifestyle, customs and habits, values and views, first in parts of Europe and then throughout the world. I use the word *culture* deliberately, and without hesitation, and in defiance of all the Eurocentrists who distinguish between the trappings of civilization, which are reluctantly granted to Americans, and culture, which is reserved for Europeans.

Getting to know America means getting to know oneself. To understand America is to understand the twentieth century. This is the singular event of this century—America's world triumph as a military power, as an economic force, as a cultural movement, and as a political idea. To grasp America means to grasp Modern Times, the transition to postmodernism, and, in turn, the contours of an emerging epoch. I believe that we, as members of Western societies, cannot understand ourselves without understanding America and recognizing the imprint it has left on us.

The title of the book alludes to the best and most famous inquiry into American political culture: Alexis de Tocqueville's Democracy in America. I have—with obvious scruples—deliberately established this almost presumptuous relationship. I have turned to Tocqueville because I believe that we are again, as 160 years ago, at a historical turning point, when it is necessary to reflect on the fundamentals of democracy. In Tocqueville's time, the idea of democracy was beginning to take root and as Tocqueville correctly envisioned was becoming so dynamic a force that it was destined to influence the course of world history. Tocqueville anticipated a democratic future for Europe and elaborated—by taking the United States as the most advanced model—its achievements and failures, its opportunities and limitations. This model was to serve as a guide for the establishment of democratic societies and governments in Europe. At present, we are witness to two major developments: One is a monumental surge in the advance of democracy, not only in Eastern Europe, but, although less dramatically, in Latin America, Asia, and Africa, too. On the other hand, especially in the United States, we observe widespread dissatisfaction with existing democratic structures, harsh criticism of the growing contradiction between democratic aspiration and democratic reality, and obvious lack of participation in the established political process. At the same time, there is a struggling development of new kinds of political institutions and initiatives bringing about a curious mixture of withdrawal and cynicism along with experiment and enthusiasm.

America is still the embodiment of democratic ideals, the model of democratic constitutions, the epitome of democratic self-awareness. U.S. leadership in political, military, and economic matters has influenced the people of the Eastern bloc to take their orientation from America, and the image of the democratic ideal, though perhaps tarnished and often more honored in rhetoric than in reality, is a genuine force. More than 200 years of democratic tradition in America itself and the strong effect and direct influence of the post–World War II American model on Western European and some Asian societies are historical accomplishments that radiate confidence and demand respect.

But the negative aspects of American political culture are, of course, also an important object for the study of democracy: America is the most developed democracy because of its longevity as the oldest practicing democracy in the world. Longevity itself, however, does not guarantee advance toward perfection. In the natural order of things, aging often means disintegration and decay. Where would one be in a better position to study this pathology of democracy than in the most developed example?

To understand the essence of democracy, it is even more important to study the importance of democracy in America in everyday life and its effect on the habits and attitudes of people. Democracy as a constitution for governance, as a system of organizing society, is no longer confined to political structures and institutions. Democracy as a way of life permeates every aspect of society. The idea of individual freedom pervades private life in the same way as self-government transforms the political order. The democratic culture of a free lifestyle inevitably leads to a democratic organization of society. Hunger for this lifestyle has been identified as a factor contributing to the revolution in Eastern Europe. It was not solely a political movement, even though the struggle was for the establishment of free representative systems of government. Neither was it merely an economic vote, although the desire for a satisfying standard of living as reward for work and initiative played a mighty role. Both of these forces are evident, but the world movement toward democracy goes far beyond them to the yearning to be able to organize one's life according to one's ideas.

It is not only by chance that political reformist and revolutionary movements have been strongly inspired by the spread of Western pop culture, especially pop music, which not even the Iron Curtain could block. Nowhere else is this break with authoritarian lifestyles and social values as obvious, whether they are communist, socialist, or fascist. This lifestyle is nothing else than what the Americans rightfully call "the American way of life." (Therein lies a real irony, of course; consider the fact that the cultural phenomena of pop culture have been organized into vast industries. They have created an egalitarian dictatorship of taste that is functioning in an almost authoritarian way.)

America not only created pop culture; it made entertainment the center of life. It promoted consumption not only as the driving force of the economy, but also as "the pursuit of happiness." In unabashed regard for money, Americans made it the ultimate measurement of values and thus broke the power of ideology over society. Although we Europeans may regard some democratic structures in America with reservations and even claim superiority in the realization of some aspects of a democratic society, there can be no doubt about the influence of America on democratic culture—not only in Europe, but throughout the world, even in countries that are politically undemocratic.

America establishes the values that other individuals and societies eagerly or reluctantly adopt or adapt as their own. Even more rapidly through the media of information, entertainment, and advertisement, the American style of life spreads everywhere, not as something superimposed but rather absorbed into the popular consciousness of local cultures. America is remaking the world in its own image as the world is remaking itself in America's image.

If Tocqueville had reason to study America in 1830, Europeans have a particular interest in the nineties because America is not merely an example to the world but a force for changing the world.

There is no way to give an all-encompassing description of America. This is true, even if the subject is narrowed to democracy in America, because democracy, especially in the broader sense, is an integral part of the essence of America and America defines itself as the concept and realization of democracy.

Furthermore, an exhaustive report on America is impossible, not only because of the vastness and the complexity of this topic, but also because we would attempt to describe something that is constantly undergoing massive and rapid change.

Finally, there is no absolute statement possible because for every observation, there is an opposite interpretation.

A description of "democracy in America" must by nature be incomplete, contradictory, and even refreshingly discordant. My idea of America derives from the "quilt," a genuinely American master-artisan tradition. Made from hundreds of colorful patches sewn together, it becomes a fascinating collage of color. Everybody is invited to dream into this combination of patches his or her own design but may also discover that it is nothing but a confusing conglomeration of colors.

It is conventional wisdom that America is the land of contradiction. This nation is unique in that it was born from an idea, the idea of democracy. Is it therefore in permanent conflict with reality?

Although Americans have always professed a pursuit of the common good and the national interest, they have tended to embrace John Locke's concept of society as an association of autonomous individuals and to fear the very structures and institutions designed to guarantee personal freedom. This remains the American paradox in what has been described as a wonderland in which "everything is true, but the opposite is too." It is not surprising that it was an American writer, F. Scott Fitzgerald, who observed ironically that the sign of a first-rate intelligence is the ability to hold two contradictory ideas in the mind simultaneously.

Although Americans persist in their naive belief that they have created true democracy, the problems plaguing American society are proliferating and intensifying in almost every aspect of human life. To consider the state of democracy in America we must also consider the state of the myriad troubles as we can identify and observe them. America-bashing has always been a sport of the European intellectual elite and is indeed the favorite national pastime of many American political scientists, politicians, and pundits. I do not wish to engage in this useless enterprise. Instead, in the spirit of Tocqueville, I want to clarify my observations and confront history in the making as directly and honestly as possible. In attempting to describe contemporary questions, I have no easy answers or patent solutions. In fact, I would consider my work to be fruitful and productive if I only succeed in posing the right questions about American democracy and its future.

There are essentially three elements of democratic substance in which America excels and leads the way: first, the openness and permeability of society and the flexibility of the people; second, their courage for change, their willingness to take risks, their inexhaustible initiative; and the third and very important aspect—their spirit of rebellion and active resistance to the encroachments of government power and influence.

Because this spirit is the heart and substance of American democracy, one cannot be indifferent to signs of weakness or flaws in the response to contemporary events or complacency and fatigue in the face of new challenges. This may be exemplified by the recent enthusiasm for the idea of an "end of history," supposedly reached by the triumph of democracy worldwide. In their well-justified democratic self-assurance, Americans tend to forget that democracy has to be expanded and amended in their own house as well. Despite their openness and flexibility, they are in a curious way blind to obvious flaws in their own system. Democracy is an always unfinished business, a constant search for deficiencies, an unending challenge to make improvements. This is especially true when the idea of democracy is not directly challenged.

Democracy can never be taken for granted. Despite a popular notion, there is no historical evidence of a deep human drive particular toward democratic forms of government. There is a desire for freedom, there is a need for self-fulfillment, but there is no inborn need for democratic institutions and democratic structures though these may better foster freedom and self-fulfillment. There must be a continuing and conscious struggle to realize democracy.

A recurrent theme of this book is the concern that democracy may perish through its own virtues, not because they have become obsolete but because they are applied in an excessive way. The desire for freedom and the urge toward self-fulfillment may become overwhelming and be made absolute goals for society. But they are only part of the whole picture of democracy. Their absolute domination is synonymous with the downfall of democracy.

A constitutional democracy is by its very nature the consequence of compromise—a middle way that thrives best on moderation. The extremes and excesses of absolutes defy the reality of human experience and the practical organization of society. Compromise is not only the work of reason but is bound up with the whole range of emotions human beings experience in the reality of daily life. The wonder of the democratic spirit is its conformity to real human experience.

Because the very essence of the democratic process is the consent of the governed entity, it is dependent on an informed and enlightened citizenry prepared to accept the burdens of self-government. It depends upon an education that not only trains the mind but also appeals to the heart and forms the heart. This applies to the electorate as well as to the elected. The fragility of this covenant demands a basic intellectual commitment that can withstand the temptations and manipulations of demagoguery and jingoism that are deadly threats to genuine democracy.

The final inquiry: What is the goal of democracy? It cannot be merely the organization of human life in society. This is often done more efficiently by dictatorial regimes. What is the essence of democracy? Americans have tried to answer the question: the pursuit of happiness of the people. But what is happiness? And what is the role of government in the "pursuit of happiness"? This most difficult question cannot be answered theoretically; the real thing must be examined. Let us take a look.

Preface

to

the

American

Edition

While I was preparing the American edition of this book, which was published in Germany just before the presidential elections of 1992, the shock waves of the midterm elections of 1994 shattered my picture of the state and the direction of American politics. I had considered the election of President Clinton a turning point in the development of American society, away from the self-centered complacency of the Reagan–Bush era, toward an energetic attitude confronting and tackling the numerous problems the nation was facing.

I had anticipated the election of Bill Clinton because in the early nineties it was obvious that the American people were in a mood of starting anew, that American society was longing for change. So when Bill Clinton appeared on the political scene and was able to present in his person and in his message these aspirations, the race for the presidency was foregone.

Then came 1994, and the political landscape changed again—this time with even more far-reaching repercussions than in 1992. It was almost unanimously considered a conservative revolution—acclaimed or bemoaned depending on the political standpoint of the commentator. Now that the dust has settled, there is more doubt and reflection about the meaning of this strong and shrill signal from the populace. How lasting the conservatism of this revolution will be, the next elections will show.

To get a better understanding, one should refrain from isolating the last election and look at it instead in correlation with the other event of 1992, even though the results are so contradictory. I don't think the midterm elections are a repudiation of the outcome of the presidential elections. Taken together, they reflect first of all the uncertainty of American society, which itself is a mirror of the uncertainty of the times and conditions America is going through both domestically and internationally. The common denominator in both events is the cry for change and the willingness to take risks in order to achieve change. It confirms the basic tenet of this book, which I adopted from Tocqueville, that Americans not only are not afraid of change but love it as a chance for betterment, and insofar are still attuned to the spirit of democracy, the energy of which is change.

These elections should be interpreted not so much from their results but rather as an outburst of deep dissatisfaction with the current state of American democracy. Even if the violent reaction to the deterioration of the political system and to the inability or unwillingness of the political actors to improve it is irrational and almost counterproductive ("throw the rascals out"), it is a healthy agitation, a rebellious uproar against "business as usual," which definitely has succeeded in setting politics in motion again.

In America, politicians are listening and reacting to the strong message from the people that there are fundamental flaws in the way democracy is working, or rather not working, and that radically new approaches have to be considered to get it on track again. The American people have responded with their seemingly erratic voting behavior to a general phenomenon familiar to all advanced Western democracies. The established political procedures and the way politicians conduct business are no longer sufficient to cope with the newly arisen problems of "postmodern" society and to satisfy the expectations and needs of its members.

Democracy is seen as dotted with so many flaws and weak spots that its problem-solving capacities are seriously doubted. That doubt, in the long run, is slowly and imperceptibly eroding even the rock-solid support democracy commands in the hearts of the American people.

We observe this phenomenon in other Western democracies in much more violent and aggressive forms, as in France, with the week-long strikes that were basically a revolt against the established system, or in Italy, with the complete breakdown of the old political order, and generally in the rise of fascist, anti-democratic movements in almost every country of the Western world.

Democracy is challenged to rejuvenate itself, to find new ways and procedures to cope with the numerous problems of mass society but also with a new self-assertion of today's generation.

Democracy is challenged to prove that it is still the political system most apt to fulfill the aspirations and desires of human beings for "the good life," which means much more than being governed by an efficient administration.

For this task it is not sufficient to exchange persons or to polish the surface with some cosmetic reforms. One has to go back to the roots of the democratic ideal. Democracy has to be rediscovered and revived through its principles, which have been buried and neglected for much too long, causing it to degenerate into something that has kept the outside appearance and structure of democracy but is losing its spirit and meaning. This book is an attempt to expose these somewhat obliterated principles of democracy, to show how they have been partially deflected and twisted in political reality, and to indicate areas where and ways how they can be revived and practiced to make American democracy again strive for its ultimate goal, "the good society."

Acknowledgments

I would like to sincerely thank all the fine people at M.E. Sharpe who helped with organizing, supervising, editing, and proofreading at various states of the publication of this work. I appreciate the advice and the support of many American friends who helped with the translation of the German original and adaptation to an American readership. I am especially grateful to three people whose help was invaluable in making the publication of this American edition possible: Thorsten Koch, who accompanied the work from the very beginning to the end; Jerry Eller, who time and again worked with me over the translation; and Utako Yokoyama, who tirelessly worked on the bibliographical research as she had already done for the German edition.

It is believed by some that modern society will be always changing its aspect; for myself, I fear that it will ultimately be too invariably fixed in the same institutions, the same prejudices, the same manners, so that mankind will be stopped and circumscribed; that the mind will swing backwards and forwards forever without begetting fresh ideas; that man will waste his strength in bootless and solitary trifling, and, though in continual motion, that humanity will cease to advance.

—Alexis de Tocqueville

SOCIETY
ON THE
RUN

Triumph

or

Resignation?

At the apex of its triumph in the world, democracy once again became a topic of concern—especially in America. Because democracy is obviously showing flaws at home, complaint, anger, and despair are apparent, side by side with confidence and satisfaction with the seemingly inevitable progress of the democratic idea worldwide.[1]

Francis Fukuyama's book *The End of History and the Last Man* presents the positive view most forcefully. Fukuyama seizes upon Georg Wilhelm Friedrich Hegel's historical-philosophical thesis of world history being the process in which the *Weltgeist* (spirit of the world) realizes itself, a process that concludes with the victory of human freedom. There is, according to Hegel and Fukuyama, no progress beyond the establishment of a political state in freedom because the *Weltgeist* has reached its destiny. History as the history of ideas would have fulfilled itself, would have brought to an end the confrontation of ideological concepts. This does not mean, in defense of Fukuyama's book against a primitive but often raised objection, that conflict between states would no longer exist. It simply states that there is no political idea beyond democracy, i.e., a society organized under the concept of freedom. With his book, Fukuyama develops not only an exciting historical philosophy worthy of discussion, but he also makes an important contribution to the understanding of the democratic idea.

The American Experiment

Fukuyama's thesis of *The End of History* has found widespread approval in America, partly due to the apparent practical confirmation of his message by the political developments of recent years. More important, however, for the American identification with Fukuyama's ideas is the author's clear acknowledgment of a noncyclical interpretation of history. This perception speaks to a receptive aspect of the self-image of Americans. America, in contrast to other nations, is not defined through its history and tradition. America is before all an idea, a design of a society that calls for its implementation. American democracy is not simply a form of government—rather, it is, as Thomas Jefferson and John Dewey called it, the "American Experiment,"[2] a step forward in the history of man, an unprecedented, singular model and at the same time an example for the rest of the world. "There still remains something new under the sun,"[3] reflects Jefferson in his emphatic statement about the rise of democracy in America.

American democracy is a utopia in reality: an ideal goal, as well as the practical road to achieve it. The idea of American democracy is a society in constant struggle to perfect itself. Belief in the capability of the democratic process to further develop the society holds the nation together. The "American dream" is not just the hope of material wealth, it is also the vision of life in a more just, more humanitarian, freer, better society. The enduring progress, the constant evolution, and the advancement toward an ideal goal is the basis of the American understanding of democracy and, even more, the basis of the American love affair with democracy.

> *"Maybe our national mindlessness is the very thing that keeps us from turning into one of those smelly European countries full of pseudo-reds and crypto-fascists and greens who dress like forest elves."*
>
> P.J. O'Rourke, Parliament of Whores

This relationship is currently strained. The present state of American democracy is being rudely criticized: The American political system is said to be paralyzed, its institutions in gridlock and its politicians inflexible. The apparent criticism of American democracy is still limited to the symptoms as the belief in the power of self-healing is unbroken. This does not exclude that, in part, radical measures for the revival of the democratic process in America are being propagated.

Doubt in the Health of the Structures

In addition to the large majority that considers the American community healthy at the core, needing only a change of personalities and a renewal of institutions, there are voices expressing serious doubts about the functional capability of existing structures. These critics see not only organizational problems in the current state of affairs of American democracy, but they also recognize an intrinsic helplessness in relation to new phenomena of democratic societies. One particular problem is the increasingly one-sided, egocentric urge for personal self-realization and the erosion of community values. The development of a society without a feeling of community is paradoxically accompanied by excessive demands from the individual citizen for government interventions to fulfill ever larger claims.

> *"Maybe [the American political system is] . . . like fast food—mushy, insipid, made out of disgusting parts of things and everybody wants some."*
>
> P.J. O'Rourke, Parliament of Whores

Criticism and praise of American democracy are linked in a sometimes rather strange way. One noticeable characteristic is a kind of national optimism, a belief in the indestructibility of the democratic spirit in America, the hope that "at the most creative moments in the American past, the nation found its true source of political energy and ideas among those citizens in unexpected quarters who took it upon themselves to renew the search [for the nature of democracy],"[4] as William Greider states in his book *Who Will Tell the People? The Betrayal of American Democracy.*

This hope feeds not only on the retrospective view of a tradition of 200 years. Greider describes the abundance of voluntary participation and spontaneous initiative outside the political establishment keeping the democratic spirit alive and balancing out, as a "reassuring anarchy,"[5] the entrenched leadership of the experts, politicians, and bureaucrats.

Greider does not consider the reform of political institutions (as important as it may be) as sufficient for the survival of democracy. "A reinvigoration of the social faith in the promise of democracy"[6] is necessary so that a democratic society is willing to work on perfecting itself. For Greider the task lies in "building something new that creates the institutional basis for politics as a shared enterprise."[7]

Comfortable Politics

There are important observers of the American political system, however, who have given up this age-old American optimism, or perhaps they never shared it. John Kenneth Galbraith, an economist with a political and philosophical emphasis, determines in his essay, "The Culture of Contentment," that in American society those who are now satisfied make up a comfortable majority (in any case a majority of those who vote). This majority has not only claimed ever more privileges for itself; it has also created a political-philosophical justification for the preservation of the status quo that adamantly prevents any thought of societal change.[8]

Galbraith draws parallels to the aristocratic society in prerevolutionary France. At that time, a political economic theory also existed—that of the physiocrats, who offered impressive arguments justifying a social system in which "all

wealth, superficial deductions for trade and manufacturing apart, was returned to the owners of the land, the aristocrats who inhabited and served the Court."[9] In democratic society, the middle class has replaced the aristocracy as the ruling class. In an aristocratic society, the principle of legitimacy was the nobility of birth. The principle of legitimacy of today's middle class society is the freedom of acquisition. One is static, the other dynamic. For the aristocratic society, the preservation of the existing order was an element of substance, whereas part of democracy's understanding of itself is that it permits change, improvement, ascent, and descent.

If democratic society, as Galbraith says, has positioned and stabilized itself so that the majority of the owners/possessors has the power to preserve the status quo and indeed to make absolute use of its power, this would point to the end of democracy and probably to the end of the middle class.

Democracy Is Motion

Greider and Galbraith, one still optimistic and the other resigned, both point to the central problem of democracy, not just democracy in America. Democracy is dependent upon development, change, and motion. Unlike in aristocratic or monarchic political systems, where social structures and relations are generally based on family origins, the structures in democracy are not clearly arranged. Democracy is a form of government of unresolved contradictions—of freedom vs. equality, of government vs. self-determination, of justice vs. solidarity. There are no final solutions. Nevertheless, democratic societies are continually obliged to find an ever new balance between these counteractive principles and thereby to make progress and to develop better structures.

Jefferson, a founding father of American democracy, put this problem at the center of his considerations. It was clear to him that the democratic spirit could indeed not be preserved through preservation of its institutions, but only through change, i.e., the adaptation of the political structures to the ever changing social needs. Change rather than preservation guarantees continuity—that was his paradoxical insight. Only by subjecting democracy to the unforgiving dynamic of time could it be saved.

> But I know also, that laws and institutions must go hand in hand with the progress of the human mind. As discoveries are made, new truths disclosed, and manners and opinions change with the change of circumstances, institutions must advance also, and keep pace with the times.[10]

The mission of constantly adapting to change for the success of the democratic concept seemed so significant to Jefferson that he developed a radical suggestion for it: the permanent revolution or, more accurately said, the institutionalization of the recommencement of a political system in regular, not too lengthy time periods. Every generation—Jefferson based his figures on the mortality rates with a span of nineteen years—should have the opportunity of a radical new beginning, when all the laws and constitutions of the society are automatically extinguished and the society either reaffirms them, reinstates them in new shape and form, or gives them up completely.[11]

Jefferson grounds this claim philosophically. It is the consequence of the "evident" fact that "the earth belongs in usufruct to the living and that the dead have neither powers nor rights over it."[12] No generation—according to Jefferson—has the right to bind the following generation to obligations for which it alone has to take responsibility. This holds true for not only constitutions and political institutions, but also for debts of the state. Otherwise the "earth would belong to the dead."[13]

Jefferson's claim focuses on the essence of democracy. It makes clear where and how freedom and self-determination are threatened in a democratic society: The structures and institutions gain a self-existence that becomes more important and powerful than the rights of those for whom they were initially created. The form becomes master over the substance, democratic formalities are nursed with care, and the democratic content becomes suppressed.

> *"This separation of powers creates a system of 'checks and balances,' which protects everybody by ensuring that any action taken by one part of the government will be rendered utterly meaningless by an equal and opposite reaction from some other part."*
> Dave Barry, Dave Barry Slept Here

Not only Jefferson, but other founders of the American nation as well, placed the adaptation of the Constitution to social developments at the center of their deliberations. James Madison, one of the great theorists of the American Constitution, saw the system of "checks and balances" as a structure in which mutual balance and reciprocal blocks against encroachments would be a means of preserving the initially established balance of freedom and governance in a democracy under changing social needs. The constitutional system that was then designed showed such flexibility and potential for development that it has not only survived more than 200 years but it has also kept pace with the enormous quantitative growth and the qualitative change of the American nation. Basically unchanged in form, the American Constitution, as it was created more than 200 years ago, still serves a society that has little in common today with the original one.

Question to America

Whether the democratic spirit has remained the same for more than two centuries—that is the subject of this book. The author does not claim to have solved the puzzle of America. Every description of democracy in America is just an excerpt, contradictory, contemporary. The purpose is not to offer a final solution but, rather, to ask the right questions about democracy in America, to pose them in a way to light the essence of democracy so that the political configuration of our time becomes clear.

Democracy cannot be judged apart from its time. The essential elements of democracy are not absolute; they are closely tied to the situation of the time in which they unfold. There is no encapsulating definition of democracy that would work like a multiple choice test superimposed on the empirical data in order to recognize right and wrong in one glance. Democracy is not a formula but, rather, an ideal always reborn in the minds of people—determined by their respective circumstances of time. The quality of democracy in a political system is contingent upon the relation of reality to this ideal; it is always dependent on the political consciousness of its time and must be measured in terms of available political chances being realized.

The realization of democracy in America, therefore, must be separated into two corresponding questions: What are the structural elements of democracy, and what are the social stipulations of our time?

Notes

1. The books by Fukuyama, Greider, and Galbraith mentioned in this chapter stand for a variety of publications in recent years dealing with the nature of democracy—especially in its American appearance, its opportunities, and the dangers with which it is confronted. This large number of publications indicates that in America the feeling is widespread that democracy has come to a turning point in its history and needs new impulses. Besides the books mentioned in the text, I would like to name a few more:

Robert N. Bellah et al., *The Good Society:* This book is the continuation of a previous work on American society.

Robert N. Bellah et al., *Habits of the Heart:* This book—as well as the new one by Bellah—is more or less an empiric study (with implications for the theory of democracy nevertheless).

Robert A. Dahl, *Democracy and Its Critics:* Dahl's recent book is of a more theoretical nature.

An important supplement to the publications in the academic field are the excellently investigated and well-written books by journalists, publicists, and members of independent research institutes:

E.J. Dionne, Jr., *Why Americans Hate Politics:* Dionne describes the antagonism between liberal and conservative ideology that dominated policies after World War II and in his opinion was the main reason for the loss of credibility of American politics.

Kevin Phillips, *The Politics of Rich and Poor:* Phillips is regarded as a political prophet because he foresaw "the emerging Republican majority" in 1967. In his book of the same name he predicted a new change brought about by shifts in and a new orientation of the voting population due to the enormous social movements as a result of Ronald Reagan's economic policies.

Charles Murray, *In Pursuit: Of Happiness and Good Government:* Murray, who with *Losing Ground: American Social Policy 1950–1980* shook the fundamental assumptions that had been valid since the New Deal, suggests a new kind of social policy to restore the dignity and self-confidence of people on welfare.

Besides the publications mentioned above and others on the general topic of American democracy there is a variety of books that deal with single aspects of American politics—especially with the changes in the economic situation during the past decade and their consequences for the future of America. I will introduce them in subsequent chapters.

2. Richard Rorty, "The Priority of Democracy to Philosophy," p. 196.

3. Jefferson to Dr. Joseph Priestley, March 21, 1801, *The Portable Jefferson,* p. 483.

4. William Greider, *Who Will Tell the People?* p. 412.

5. Ibid., p. 407.

6. Ibid., p. 413.

7. Ibid., p. 410.

8. John Kenneth Galbraith, *The Culture of Contentment,* p. 2.

9. Ibid.

10. Jefferson to Samuel Kercheval, July 12, 1816, *The Portable Jefferson,* p. 559. This programmatic declaration is one of the four texts (another is the beginning of Jefferson's Declaration of Independence) that are chiseled in the walls of the Jefferson Memorial in Washington, D.C.. Obviously, Americans are well aware of the importance of these words, but it is another thing whether they are observed.

11. Ibid., p. 560. The idea itself is—even down to the details—much older: See letter to James Madison, June 8, 1789, *The Portable Jefferson,* p. 447. Jefferson's thesis has been well discussed in Richard Matthews's book *The Radical Politics of Thomas Jefferson,* p. 19.

12. Jefferson to James Madison, August 6, 1789, *The Portable Jefferson,* p. 445.

13. It is characteristic for the spirit of democratic revival in America and the search for the true nature of democracy that the Democratic party in the election year 1992 rediscovered Jefferson's ideas and professed them. The platform of the Democratic national convention began with the words: "Two hundred summers ago, this Democratic Party was founded by the man whose burning pen fired the spirit of the American revolution—who once argued we should overthrow our own government every 20 years to renew our freedom and keep pace with a changing world. In 1992, the party Thomas Jefferson founded invokes his spirit of revolution anew." Leslie H. Gelb, "The Democrats Need to Come Clear on the Means," *International Herald Tribune,* July 13, 1992.

(Post-)

Modern

Democracy

During the past fifty years since World War II, the United States underwent the most far-reaching and rapid social changes in its more than 200-year history.

These transformations fundamentally altered the landscape and the soul of the United States. The migration from the country to the city, and from the city to the newly developing suburbia (and again to the so-called "edge cities" close to highway intersections[1]); the slow decline of the family as an institution, a cornerstone of American society; the decay of other pillars of the political system such as labor unions, political parties, churches, and public schools; sexual liberation and change of moral values; the growing prosperity of the middle class (in decline again); the evolution of a society accustomed to waste and the simultaneous collapse of the public infrastructure; the automobilization of society; the changes in lifestyles and in the political culture caused by television; the dominant role of consumerism and entertainment in private life and in politics; the global role of the United States as a superpower; the militarization of politics; the enormously increased significance of federal politics and the concurrent centralization of the government; the end of racial segregation; the triumph of pop culture. These developments of the past fifty years—the list is by no means exhaustive—have shaken the traditional system of values and are constantly changing it further.

Within the American society, this process is not homogenously developed but has varied, according to geographic region, age, ethnic origin, education, religious persuasion, and social status. In some parts of the United States, especially in the vast rural areas of the plains, the traditional values established during the nation's pioneer days are deeply rooted and still alive. Other parts, such as Southern California, seem to have been living mentally in the twenty-first century for some time.

Some of these phenomena are aftermaths of the industrial revolution. Most, however, mirror the effects of the transition to a postindustrial society. A definition of this revolution is complicated because we are in its midst and as yet lack a perspective. What can be said with certainty is that this economic revolution is accompanied by an upheaval of ideas and a change of values that splinter and leave behind the structures of the modern industrial era. Thus it is perfectly appropriate to use current jargon and talk about a postmodern society that is in the process of discovering its own options of democratic life.[2]

Changes of Meaning in Democratic Principles

There is no doubt that American society is most advanced on the path toward this new age. That does not mean that America has also developed the democratic principles suited for this new age. It is by no means unimaginable that the form of democracy practiced in the United States has not kept pace with the changes in social conditions and, therefore, misses the essence of democracy.

There is no way to determine the functionality and legitimacy of the present American democracy by external definitions. One has to look at American democracy from the inside, observe it in action, and relate these insights to our knowledge of fundamental democratic principles.

> *"It is remarkable, on close inspection, what a lousy way to get things done democracy is."*
>
> P.J. O'Rourke, Parliament of Whores

While monarchy ordained by God was considered the natural order in its time, no serious defender of the democratic idea will claim that democracy is endowed with sacred blessings. Democracy is not defined by inherent goodness. It is justified by the as yet unproved assumption that it is the most reliable of all systems to protect and promote the property and interests of the largest number of individuals affected by government decisions.[3]

How does democracy fulfill this promise? Which instruments are used to further this claim? The answers to these questions reveal the complexity of structural elements of which a democratic system consists. The freedom of the citizens' vote for or against a government; the basic right of free speech; the guarantee of equal rights and equal opportunities; the right to equal justice under the law: all this and much more are building blocks of a democratic system, but in order to gauge their real substance and relevance in shaping a democratic culture, one has to ask what practical importance they have for the average citizen of modern mass societies. Today more than ever this kind of inquiry is of particular significance because every realm of society is in a state of transition. It is quite possible, even likely, that some shining beacons of democracy have become meaningless as far as democratic spirit is concerned. Thus we may be in danger of overestimating political institutions and civil rights that are no longer appropriate and important. On the other hand, we either underestimate or simply do not recognize the relevance of new political attitudes, new demands by the citizens, and new structural elements of society created by change. Certain modes of measuring the quality of a democratic system are probably outdated while important questions that could reach the core of democratic self-understanding have either not yet been formulated or have already been suppressed.

Possible Fissures of the Democratic System

Whether a system—be it organic, mechanical, or social—is in good working order is often difficult to determine for lack of positive criteria. Is it possible for a doctor to claim with absolute certainty that a patient is healthy? He can only state the absence of illness. The procedure used in medicine could be used to explore the internal state of a political system, too. One examines the body politic and checks for possible weak spots, thus finding out whether there are symptoms of decay and degeneration in the pillars of the system, in the mechanisms crucial for operation, and in the energy sources that keep the democratic organism going.

We can summarize the possible dangers to a political system, especially a democratic one, in three problem areas:

1. *Erosion of Substance* Institutions remain intact but no longer have any significance or no longer fulfill their function within the framework of the system.
2. *Overextension of Principles* The values providing the system with stability and energy are driven to their extreme and in their exaggeration lose their positive character. They are transformed to their opposite.
3. *Inability to Respond to Value Changes, Ossification* Certain structural elements of the system become irrelevant. The methods needed to cope with new social problems are lacking.

In the United States there are numerous signs of the *erosion of the democratic substance* behind erect facades. The division of power, an indispensable element of democracy that, in America, has developed into the particular form of "checks and balances" (the mutual control of the three powers within the state) seems intact and functioning on the surface. The legislative and the executive powers, Congress and the president, guard their share of the power base and prevent its one-sided accumulation. This impression may be accurate in internal politics, but it no longer applies to foreign politics and questions of war and peace where the president often claims absolute authority.

Freedom of speech and freedom of the press are securely and incontestably established in the United States and the Western democracies. The question is whether the original function of this freedom for the democratic process has been retained. What if everyone could express his or her opinion but whether it had any importance depended entirely on that person's access to the media? If we define freedom of expression not only as accessibility of information but also as a right to participate in the formative process of information and opinion, then this freedom applies primarily to those who control the media by economic power.

Universal suffrage to vote is a particularly interesting example because in this area the inner erosion has been accompanied by an external improvement. The principle of universal participation in the political process has been nearly perfected. This has been achieved by granting the right to vote to many segments of the population formerly banned and by abolishing procedural obstacles that excluded certain minority groups such as African Americans from voting. Until a few decades ago there were voting taxes and literacy tests in parts of the United States.[4] But while the right to vote has been extended, participation in elections has dramatically dropped—an indication that citizens no longer consider the right to vote a great achievement and that this right is steadily losing significance in the political system.

The disease that lies in *straining and stressing democratic values* can best be demonstrated by observing the principle of individual self-realization. This principle is the secret source of the inner dynamic operating within a democratic system. Tocqueville observed:

> Democracy does not give the people the most skillful government, but it produces what the ablest governments are frequently unable to create: namely,

an all-pervading and restless activity, a superabundant force, and an energy which is inseparable from it and which may, however unfavorable circumstances may be, produce wonders.[5]

The individual's liberation from governmental interference in favor of the pursuit of his or her private interests is not just a value in itself for Americans. It is considered a premise for society's achievement of wealth and satisfaction. There is hardly any political cliché as deeply imbedded in American society as the belief in the wonderfully beneficial effect of an unrestrained pursuit of individual interests. This highly developed faith in individualism is valid only to a limited degree; an excessive egotism not only poses a danger to the community, it often turns against the individual in damaging ways. In their book *The Good Society*, which discusses those aspects of "American individualism" threatening society, Robert Bellah et al. illustrate the phenomenon with the example of Los Angeles. Once one of the most beautiful regions of the world, Los Angeles today, after decades of unlimited individual mobility, is so threatened by air pollution that it is no longer the individual but the city administration that decides about everyday life—whether factories will be permitted to be in operation, whether cars are permitted to be used, even whether you are permitted to use your garden grill.[6]

> "Between Mets fans, what difference does it make who's President of the United States?"
>
> *Victor Gold and Lynne Cheney*, The Body Politic

The effects that *change in value concepts and attitudes* have upon democracy are difficult to determine because the contours of the evolving postmodern society are not yet clearly visible. But it is within the range of imagination that one of the central tenets of democracy—citizen participation in institutional processes—will eliminate itself in a society that considers events that occur on the so-called political level increasingly unimportant. Does this mean that the much bemoaned lack of political participation is no reason for concern at all but, rather, a natural assimilation of democratic structures to social changes? The thought is apt to spread discomfort.

One of the structural principles of democracy—the election of the government by its citizens—is being undermined by the fact that it is no longer the elected government but a permanent power elite of professional politicians connected to the official bureaucracy that makes policy decisions. On the other hand, there are social movements attempting to abolish the monopoly politicians hold within the political realm. Media stars, famous athletes, and personalities in show-business today have more "political" clout in the sense of influencing political convictions and political actions than do elected politicians.[7] Political issues of real impact on the average citizen's life are discussed and presented to the public expertly and comprehensibly by radio and television rather than by Congress.[8]

Democracy at the End of the Age of Rationalism

The old democratic structures and decision-making processes have come under pressure from two sides. On the one hand, problems haunting economic growth and technical progress have grown so large and urgent that they more and more exceed the problem-solving capacities of traditional democratic mechanisms. On the other hand, citizens' demands upon the state have dramatically increased, as have their skills to get these demands fulfilled within the political system at the cost of the community's well-being. More and more the democratic system loses the capacity to protect the interests of society against individual and group interests.

It is quite possible that what we are facing is not at all a perfection of the democratic idea. Rather, it could be a kind of dawning of the gods, a false radiance, a deceptive mood of jubilation, similar to the situation at the end of the ancien régime. The beginnings of democracy had their origin in a new way of thought, in a new perspective on the world and its order. The renaissance of democracy after the Middle Ages evolved simultaneously with the Enlightenment. It was firmly wedded to the triumphal victory of reason over faith and tradition. Only when "ratio" was established as the real ruler of the world was the path free for the development of political ideas that were to justify modern democracy.

We cannot ignore the fact that the age of self-confident rationalism in its undiluted form is coming to an end or has already ended. The limits of rationalism as an instrument for knowing and governing the world are becoming ever more obvious. New methods of analysis and thought—albeit chaotic and incomprehensible—have been offered. We are facing an epochal change of paradigm, a new *Weltanschauung* is emerging.

A new irrationalism, partly helpless, partly confident, partly stupid, partly illuminated, partly mystical-utopian, partly earthy-savvy, disputes the sovereign rule of the old rationalism. People have developed a fundamentally new attitude to the world and to themselves, an attitude not captured solely by the categories of rationality. As modern science, another offspring of rationalism, is affected by its relativity, so surely is democracy. The values of this emerging new political culture could be compassion instead of egoism, solidarity instead of competition and domination, moderation instead of growth and progress at any price, values of the heart instead of those of the head. This is not just blue-eyed utopia. Value changes in this direction are happening. One only needs to look at the decline in the social value of war from the early decades of this century when the outbreak of World War I was enthusiastically greeted by the people, up to now, where it is abhorred and utterly disqualified as a means of politics.

It is an open question: Is democracy merely being refreshed under the impact of a newly defined world view that in the end will prove to be just a further advancement of the old ideas, or will this new thinking produce a force that will explode the existing political structures, just as the incipient rationalism did to the ancien régime at the end of the eighteenth century?

At any rate, rather than to relax and to enjoy the momentary triumph of democracy it seems to be more relevant and interesting to explore the direction in which things are moving. Perhaps American democracy has already traveled a little farther on this path than other democracies. Perhaps it could even serve as the model for a political system that is "irrational" in a totally neutral sense of "not-solely-rational."

In his book *Contingency, Irony and Solidarity*, Richard Rorty outlines the intellectual foundation and order for a society no longer able to rely on the basic premises of the Enlightenment. According to Rorty, society has given up faith in ultimate ratios, in absolute truths. The author declines to expand upon the indissoluble opposites—absolute and relative, rational and irrational—that contribute nothing to the orientation of a modern society. He simply shunts them aside and introduces a new vocabulary for understanding the foundations of human community, especially the concepts listed in the book's title: contingency, irony, and solidarity.

Rorty deliberately does not design a new *intellectual foundation* for liberal democracy. In his view, an *improved self-definition* is more necessary and suited for our times.[9] According to Rorty, the idea of justifying a culture belongs to the intellectual realm of the Enlightenment, which sought to relate the decisive cultural development of its time to the sciences. That may have been of value then, but it has lost its importance today. In Rorty's view, science is no longer the most interesting, most promising, or most exciting area of human culture. Thus, Rorty advises us to turn our attention to those areas belonging to the cultural avant-garde and stimulating the imaginative powers of our young people: art and political utopia.

> We need a redescription of liberalism as the hope that culture as a whole can be "poeticized" rather than as the Enlightenment hope that it can be "rationalized" or "scientized" . . . an ideally liberal polity would be one whose culture hero is Bloom's "strong poet" rather than the warrior, the priest, the sage, or the truth-seeking, "logical," "objective" scientist.[10]

Notes

1. The expression was coined by Joel Garreau who has written a book about this phenomenon, *Edge City: Life on the New Frontier*. See also Joel Garreau, "Life on the Edge: Urban Snobs Hate American New Fringe 'Cities': Do They Understand Them?" *Washington Post*, September 8, 1991.

2. Fukuyama speaks—in consequence of his theory of the end of history—of a

posthistorical society (e.g., p. 276). More important than the term, however, is the fact that self-assessment, values, and goals of today's society have drastically changed in comparison to preceding stages of *modern* societies.

3. Compare with, for instance, Robert A. Dahl's statement: "In my view, neither political equality nor the democratic process is justified as intrinsically good. Rather, they are justified as the most reliable means for protecting and advancing the good and interests of all the persons subject to collective decisions." *Democracy and Its Critics,* p. 322.

4. The voting tax was abolished in 1962 by the 24th Amendment to the Constitution, the literacy tests by the Voting Rights Act of 1965.

5. Alexis de Tocqueville, *Democracy in America I*, p. 252.

6. Robert Bellah et al., *The Good Society,* p. 270. The American individualism and its effects on modern society was the main theme of Bellah's first book, *Habits of the Heart,* and is investigated in this book from a different perspective. Bellah et al. strongly insist that the American problem is individualism and not so much the struggle for equality as Tocqueville supposed. However, Tocqueville also discussed extensively the effects of individualism on a democratic society—especially in the second volume of *Democracy in America.*

7. William Greider, *Who Will Tell the People?* p. 321. Greider reports how movie star Meryl Streep forced the Environmental Protection Agency to prohibit a certain pesticide with only one television appearance.

8. Alexander King and Bertrand Schneider, *The First Global Revolution,* p. 110.

9. Richard Rorty, *Contingency, Irony, and Solidarity,* p. 52.

10. Ibid., p. 53.

Pursuit

of

Happiness

The most remarkable aspect of the American Declaration of Independence is the concept of happiness for the people as a touchstone for the legitimacy of a government. In the first sentences of this declaration, it is written that governments are installed for the sole purpose of securing for their citizens "life, liberty and the pursuit of happiness."[1]

> " 'This is living!' 'I gotta be me!' 'Ain't we got fun!' It's all there in the Declaration of Independence. We are the only nation in the world based on happiness. Search as you will the sacred creeds of other nations and peoples, read the Magna Charta, the Communist Manifesto, the Ten Commandments, the Analects of Confucius, Plato's Republic, the New Testament or the UN Charter, and find me any happiness at all. America is the Happy Kingdom."
> P.J. O'Rourke, Parliament of Whores

The author of the Declaration of Independence, Thomas Jefferson, used the idea of happiness deliberately and emphatically. The triad of constitutional goals evolved from John Locke's political philosophy, which was the source of many ideas and arguments for the American founding fathers. Locke's words, however, were *"life, liberty and estate,"*[2] and in this form it was known not only to Jefferson but throughout the intellectual elite of early America.

This change of words does not mean that "estate" or "property" were of minor importance for the people of the American colonies. The word *revolution* for the secession from the British crown should not be taken to mean that a deprived proletariat revolted against a dominant class of property owners. The American "revolution" took place in a society in which property was in abundance and widespread. The leaders of this "revolution" were well-to-do property owners, and the protection of property was indeed one of the central topics of the discussions about the new constitution for the thirteen states.

For Jefferson, however, property obviously was not sufficiently important to be put on equal status with life and liberty. He exchanged it for something that since Aristotle had been valued as the ultimate goal of human striving, indeed the meaning of life itself: the pursuit of happiness. Jefferson did not invent the "pursuit of happiness." It was an established term of the political philosophy of eighteenth-century Enlightenment. But Jefferson wrested it away from the sphere of philosophical or academic talk and put it into the political arena where it evolved its dynamic character.

The Real American Revolution

With this declaration, Jefferson distinctly and unalterably placed the human being and his aspirations at the center of all governmental efforts. This was a revolutionary act at a time when in Europe and its dominions the citizen was thought of as the subject of the state whose only reason for existence was to work in the service of king and nobility who not only represented the state but incorporated it. Happiness had been the sphere of the church, which for the promise of a better life after death asked for spiritual submission and material sacrifices in this world.

Jefferson and the cosigners of the Declaration of Independence, by making the happiness of the people the proof of legitimacy for a government, gave the final blow to the until-then unchallenged rule of absolutism. By introducing the pursuit of happiness as a fundamental right for every member of a democratic society, the definition of democracy was substantially enlarged beyond the mere formal principles of majority rule and equality under the law. A government is legitimated if and only if it renders possible the pursuit of happiness or, to put it into modern terminology, if it serves the aspirations of its citizens for self-realization.[3]

There is an important difference, however, among life, liberty, and happiness. Whereas government according to the Declaration of Independence is obliged to guarantee life and liberty of its citizens, happiness itself is not its responsibility—this would indeed be an impossible obligation. It is only the "pursuit of happiness" that ought to be protected by governmental action.[4]

There are many utopian political theories and practices (such as Marxism) that go beyond this natural limit for political potentiality and put the state into the role of creator of happiness for humankind. But modern democracy, too, in its configuration as welfare state, is in danger of giving up the prudent constraint of the American founding fathers to present itself as a source of happiness. By obliging government only to provide the basis for the "pursuit of happiness" so as to give everyone the potential to actually pursue one's personal happiness, the political promise in the Declaration of Independence becomes realistic, concrete, honest, binding.

There is yet another revolutionary aspect in the declaration of the "pursuit of happiness" as a fundamental and inalienable human right. It liberated not only the citizen from the pretensions of the absolutist state, it released the individual from the ties to "the other world." By declaring the pursuit of happiness as a basic right under the protection of the state, this political philosophy set men free to love life in itself and for itself. Friedrich Nietzsche's fight of a century later against a predominant religion, which in effect tied human beings like slaves to the other world, was already decided in America by the founding fathers in favor of this life without much argument against religion. The religions may preach whatever they want; the state sends the message to its citizens that they are here on earth to be happy.

This revolutionary view of man as a private and political being is of utmost importance. It is the driving force that has disentangled the development of American society from its European counterpart. It is the source of its advantage in forming the structures of a modern society. It is the reason for the American view of the world as something that is theirs to be formed and to be enjoyed. It is the basis for the lightness of American life that is both fascinating and shocking for Europeans. It is the source of the self-assurance and lack of constraint that is part of the American habit. It is the core of the "American way of life," the philosophy of the nation. Jean Baudrillard in his reflections about America remarked that only the Americans are really modern because here and nowhere else modernity is original.[5] One important aspect of this modernity is certainly their ease with the world and toward themselves because in the beginning of their history there was not a prohibition but an invitation to be happy.

The Far Side of the American Way of Life

> *"Don't worry, be happy!"*
> *Popular song of the late eighties and official song for the*
> *presidential campaign of George Bush in 1988.*

The invitation to pursue happiness is, on the other hand, the root of many repulsive and dangerous developments of American society: unbridled greed for material property, impetuosity in the exploitation of the environment and of other people, egoism and ruthlessness in pursuit of one's own personal goals, consumer frenzy, inability to say no, demand for instant satisfaction, search for ever new stimulations.

But it is not only the excesses that upset the pursuit of happiness, turning it into a negative phenomenon, it is the single-minded fixation on a material definition of happiness. The author and the cosigners of the Declaration of Independence did not define happiness. Rightfully so, because it cannot be defined, at least not by proxy for somebody else. Nevertheless, it is important to know how these people viewed happiness and why they gave it such a central place within the American political philosophy.

For Jefferson, happiness was identical with the "good life," which in his voluminous work he described quite extensively. It was above all a life of moderation.[6] Jefferson was strongly influenced by Greek philosophy, mainly by Epicurus and Aristotle. He agrees with Aristotle in defining happiness as the central and ultimate value of human life.[7] Aristotle's theory of the golden mean[8] as the peak between two extremes is reflected in Jefferson's philosophy. His ideal of a good life in the country among a circle of good friends[9] (also an Aristotelian thought) with leisure for intellectual reflection[10] (again a parallel to Aristotle's ideas) tries to strike a happy medium between the primitive state that lacks cultural achievements and over-civilization that had already taken place in Jefferson's times.[11]

The proponents of an ideal of happiness that is oriented in material well-being cannot claim Jefferson as their advocate. On the contrary, he emphasized time and again nonmaterial goods such as friendship, leisure, spiritual occupation, family life, and political involvement, although he saw a sufficient, even generous material basis as a natural fundament for a good life—here, too, in agreement with his great predecessor, Aristotle.[12]

The Influence of Alexander Hamilton on American Self-Awareness

Jefferson's concept of happiness has not made great imprints on the value system of American society. Alexander Hamilton, another of the founding fathers, was much more influential in shaping its political philosophy and value orientation. In the early stages of the birth of the nation, he gave direction to its economic course and political self-awareness. His was the decisive voice in favor of a dynamic industrialization over the self-sustained agrarian economy preferred by Jefferson. As a political writer with his numerous essays in *The Federalist Papers,* which soon became the quasi-official interpretation of the Constitution, and later on in politics itself, as the first Secretary of the Treasury of the newly born state, he strongly promoted the triumphal march of capitalism in America. Even though Hamilton's essays in *The Federalist Papers* are less concerned with problems of constitutional philosophy—as compared to the contributions of James Madison—and deal more with issues of practical importance, his views are based on a political philosophy in which the happiness of the people plays a central role. In the programmatic first essay of *The Federalist Papers* he states:

> I am convinced that this [the ratification of the Constitution] is the safest course for your liberty, your dignity and your happiness.[13]

But Hamilton's political philosophy is based in two decisive aspects on different assumptions from Jefferson's: First, he is convinced that only a strong and powerful state is able to guarantee its citizens wealth and happiness, and for this reason he not only preached the idea of a manufacturing and merchandising America, but he was also a strong advocate of a militarily predominant state able to protect sea-lanes and markets.[14] Hamilton was deeply convinced that everything that contributes to the creation of a solid and permanent state organization and to the strengthening of the industrial and financial base of the country would trickle down a blessing to everyone within the community:

> It is a truth as important as it is agreeable, and one to which it is not easy to imagine exceptions, that everything tending to establish substantial and permanent order in the affairs of a country, to increase the total mass of industry and opulence, is ultimately beneficial to every part of it.[15]

It is an open question whether Hamilton really was interested in the happiness of the individual citizen, which he believed could only be gained in a wealthy and powerful state, or whether he was genuinely enthralled by the concept of a mighty state. There are reasons to believe it was the latter, but it is of no importance for the development influenced by his ideas and policies. The decisive aspect is the change from self-contained to dynamic ideas of happiness and the narrowing of the idea of happiness to mere material well-being. This was due to another of Hamilton's basic philosophical assumptions in which he differed most strongly from Jefferson. In contrast to Jefferson's positive and optimistic view, his concept of the nature of man was deeply skeptical and pessimistic:

> The passions of men will not conform to the dictates of reason and justice without constraint.[16]

Whereas Jefferson emphasizes the positive aspects of human aspirations, Hamilton draws his conclusions from the negative ones. He sees human beings as ambitious, envious, greedy. But these bad habits can become quite beneficial both for the individual and for the community within the framework of a well-organized and powerful state.

"Greed Is Healthy"

> *"A vast amount of the pathetic hope, if not assumption, that you can buy a good life resides in a statement like 'Those people are so lucky: they live in a million-dollar home.' "*
>
> *Paul Fussell*, BAD

In the eighties, this American belief in the virtue of greed was widely preached and enthusiastically accepted. The Wall Street arbitrageur Ivan Boesky, one of the most flamboyant figures of the times, gave this message in a commencement address at a major university: "greed is healthy."[17] Greed became the key-word for the attitude of American society during the Reagan years. There has been a sobering since; Ivan Boesky went to jail, and the speculative empires of his peers collapsed and ruined the savings and loan, banking and insurance business, the real-estate market, and dozens of giant companies. They plundered the American economy and left it in serious disrepair. There is profound reflection and heated discussion in America over the excesses and the consequences of the "economy of greed."[18] It is doubtful, however, that the disenchantment and indignation will lead to a general reorientation of the value system. The heritage of 200 years of unbroken experience within a society cannot be easily cancelled.

Besides, has America not been very successful with her philosophy of enrichment, perhaps not very noble but definitely reliable? Could it be that one has to accept periodic excesses like the ones of the eighties as the price for a dynamic development that in the end is to the benefit of everybody?[19]

The capitalist system based on the striving for wealth, cannot be repudiated out of hand because of its excesses and exaggerations, but it is shortsighted to view these excesses as lamentable slips of a basically balanced order. These excesses are endemic. By narrowing man's natural aspiration for happiness into a striving for wealth, happiness becomes a material category and is looked at in terms of quantity instead of quality. If happiness is quantifiable, it can theoretically be increased boundlessly. So the virus of wantonness intrudes into the human aspiration for happiness. The lack of moderation in the pursuit of enrichment is no aberration, no accident; it is part of the system. The aspiration for individual happiness in the form of material wealth is without limits and restraints—a dangerous element in a democratic society that is based in principle on the idea of equality and is dependent in its function on at least a minimum of solidarity.

But it is not only the faults and excesses of the conventional notion of happiness that cry out for a nonmaterial interpretation of happiness. There are many positive elements in Jefferson's theory of happiness that have been overlooked or consciously suppressed. His ideas are by no means naive, overly optimistic, and impractical.

Jefferson does not deny the need for a material base for happiness. On the contrary, property in the form of a sufficient piece of land to support oneself is the inalienable condition for a happy life, not as a goal in itself, but as a means for independence that is a necessary element of happiness. If one lays out these conditions, the chances are slim a member of modern mass society will find happiness. Not so much because he or she can no longer live from the fruit of his or her own soil, but because his independence is lost to outside forces—his work is determined by an economic system in which he is both exploiting and exploited. He is even forced to exploit himself by working more than is necessary for a good life. Even the distribution of his income is determined from outside by an ineluctable consumer atmosphere that imperceptibly, but forcefully, dictates "that" people have to consume and "what" they have to consume. Not even the growing amount of leisure time offers relief because industry that sees people's free time as a promising market has been very effective in turning it into a consumer world.

Public and Private Happiness

Jefferson's goal was not only independence for the individual in his private life, but also his political independence, which he considered an indispensable aspect of human happiness. Here the decisive difference becomes clear between the individualistic, consumer-oriented philosophy of happiness that is the trademark of today's American society and Jefferson's "pursuit of happiness" that is oriented toward higher aspirations.

For Jefferson, "private happiness" was unthinkable without "public happiness"; there could be no happiness for a member of a society without participation in public affairs. Jefferson sensed that human beings trying to organize community life were bound to restrain their egoistical recklessness and their instincts for enrichment. The daily experience of dealing with one another creates an awareness of other people's rights and needs; it teaches imperceptibly, but inevitably, an attitude of compromise and moderation. Constant participation in the political process, of course, is only possible within small entities, but Jefferson with his model of the ward republics[20] made a practical proposal for the realization of his theory of "public happiness."[21]

Moreover, participating in the political process is a sure way to get a sense of self-determination. According to Jefferson's philosophy, the independence as an individual that comes with the ownership of a small estate has to be supported and perfected by the political independence of the citizen. There is no doubt that people cannot really be happy if their every need is satisfied but they have no voice in the organization of their own affairs. Modern mass democracy comes closer and closer to this state. Aldous Huxley in *Brave New World* vividly described how such a society looks in its final stage when its members get instant satisfaction for all their desires but are excluded from all responsibility.

There is reason to believe that determination from outside is intolerable in the long run, even if it is handled quite imperceptibly. There will be rebellion against it. Just as adolescents want to search for their own happiness, even if they have the paradise on earth in their parents' home, citizens of advanced democracies cannot bear for an extended time the determination of their private and political life by outside forces. The escape route is a way back to a more difficult, but also a more accomplished, life in which less is offered but more can be realized. It is a big mistake to assume that Jefferson's concept of happiness is oriented toward idling and leads to a *dolce far niente* mentality. Compared to such a caricature, Hamilton's concept of striving for property and wealth, which brings dynamism and tension into society, looks like the better alternative. But the "pursuit of happiness" is not a passive waiting for happiness to come along. It is activity directed not toward external property but toward self-realization.

It is *energeia* in Aristotle's terms: "activity of the self in order to accomplish its destiny." Or to express it in political terms with Charles Murray who writes in his book, *In Pursuit: Of Happiness and Good Government:*

> The pursuit of happiness means making life deliberately difficult in certain ways—not so difficult that we cannot cope, but difficult enough, in certain important ways, that coping is an authentic accomplishment.[22]

Notes

1. "We hold these truths to be self-evident: that all men are created equal; that they are endowed by their Creator with CERTAIN (inherent and) inalienable rights; that among

these are life, liberty and the pursuit of happiness; that to secure these rights, governments are instituted among men, deriving their just powers from the consent of the governed; that whenever any form of government becomes destructive of these ends, it is the right of the people to alter or to abolish it and to institute new government, laying its foundation on such principles, and organizing its powers in such form, as to them shall seem most likely to effect their safety and happiness."

This is the beginning of the second paragraph—the first after the Preamble—of the American Declaration of Independence. (Jefferson's original version *"with inherent inalienable rights"* was changed to *"certain inalienable rights"* by Congress.)

2. John Locke, *Second Treatise of Government*, p. 66.

3. In Jefferson's opinion, this is not only a matter of "private happiness." I'll enter more details into the distinction between "private" and "public happiness" and the necessity to connect both at the end of this chapter and at the end of this book. Compare with: Hannah Arendt, *On Revolution*, p. 126; Richard Matthews, *The Radical Politics of Thomas Jefferson*, especially chapters 2, 4, and 7.

4. Aristotle, *Nichomachean Ethics* I. 2.1095a11.

5. Jean Baudrillard, *America*, p. 81.

6. Matthews, *The Radical Politics of Thomas Jefferson*, p. 37. Compare with "The Syllabus of the Doctrines of Epicurus," whom Jefferson calls "our master Epicurus." There he emphasizes that virtue consists of 1. Prudence, 2. Temperance, 3. Fortitude, 4. Justice. Jefferson to William Short, October 31, 1819, *The Portable Jefferson*, p. 567.

7. Aristotle, *Nichomachean Ethics* I.5.1107b20.

8. Ibid., II. 6.1106b36.

9. Compare with the invitation to James Madison to move to the area of Monticello. Jefferson to Madison, December 8, 1784, *The Republic of Letters*, p. 354.

10. Matthews, *The Radical Politics of Thomas Jefferson*, p. 90; Aristotle, *Nichomachean Ethics* X. 7.1177a12; Jefferson to Madison, June 9, 1793, *Writings*, p. 1010; and Arendt, *On Revolution*, p. 128.

11. Leo Marx, *The Machine in the Garden*, p. 139.

12. In his draft for a constitution for Virginia (his home state), Jefferson planned that every man should get fifty acres of land from the state, if he did not own a piece of land of this amount already. *The Portable Jefferson*, p. 248.

Compare with Aristotle, *Nichomachean Ethics* X. 9.1178b33; I. 9.1099a31; and I. 1101a15.

13. *The Federalist Papers*, No. 1, p. 36; compare also with *Federalist*, No. 15, p. 105 and *Federalist*, No. 30, p. 191.

14. Compare especially with *Federalist*, No. 11, p. 86.

15. Alexander Hamilton, *The Reports of Alexander Hamilton*, p. 164.

16. *Federalist*, No. 15, p. 110.

17. Ivan Boesky at a University of California, Berkeley, commencement; quoted by Paul Slansky, *The Clothes Have No Emperor*, p. 176.

A similar remark is quoted by the businessman Julius Dart, one of the members of Ronald Reagan's Kitchen Cabinet.

"I have never looked for a business that's going to render a service to mankind. I figure that if it employs a lot of people and makes a lot of money, it is in fact rendering a service to mankind. Greed is involved in everything we do. I find no fault with that." Bellah et al., *Habits of the Heart*, p. 264.

This attitude in America became a philosophy that is attributed to Ayn Rand. She founded the "objectivist" school and taught the "virtue of selfishness"—the title of her best-known book. She fights against all forms of altruism in private as well as in public life. Her interest was not confined to writing books; she even led an "Objectivist Movement" that found many followers throughout the country. This movement still exists, although Ayn Rand died in 1982.

18. Meanwhile, many books, articles, and television documentaries describe all the disgusting details of so-called "megadeals" of finance jugglers. A lot of books have also been published that investigated the reasons and the consequences of the economic policy of the eighties.

A few books were especially successful and/or informative:

Michael Lewis, *The Money Culture:* The book offers interesting insights from the point of view of a young, disrespectful manager.

Michael Lewis, *Liar's Poker:* Another book by the same author about his experiences at Salomon Brothers, one of the biggest brokerage houses.

Bryan Burrough and John Helyar, *Barbarians at the Gate:* They describe the biggest and most spectacular leveraged buyout—the case of RJR Nabisco.

Other books that deal with economic and political consequences of the wild eighties: Donald L. Barnett and James B. Steele, *America: What Went Wrong?;* Paul Krugman, *The Age of Diminished Expectations;* and Robert Kuttner, *The End of Laissez-Faire.*

19. William Greider quotes the financier Andrew Mellon: "The prosperity of the lower and middle classes depends upon the good fortune and light taxes of the rich." *Who Will Tell the People?* p. 87.

The robber baron Jay Gould strikes the same chord, when he says: "We have made the country rich, we have developed the country." Richard B. Hofstadter, *The American Political Tradition,* p. 167.

20. The essence of this theory is that as many political decisions as possible should be made in wards of a manageable size. I will elaborate on this theory in more detail in the chapter "Plebiscite and Participation."

21. Jefferson to Samuel Kercheval, July 12, 1816, *The Portable Jefferson,* p. 556.

For the importance of the ward-republics as places for political participation and therefore as a means for public happiness, compare with Matthews, *Radical Politics,* p. 81 and Arendt, *On Revolution,* p. 248.

22. Charles Murray, *In Pursuit: Of Happiness and Good Government,* p. 270.

Money, Part I

Motor

and

Nemesis

of

Democracy

"I know of no other country where money plays an equally significant role in people's minds," Alexis de Tocqueville writes about the America he observed. But this remark is obviously not intended to be pejorative as one would expect from a French aristocrat burdened by the century-old tradition of disdaining money. For this is how Tocqueville continues his observation: "and where there is more deep-seated contempt for wealth that does not increase." [1]

It is evident that he sensed the connection between money and the democratic spirit that expresses itself above all in the aspects of mobility, of freedom and restlessness, of enterprise and capacity of development.

The Emancipatory Character of Money

Taking the most advanced, the first "modern" society as a model, Tocqueville discovered and described what the philosopher Georg Simmel wrote about in theoretical terms half a century later in his *Philosophy of Money:* Money is one of the strongest motors of modernity; progress of the monetary system parallels the growth of individual freedom. The monetary system created and strengthened a new class of citizens beside and later surpassing the land-owning aristocrats. This newly emerging class, in turn, made democracy imperative by demanding a share of political power. For individual self-esteem and social position, money remains a great emancipatory force at work. Century-old traditions, values as firm as rocks, practically indissoluble ties have been destroyed or, to use a term coined by Joseph H. Schumpeter, *vaporized* by the advance of money.

The congruity of money and freedom is nothing new for those who have money—their lives are direct proof of this equation—and even have-nots identify money with the liberty to spend. This philosophical recognition and justification of the relationship by Simmel is of great significance for philosophy itself, which could finally shed its suspicion of money. For centuries, serious philosophers dealt only in a superficial and condescending manner with one of the most important aspects of human existence. Simmel's thesis, however, assigns money the status it deserves in "the realm of the mind." Even more important, Simmel's theory opens up a new and fruitful approach to the phenomenon of money by drawing on the rich heritage of philosophical reflection and knowledge on the notion of freedom.

The liberating role of money goes beyond the economic-financial realm and reaches into the core of social structures. The advance of the money economy, more concretely the participation of more and more social classes in the money economy, has broken up rigid social orders and has made them flexible and porous. By way of money, more and more new groups have become equal players in society. The latest dramatic development that lets us observe this process in concrete fashion is the emancipation of women. When women decided voluntarily or involuntarily to switch from the self-supply economy of their households to the money economy of professional life, they drastically changed the face of society. They also garnered for themselves a momentous growth in political and social rights.

However, the evolution of the money economy and of social emancipation have not always proceeded at the same pace. Women today still lament a lack of emancipation in many areas of life. Other cases are even more blatant. The inhabitants of rural areas in Europe who were freed from slavery in the early stages of capitalism initially experienced a loss of freedom, social equality, and political clout in the transition to a money economy.

But these obstacles and delays do not counter the argument that, on the whole and in the long term, the development of a money economy and a democratic society run parallel. Here lies the seed for the failure of totalitarian regimes in modern societies. The only societies in which these totalitarian systems can be stabilized are those operating on an agricultural self-supplying basis. The political upheavals in Eastern Europe were possibly the first revolutions in human history that derived their impetus from the fact that people had too much money and knew—through the media—on what to spend it, but there was not enough to buy.

The Equalizing Function of Money

Besides its emancipatory character, money has an equalizing effect that contributed to spreading democratic culture. Money as an abstract means of barter strips material goods of their qualitative individuality, those special qualities knowable only by the experts and connoisseurs. Money reduces material goods to a commodity that everyone can compare by price. Not only does the exchange of commodities become universally accessible because it does not require any expertise, money also creates, as F. Fürstenberg formulates, "a formal equality of the individuals participating in the economic barter business. It dissolves class distinctions. Money does not show its origin. Personal values and the motives for payment are not visible in the financial transactions. The exchange of goods is being set free from social accessories and is reduced to its purely economic function, but by this is also being organized especially effective."[2]

This quotation speaks to the third important contribution that money makes to the democratization of society. The advance of the monetary system laid the foundation for the economic growth taken for granted in Western democracies today. This happened within the states as well as worldwide between the states through increased commerce made possible and facilitated by the advance of money. Growing prosperity among a wide range of the population contributed most to the stabilization of democratic institutions. Conversely, the desire for a similar standard of living was one of the strongest forces driving the most recent movements toward democratization.

Freedom, equality, prosperity, money as a messiah—this sounds alien to Europeans who have traditionally been taught about the shameful and damaging effects of money by poets, philosophers, religious founders, and folklore. This may ultimately have to do with the fact that money indisputably is a product of modernity and that the romantic wise men are attached more to a mythologized past.

America's Affirmation of Money

America was "modern" in this respect from the very beginning and unabashedly affirmed its faith in money. The most remarkable aspect of this orientation toward money is the use of money as a measurement in nearly all areas: professional success, social position, personal happiness.

This is only the most recent consequence of quantifying and materializing the world where all qualities find their price. It is a logical sequence of the total rationalization of all social processes. What better measure is there for human reason than a criterion free of all subjective influences, understandable to everyone, and calculable in numbers? Money is the absolute objective value.

If money is firmly established as a measure of success, then earning it is not contemptible but is praiseworthy. Americans are driven by a "burning desire for success," and money is "the stamp and seal of success." This is the reason for the naïveté with which Americans declare moneymaking as the true sense of life. Though tempting, it would be wrong to make fun of this "primitive materialism." As long as Europeans have no reliable measuring stick for values—and it might be difficult to come up with one—criticism of the American faith in moneymaking remains irrelevant. On the contrary, the American attitude to money is not only logical but in the final analysis is morally more consistent because it is free of hypocrisy.

The advancement of money, considered typical for modern society by Simmel, began in America and made its greatest progress here because this nation was able to construct a social value system unfettered by traditional values and social status symbols. Tocqueville remarked:

> In America, in the absence of all material and external distinctions, wealth appeared as the natural test to measure men's merit. Besides, the Americans are a people with very little feeling for the pleasures of the mind. Exclusively occupied in making their fortunes they must naturally have a sort of veneration for wealth.[3]

Monetarization of Society

America has begun to monetarize most social aspects and activities, a development that has spread to other Western nations and to a lesser degree permeates the whole world. A few decades ago, there were only amateurs in sports with the exception of a few top athletes. Today, even the most obscure sports have become professional and have been commercialized. There are no longer any sports stars without sponsors and lucrative advertising contracts.

"The perfect marriage of art and commerce."
Celebrity Madonna's comment on her $60-million contract
with Time Warner

The art market—even the name is an indication of a novel development—is also an American initiative. Of course there always were galleries that sold paintings for money, but the cool and deliberate retooling of the work of art into an object of speculation is an essential developmental leap toward the total monetarization of art.

Though books are still written by writers, poets, journalists (and ghost writers), in America, as everywhere else, book "production" is no longer predominantly an artistic process. Rather, it has become increasingly a matter of marketing—from the thematic idea via the search for the author up to the careful orchestration of an integrated media campaign on the occasion of publication. Borrowing from a well-known expression, Americans have already created a "literary-industrial complex."

> *"Erich Segal's spellbinding drama 'Act of Faith,' $23.00 at most bookstores, only $18.40 at Crown Books." Daniel Luria is the only son in a family that has produced great rabbis for nearly two thousand years. His domineering father molds him to be his successor, at the same time that he tries to raise his brilliant daughter to be docile and dutiful—the perfect rabbi's wife. 'Acts of Faith' is a novel of piety, politics, and passion that rivets our attention and will reverberate forever in our memories. So remember, if you paid full price, you didn't buy it at Crown Books."*
>
> *Advertisement by Crown Books*

It is a sign of the enormous vitality and versatility of the American society that literature has been able to hold its own in this unholy alliance. But the dimension of quantity, which money imprints upon everything so unremittingly, is beginning to overshadow traditional characteristics of quality. Clear evidence of that can be seen in the fact that an author's significance is measured by the number of book copies sold. Europeans have internalized this attitude to a large degree as evidenced by their equally unqualified use of bestseller lists, adopting this very term *bestseller* in their language.

A development that is only in its initial stages in book production and the performing arts, it is already a fait accompli in the area of the so-called pop-culture—the unchallenged replacement of proof of quality by quantity. Michael Jackson is the "biggest," the "greatest," the "best" pop artist because 37 million copies of his records have been sold.

Professionalizing All Social Activities

The monetarization of society is evident in the increasing professionalizing of social activities that formerly used to be carried out through private or volunteer services. Baby-sitting may not be the most significant but certainly a very telling example of this development. Things have been taken to new heights in this area: Now you can hire someone to walk your dog. This can mean an immeasurable relief in cities like New York where the removal of dog feces by the owner is a law observed in the strictest terms.

Socially more relevant is the evolution taking place in social services—in such areas where traditionally help was provided by families and neighbors, like looking after and caring for sick and elderly people, baby-sitting and day care, and even in organizing a family reunion. In all these activities, you now may hire professionals for money to provide the services. These social services companies often exhibit structures and sizes of large corporations, a sign of the unconfined dynamics of monetarization.

There is definitely a positive aspect of this development. For hiring and paying others to perform domestic services was not unknown in former days. It was, however, limited to the ruling aristocratic class that freed itself from everyday labor with the help of a large staff. Those without wealth had to rely on the help of family members, friends, and neighbors, or were left to their own devices.

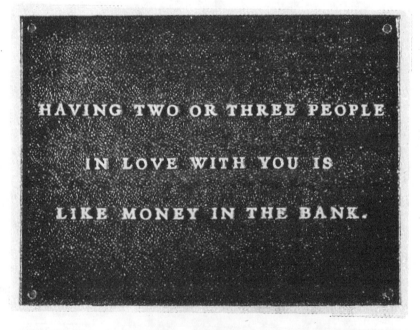

Professionalizing social services and analogously monetarizing social structures have resulted in increased independence. People no longer have to rely on the help of others. With the aid of money, people can obtain what used to depend upon the tentative nature of human relations. Yet it is obvious that this increased freedom, reliability, independence, is accompanied by a loss of human relations, emotions, warmth, spontaneity. Money isolates through its capacity to render independence.

> *"Money poisons you when you've got it and starves you when you haven't it."*
>
> D.H. Lawrence, Lady Chatterly's Lover

As liberating as the rise of money is, there are dark sides, a price to be paid for the way in which money governs more and more areas of social and personal life. It displaces other qualities that infuse human existence with soul, stability, and joy. Not only is this impoverished state in itself sad. More threatening for human existence is this vicious cycle: The more aspects of human life money determines, the fewer are the nonmonetary alternatives, the stronger then the drive becomes for the acquisition of money, and so forth, ever more narrowing, foreclosing any escape.

This is the dilemma: There is no natural end to money's ever-growing influence and significance in society. Money itself has no built-in self-discipline that would assign it natural limits or taboo zones. Nor are there any signs that money's dynamics of domination will have exhausted its energies anytime soon and will come to a halt all by itself.

Money, like power, has an inner law that urges it on and forces it to grow larger and spread further. Like cancer cells it has lost its genetic code that stops the process of cell multiplication at the point of its natural perfection; without this internal signal, the process continues ad infinitum. Has modern society reached this phase of metastasizing where money is concerned?

Money in itself is absolutely meaningless, just like freedom to which it is related. Taken by itself, money has no usefulness at all; it has no objective in the sense of a final goal where it would reach its destination. Without internal destination, left to its own device, money follows only its inner law—the urge to procreate.

Interest is the perfect personification of the nature of money. Simmel writes: "The rejection of the rate of interest in Canon Law reflects the general rejection of money as a whole, since the interest rate represents monetary transactions in their abstract purity."[4]

Economists may eloquently deduct the significance and function of interest from the nature of capital that is characterized by scarcity and from the need to utilize it as profitably as possible. The existence of interest as payment for nonservice, for its mere presence, can only be justified by contemplating the nature of money that is defined by nothing but growth.

Folklore has recognized and formulated this essential core of the nature of money most fittingly: "The devil will always shit onto the largest heap." There are more elegant ways of expressing this in Aristotelian terms. Money's *energeia,* its natural activity, is growth, but growth without ultimate goal. There is no *entelecheia* in money proper because there is no goal (*telos*). Money is pure energy. It is totally meaningless by itself and can be assigned meaning only from the outside. Sadly, money has become more and more powerful and is continuously subjecting, destroying, and excluding other values. As a consequence, it is difficult today, if not impossible, to mobilize substantive values other than money that could be used to give money direction and orient it toward a goal. Because external goals are lacking, money's pure energy—growth—has itself evolved as the fundamental idea.

No Relation between Money and Service

> *"How do you distinguish between money earned and money merely taken."*
>
> George F. Will, "Ripping Off Capitalism"

In 1986, Michael Milken, the inventor of so-called "junk bonds" received an annual bonus of more than half a billion dollars from his company Drexel, Burnham, Lambert. Time Warner's chairman of the board received a consolidated package of $78 million including salary and shares for 1990. Reports of this generous remuneration came simultaneously with the announcement that the company was firing 600 members of the editorial staff in order to minimize the company's losses of $200 million.

Payments to the top earners by themselves explode any relationship to logically understandable criteria for measuring achievement; nor are they in any way related to the company's profits. The president of the athletics goods manufacturer Reebok got $40.9 million for the years 1988–1990; during this time, the company's stock prices rose only moderately. In contrast, these same years were an era of stormy growth for the competitor Nike while Nike's chairman had to content himself with a meager $1 million for the whole three years.

In a column where he presents these numbers under the telling title "Ripping Off Capitalism," George Will asks this rhetorical question:

> Perhaps Reebok's CEO was worth $14.8 million in 1990, but why precisely? Would he have done his job less well for a piddling, oh, $7 million? Would he have left the company if paid less? Would the company have done worse with a $7 million—or even $1 million—replacement?[5]

Unfortunately, George Will, one of the most intelligent observers of American political culture, shies away from the ultimate consequence of his own realizations. He does not equate this nonsense to the loss of reality; instead, he shifts the problem to the moral realm by talking about a pillaging of the companies by their managers. But we are not dealing with a few mischievous pranksters who play foul in an otherwise orderly system; the phenomena show up the nature of the system itself that leaves behind all connections to a real external world and constructs its own reality.

Do we need to mention the fact that there is absolutely no rationally comprehensible relation between the pay for those who feed directly from the trough and the remaining staff? But the numbers—after all they are the medium of money—remain a revelation nonetheless. The president of United Airlines was paid $18.3 million in 1990, a year in which profits sank by 71 percent. That is 1,200 times the starting salary of a stewardess. Compared to this, the chief executive officer of Disney is much more modest: According to a report in *Business Week,* he only earns in one day what the average employee makes in one year. The relation of executive to employee salaries is between 85–100 to 1 in the United States.

Looking at international figures, the relationship in Japan is 17 to 1, in France and Germany it is 22–25 to 1, and in Great Britain it is 35 to 1. These numbers not only carry economic and social implications, they confirm the greatly advanced monetary culture in America. Here, as nowhere else, money has freed itself from all ties and now follows only its own law, the law of excess.

We could round out this enumeration by adding athletes' salaries, the prizes they win, and the fees they get for commercials. We could further add the income of rock and pop giants and other show-business megastars. They are indicators of money running amok in modern society, a phenomenon that cannot be grasped by rational categories.

> *"SAVE—the shrewd business person's favorite four-letter word."*
> *Advertisement in the* Washington Post *by Computerland* [6]

But "money fever" is not only an epidemic in America's board rooms, society in its totality is permeated by the money game. It is the same attitude the other way around—motivating the American consumer to buy for the mere sake of buying or, to pursue this line of thought even further, to buy for the sake of saving money.

People don't buy what they need but what is offered as a special value. American ads do not invite consumers to buy but, rather, to save. The term used most often in commercial spots is *Save!* The act of saving money, not the merchandise, is the source of real enjoyment. The temptation to buy things one does not need would obviously fail without this monetary appeal.

The most telling symptoms of the uncontrolled monetary culture are the junk bonds mentioned earlier and the so-called leveraged buyouts, for whose benefits these financial instruments were designed. Small wonder that these structures exhibit signs of total irrationality and autonomy from any external, traditionally applied conditions. In the case of an LBO (leveraged buyout), so-called raiders—Americans use this term with great equanimity—get loans that are guaranteed by the very object that is to be purchased.[7]

> *"And you don't make anything."*
> *"No."*
> *". . . and you don't build anything."*

"No."
"So, what do you do with the companies once you buy them?"
"I sell them."
"You sell them!"
"Well, I don't sell the whole company. I break it up in pieces and sell them off because it's worth more than the whole."
"So it's sort of like stealing cars and selling off the parts, right?"
"Yeah, sort of, but legal."
>   Dialogue between the call girl Vivian Ward and raider Edward
>   Lewis, from the film Pretty Woman.

In effect, the raiders' real objective is not long-term ownership, but the opportunity to break up these companies into pieces and to sell them at the highest returns possible. This same procedure is being used in the real estate business where houses are bought and then sold as condominiums. But for real estate speculations, the same is true that they are not connected with a growth in social productivity.

If the raiders cannot break up companies into various pieces, they proceed in the following manner: Having first bought the firm below value, and after having made some cosmetic improvements, they offer large stock packages back on the market. In spite of the great indebtedness due to the mortgages—or rather because of this condition—the stocks of these companies will have increased tremendously in economic value after said maneuver. Because interest decreases any profit it makes, the company does not pay taxes for years. As the self-nominated "world's greatest investor" Warren Buffet declared that a deal is a lot more profitable when the state can be eliminated as a 46 percent partner.[8] That was, of course, before the maximum tax was lowered to 32 percent.

Economic Ruin through the Prevalence of Purely Speculatory Deals

> *"The stock market of the 1920s was very different from the stock market of today. Back then, the market was infested by greed-crazed slimeballs, get-rich-quick speculators with the ethical standards of tapeworms, who shrieked "buy" and "sell" orders into the telephone with no concern whatsoever for the nation's long-term financial well-being. Whereas today they use computers."*
>   Dave Barry, Dave Barry Slept Here

The method of purchasing a company by paying the former owner with monies drawn from the future possession reminds us of the story of Baron von Münchhausen who pulled himself out of the swamp by his own hair. It is fairly easy to call the liar baron's bluff without exactly knowing the law of physics prevailing in his story. Likewise, one does not have to be an economist to recognize that the growth in the company's value attained through this ploy does not come out of the blue, but that somewhere there are victims who pay for it.

> *"The good Lord gave me my money."*
> John D. Rockefeller quoted by Richard B. Hofstadter,
> The American Political Tradition

If the company survives, it is the taxpayer who suffers because the company will not pay taxes for many years due to its large interest payments; if it goes bankrupt, it is the investors who have financed the LBOs by buying the junk bonds.[9] They are the ultimate sources of the raiders' wealth created "out of nothing" by the purchase. Pension funds, insurance deposits, and savings and loan associations (S&Ls) assets have been poured into junk bonds. The S&Ls have already collapsed and are being supported by the taxpayer at a cost estimated so far to be $500 million (and growing). Many insurance companies and pension funds are at risk because they bought too many junk bonds issued by companies in trouble or already insolvent.

Many companies have perished as a result of these raiding strategies.[10] But it is not only the loss of thousands of jobs and the social problems of the unemployed that have a damaging effect upon the economy. An economic crisis develops whenever there is an extended period where pure financial transactions promise higher profitability than innovative and productive activities. Thomas Jefferson pointed out this danger in urgent—though resigned—terms:

> The wealth acquired by speculation and plunder is fugacious in its nature and fills society with the spirit of gambling. The moderate and sure income of husbandry begets permanent inprovement, quiet life, and orderly conduct.[11]

This quotation is from a letter to George Washington from the year 1787. A few years later, in 1792, Jefferson warned anew.

> Agriculture, commerce and every thing useful must be neglected, when the useless employment of money is so much more lucrative.[12]

The United States has often gone through such phases of pure speculation. Until now, the country has always been able to overcome them because the speculative character of American capitalism has remained embedded in a work ethos based on achievement and productive transactions. But this is in no way guaranteed for the future. Speculative tendencies could acquire such proportions that the whole economy is immersed. Present developments do not make the possibility of such a decline appear totally unfounded.

Money Enjoys Itself

It is surely no coincidence that the figure most aptly symbolizing money was created at the place where the nature of money not only has been most clearly understood, but also where it has been most thoroughly turned into reality. By introducing the figure of "Uncle Scrooge," Walt Disney not only gave life to the image of the super-rich in the world of comics, by creating this image, he offered insights into the nature and the effect of money that may be superior to all theoretical reflections on this topic.

Scrooge's experiences, his actions and thoughts, are reflections upon money. A point of climactic happiness and the core of his existence for Scrooge consists of a bath in his money safe: It is a source of endless delight for him to jump in head first, to dive into the money, and to toss the coins into the air in such a manner that they rain down on his head and back like a shower.

I can think of no representation of money that would show its nature in a more revealing manner: It isn't a means to an end; rather, it is self-sufficient in its innermost core. It is like God, whose place it has taken, the final goal, the highest value. Money in itself is totally without meaning, as Scrooge symbolizes with childish delight; it wants nothing but to exist and to grow. As philosophers and folklore claim, money is meaningless. In a world that has lost its meaning, this pronouncement assumes a totally new significance. If the world has lost its meaning, the absolutely meaningless that exists only for its own sake necessarily assumes the highest rank. Money is the most perfect representation of the world not because its meaning is so complex but, on the contrary, because it is empty.

Scrooge is helpless because the safe fills more and more and because he does not know how to cope with this growth. In a desperate attempt to break the iron law of growth, he goes on a trip to spend money extravagantly. Returned from his travels, he has to watch helplessly as his employees ferry money in wheelbarrows to the safe. They inform him that "some crazy type" lived and ate in his hotels and restaurants during the last few weeks, that he used his railroads and airlines, that he emptied his gift shops, and that he generally left a fortune in Scrooge's economic empire. Scrooge—the money—has no chance to come to rest. There is no alternative to growth. You cannot leave it lying at rest; it needs motion; it seeks operation.[13]

Notes

1. Alexis de Tocqueville, *Democracy in America I*, p. 51.

2. F. Fürstenberg, "Art. Geld III, Soziologisch," in: *Die Religion in Geschichte und Gegenwart*, 3. Auflage. Tübingen: J.C.B. Mohr, 1958, Bd. II, p. 1317.

3. Alexis de Tocqueville, *Journey to America*, p. 260.

4. Georg Simmel, *The Philosophy of Money*, p. 237.

5. George Will, "Ripping Off Capitalism," *Washington Post*, September 1, 1991. Compare with Richard Cohen, "Greed Inc.," *Washington Post*, September 24,

1991, and Peter Carlson, "How the Rich Get Richer. Everything you ever wanted to know about executive compensation—but were too angry to ask," *Washington Post Magazine,* April 5, 1992.

   6. Advertisement in the *Washington Post,* September 4, 1989.

   7. The main difference from a real estate purchase by mortgage is that the "raider" not only takes a mortgage, but also speculates on the reserves of the pension funds of the enterprise that he will use to pay for the purchase.

   8. Quoted by Michael Lewis, *The Money Culture,* p. 69. Barlett and Steele document in their book *America: What Went Wrong?* that the relationship between taxes paid by corporations and taxes they escaped from paying due to interest deduction was reversed in the eighties for the first time since World War II. Although this relationship has continuously shifted in favor of taxes saved since the 1950s, it was the eighties that brought the big explosion of debts and lost taxes. During the seventies, $42 billion of taxes were paid and $22 billion saved through depreciation and interest. Today it is $67.5 billion paid versus $92.2 billion saved. It is obvious that these lost taxes have to be paid by others who do not have the privilege to save money this way. The tax rules for interest payments for the purchases of company stocks have often been criticized because they have the effect of a subsidy for leveraged buyouts, but efforts to change the legislation have never been successful (compare with Barlett and Steele, pp. 40, 190). The corporations and investment houses even advertise frankly with the argument that investors can escape paying taxes thanks to interest deductions (compare with Barlett and Steele, p. 59).

   9. Lewis, *The Money Culture,* p. 70.

   10. A well-known example is Eastern Airlines. Many commercial and fashion houses, like Bloomingdale's, Brooks Brothers, and AnnTaylor, have been involved in the bankruptcy of the Canadian raider Campeau. The famous commercial house Macy's is nearly ruined due to the buyout by its own director. Another example is the big publishing house Harcourt, Brace, Jovanovich. Barlett and Steele list many more of these spectacular cases.

   11. Jefferson to George Washington, August 14, 1787, in *The Papers of Thomas Jefferson,* vol. 12, p. 38.

   12. Jefferson to Plumard DoRieux, January 6, 1792, in *The Papers of Thomas Jefferson,* vol. 23, p. 27.

   13. How close the figure Uncle Scrooge is to reality is shown by a comment by a billionaire that Wolf von Lojewski quotes in his book on America. This billionaire has been asked in a television interview: "You have earned in a rather short time two billions. Two billions. What are you going to do with such a lot of money?" He didn't think for one second and said plainly: "The third billion" (*Amerika,* p. 145).

Money, Part II

Democratizing Money

Will modern society be helplessly victimized by the process of monetarization in America and imitated all over the world? Neither utopian economic systems nor appeals to the supposed intrinsic good in human nature are meaningful alternatives. Devices to control money's destructive dynamics must be derived from its inherent structure. Money and freedom are closely related. Like money, freedom is meaningless in itself; it is pure motion away from something, a severance. Freedom like money seeks to expand if no outside forces interfere. But an expansion of freedom paradoxically yields not more but less freedom. In his treatise on ethics, Aristotle defined the principle of *mesotes,* the median that governs all human actions. According to this thesis, increased good does not continuously result in something better but at a certain point turns into its opposite. In Aristotle's view, human values are not something one-dimensional that can be attained with the simple equation "more = better." Rather, they are located in a median position between two extremes (= nonvalues). In figurative terms, their structure is not represented by a straight line that rises into infinity, but by a wave with an optimal zenith. Once this high point is reached, there is no increase in value, only a renewed decline into the other extreme.[1]

This law applies to freedom as well. Unlimited freedom, freedom that transgresses borders, does not lead to more freedom but rather to the loss of its actual content: One loses the capacity to set goals, to be self-determining. Freedom, the optimal zenith, is threatened from two sides: the condition of bondage from which it emancipated itself and the inability to make use of freedom, i.e., to

43

develop voluntary ties. Freedom from something is empty and destructive if it is not linked to freedom toward a specific objective.

The same law applies to the nature and the effects of money. The freedom that modern societies enjoy by virtue of the money culture threatens to reverse to its opposite if it is taken to extremes and not given direction. It may be initially liberating to dissolve all value concepts, but this process deteriorates until it destroys all ties. Emancipation without an individual or social value system turns into rootlessness. In his *Philosophy of Money,* Georg Simmel explored this as the core of money's nature:

> An extraordinary amount of freedom is realized by the fact that, where all this [—businesses and factories, works of art and collections, landed property, rights and positions of all kinds—] remains the property of one person for an increasingly shorter period, the person changes the specific conditions of such property more quickly and frequently. However, since money with its indeterminateness and its inner lack of direction is the other side of these processes of liberation, they often do not advance beyond this uprooting, and fail to sink new roots. In fact, since under very rapid money transactions possessions are no longer classified according to the category of a specific life-content, that inner bond, amalgamation and devotion in no way develops which, though it restricts the personality, none the less gives support and content to it. This explains why our age, which on the whole, certainly possesses more freedom than any previous one, is unable to enjoy it properly.[2]

Thus, modern man in his freedom—"free because he can sell everything, and free because he can buy everything— . . . now seeks in the objects themselves that vigor, stability, and inner unity that he has lost because of the changed money-conditioned relationship that he has with them."[3] The objects that money has exposed in all their *indifference* now are assigned "a new importance, a deeper meaning, a value of their own."[4] This is the core of cultivated materialism, of consumer ideology, wherein the act of acquisition itself looks for a compensation of lost values. This is done in vain because with "the hoped-for satisfaction that is connected with new acquisitions, and immediately grows beyond them, . . . the core and meaning of life always slip through one's hands."[5]

When freedom deteriorates and turns into mere uprootedness, it no longer contributes to the individual's self-realization that it initially spurred. On the contrary, it now leads to a loss of orientation and to other-directedness. Similarly, the severance of money from all values connecting a democratic society is not propitious to the democractic progress once spurred and advanced by money.

Freedom itself can never be the source of self-determination because freedom—like money—only enjoys itself. Freedom, if it is to mean self-determination, needs a connection to values outside of itself. Self-determination means being tied to a personal value system, to a personal ethic, that determines the use of freedom and necessarily limits its use. Money, as a socially determining factor, must analogously be tied to an external value system. Obviously, in a democratic society these values are those which constitute the essence of democracy: justice, equality (or at least equal opportunity), solidarity, liberty, right to participate, etc. Money is the formative force of the bourgeois society, just as nobility inherited by birth determined the aristocratic order. Both possessed a social legitimation. Class differences in aristocracy could be traced to the protective function of nobility in the fight against hostile neighbors. It was only when this raison d'être was lost and when birth privileges nonetheless continued to govern the social strata that the aristocracy became obsolete.

A similar fate threatens bourgeois society when money becomes disconnected from its legitimizing basis as emancipatory principle and dominates the social order absolutely.

One may argue that in practical terms modern society is not empowered to subject money to democratic principles. But why? Because no serious effort has been made to try it? If a democratic society fails to control money in a democratic fashion, this is not necessarily proof that money cannot be checked. On the contrary, the role of money in a democratic society depends upon how clearly and self-confidently society understands democracy and its ruling principles. If a society clearly professes its allegiance to a "democratic ethic," to the integral values of democracy, then the process of democratizing money is no unsurmountable problem. Money is not as almighty as it appears.

A Public Philosophy of Money

Because money owes its existence and its value to the backing of the state, the state can easily exercise restraint. Without the guarantee provided by the state, money is not worth the scrap of paper on which it is printed. This allows the state to exert a great influence on the impact of money in society. Because of liberalized trade and the free movement of money, the states have lost many of the mechanisms that traditionally exerted influence. But that does not mean that they have to resign themselves to helplessly watching the erratic flow and ruthless reign of international money development. It could also be a call for more intensive international attention and control.

The state's decisive weapon in the battle against the power of money is taxation. It ultimately regulates the course of money in a society. The development of American society in the eighties and the ways in which money ran amok here can be clearly traced to the Reagan government's changes in tax laws,[6] many of which were also supported by the Democrats. Tax laws reflect a society's political philosophy; more than an economic instrument, they are indicators of the fundamental political principles to which a society subscribes.

In his 1955 book, *The Public Philosophy,* Walter Lippmann, one of America's most prominent journalists, devised an exciting modern theory about private property and public philosophy. Here he points out a congenital defect of capitalism following from the fact that property is no longer tangible (land), but has been replaced by intangibles (money, stock). Lost in this change was the public philosophy, natural and obvious until then, that both rights and duties were connected with property.[7] Lippmann occasionally calls this public philosophy the natural law, although he makes it unmistakably clear that, unlike natural laws, these laws do not determine what is but what should be.

> They are the principles of right behavior in the good society, governed by the Western traditions of civility.[8]

In the context of these principles, private property is not meant to satisfy primitive human instincts for acquisition and ownership. Rather, it is designed to foster the great ideals of a civilized society, which include peace and security for individuals.[9]

According to Lippmann, the modern state has broken with this tradition. It has not incorporated the concept of property into a public philosophy, but has left it entirely to the fluctuations of the market. In Lippmann's presentation, William Blackstone and other thinkers at the end of the eighteenth century had already developed a theory of property discrediting "exclusive and unrestrained disposal over property." But this "public philosophy" was based upon the familiar form of landownership, a model where the duties of ownership were obvious. In Lippmann's view, people at the turn of the eighteenth century either were not aware of the problem or were not up to the task of defining the "duties" connected with the possession of stock, shares, and money. Thus, he claims, the concept of property as a limited right deteriorated to an absolute right. To bring Lippmann's position to the point: The way modern societies shy away from putting restrictions on the disposition of money is alien to the Western tradition of civility.

In its crudest form, this concept of ownership of money as an absolute right applies chiefly in the United States, but the dynamics of money threaten the limitations still accepted in other parts of the world. It is the task of political philosophy to discover the mechanisms by which a society exercises its rights to govern money and to strengthen the checks and balances needed for the survival of civilization in modern democracy.

Without claiming to generate such a "public philosophy" at this point, we should consider the relation between money and democratic principles as well as the possibilities of translating these values into reality within six major areas: money and pluralism, money and justice, money and freedom, money and property, money and solidarity, and money and equality.

Money and Pluralism

It is a mortal sin committed against the spirit of democracy to accept money as the absolute determinant of all social processes and norms of behavior. The life of democracy is control, compromise, checks and balances. It follows then that the totalitarian tendency by which money transforms all aspects of society in its own image slowly undermines democratic variety and pluralism.

It is interesting in this respect to look at the parallels between the ascendancy of money in the modern society and the ascendancy of power as an absolute toward the end of the seventeenth and in the eighteenth centuries. In both cases, these mechanisms evolved without reason, for their own sake. Neither then nor now is there any justification for society to be so completely overwhelmed by political power in one case or by the influence of money in the other.

In the case of political absolutism, power was exhausted simultaneously with its climax. Absolutism contains the seed of its own decline and a total reassessment of political values. Absolute power, not merely tolerated but also accepted as divine revelation, was replaced by a division of powers and ultimately by democracy. Perhaps in some not too distant future, people will look back with amused incredulity at the ways in which we accepted the totally unjustified arrogance of money, just as predemocratic people considered it natural to obey unconditionally any cretin who happened to be born by God's grace as the son of a king.

Money and Justice

In the long run, the salary differences between the mass of wage earners and the power elite that have developed in the United States are incompatible with the ideal of justice. They can and must be eliminated without interfering with the spirit of the free-market system. There are interesting innovations under way in the United States. A very successful company in Vermont, Ben & Jerry's, designed a salary structure under which managers earn a maximum of seven times the salary of the lowest-paid employee. There is no economic or political reason why a democratic society cannot design for itself a set of regulations to limit differences between income levels.

In America, public outrage over business executives' excessive monetary rewards and perquisites exerted so much pressure that a wide array of corrections are being made. It can be said without irony: Democracy is working. Unfortunately, however, only the symptoms are being addressed; what is needed is a thorough confrontation with the money culture at the root of these excesses.

Money and Freedom

The value system of a society to a large degree regulates the rank and power of money. This is evident from the widely different priorities assigned to capital and labor in developed Western democracies. The strategy of downsizing in order to keep a company sound is possible in Germany only after expensive benefit plans for the involuntarily retired workers have been designed and financed. In the United States, companies that file for bankruptcy under chapter 11 are even permitted under reconstruction to stop their payments to the company's pension funds. While the state watches unperturbed as thousands lose their jobs in banking institutions and related businesses as a result of the savings and loan catastrophe, everything possible is done to save the investments of stockholders and speculators.

Other highly developed capitalist systems operate quite successfully with a limit placed upon the extent to which capital dominates employment. Furthermore, the ruthless preference granted to capital did not create a greatly improved or particularly efficient economy in the United States.

The wild tactics of buying, raiding, and reselling companies with the help of gigantic stock transactions that became the trademark of the eighties ended up costing hundreds of thousands of jobs. The reduction in the labor force did not, however, lead to healthier companies. Rather, it was the sad consequence of their emaciation due to their huge debts run up to finance their purchase. Not only individual companies, but the entire American economy as well was undermined by the piracy of capital. Barlett and Steele in their 1992 book, *America, What Went Wrong?*, examined the correlation between the liberation of money from all legal and social controls and the destruction of America's economic and social infrastructure.[10]

Money and Property

Farmland is currently being sold at a tremendous rate in the United States. In this process, personal property becomes corporate property. Owning a piece of land has always meant more than can be expressed in monetary value. It made life stable and meaningful; it provided life with a goal, a task, and fulfillment. It seems as though the Western idea of landownership is finally being confronted with its metaphysical contradiction of declaring something as one's possession that is the common property of the human race[11] as was the "primitive" concept of land by which the Native Americans, among others, lived.

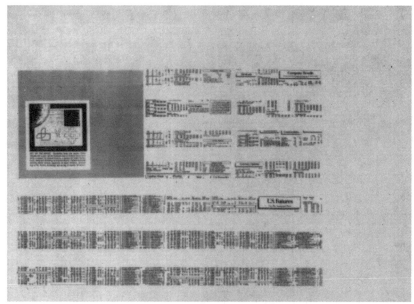

"US-Futures"

Landownership in the emphatic form with personal ties is becoming more and more outdated; the land as real estate becomes merchandise like any other, a certificate, a stock, a piece of paper. With this process, however, the Western concept of ownership loses its sole justification against a "primitive" value system that considers land to belong to no one.

There will be no return to the Native American philosophy of ownership, but the ever evolving monetarization of landownership forces a rethinking of its social rank and value. A hereditary lease instead of landownership might very well be the instrument more fitting for this new situation, an instrument that would better regulate the relations between the individual and the land that "belongs to all." This would also take into account the transitory character of human existence as opposed to the immortality of the soil.

Money and Solidarity

There are enormous philosophical differences between Europe and the United States about how much social responsibility those owning property should exercise. While this principle has been highly internalized in Europe—in Germany it is even protected by the constitution—such deliberations are alien to Americans. The rich and the property owners in the United States do indeed have a moral obligation to help the community with generous contributions and foundations, and not only do they take this responsibility more seriously than in any other country, but they also act on it with greater urgency. But the thought that money-making in itself should be socially responsible does not occur to Americans easily with the exception perhaps of such mavericks as Walter Lippmann.

Let us not forget, however, that we are not dealing with two different economic orders, but with two variations of the same capitalist system. The Americans exemplify one extreme that seeks the greatest possible benefit—for society as a whole as well as the individual—in the unimpeded development of money; Europeans, on the other hand, mistrust the power exerted by money and place limits on it for the benefit of the community. Yet, the legal or, in the case of Germany, constitutional obstacles facing money as a power are only as strong as their support in a corresponding social consciousness. At this point in Europe, traditional value concepts still shore up this limitation of money's reign, albeit unconsciously. But they are fighting an uphill battle against the firm demand that money reign supreme in society. If the idea that money carries certain social obligations is to gain larger support or at least to survive, it will have to be spread wider and more intensively within democratic societies.

Money and Equality

Finally, there is another instrument for breaking or at least taming the power of money—placing limits on inheritances. Concerning this issue, it is again helpful to observe the battle mankind has been fighting to limit political power and to increase individual and social liberties. An outgrowth of the democratic idea is the thought that power—from a certain point on, wealth is power—should not be inherited. If drastic limits are placed on inherited wealth, it would neither result in a paralysis of capitalist impulses nor would it restrict democratic liberties excessively.

In its time, it was the most natural thing in the world that the king and the nobility would bequeath their children political power. Today, that seems like an intolerable situation, something we would never live with anymore. However, we accept the handing down of economic power just as unquestioningly because we have become accustomed to this practice and don't know any differently. Is there any reason why we should not apply the laws about economic power with the same decisive effect upon humans as we habitually use them in relation to political power? The democratic principle concerning the equality of opportunities requires that conditions with which people start their lives be equal: This is impossible when huge inheritances create vast differences.

Nor would a restriction of inheritances greatly strain the principle of freedom. If everyone begins with equal opportunities, everyone is at liberty to make the best of these opportunities offered in the course of his or her life. Of course, the freedom to decree what is to happen to one's possessions is limited after death, a realm in which one should not want to conduct further business anyway.[12]

An Ideology of Generosity

These outlines of a public philosophy of money are not even remotely close to any political realization. On the contrary, we find ourselves in the reverse situation, where politicians do everything to accommodate the highly developed orientation toward money. But does it mean it is utopian to work toward the goal of putting reins on the money culture, to keep money, one of the generating forces of democracy, from becoming the source of its destruction?

It is a fatal mistake to use money as the supreme orienting force. By this everything falls under the law of reciprocity, the counter-deal. Every act is examined under the premise: Do I get back—directly or indirectly—the same value I spent or—even better—more than I put in? It is not difficult to see where this principle—taken to extremes—will lead: If the law of strict reciprocity, of cost orientation, is taken too far, any community life will freeze to death.

One possible solution for escaping the stranglehold of reciprocity would be a system of thinking in greater dimensions, in terms of time, place, and content. It could be called an ideology of generosity, of magnanimity, and it would have its place between money's petty calculations and altruism's boundless scope.

The word *generosity* contains both the word for species (*genus*) and generation; indeed, this is an attitude that applies to a reciprocity of far-flung dimensions. Nor is it in any way a new attitude; rather, it was the behavior that for centuries controlled the so-called traditional societies. One generation gave to the next because it had been the benefactor of the previous one. People donated to others without expecting from them anything other than that they would be generous in turn. This is how an attitude based on charity and assistance develops; whatever a person invests in society is no longer returned in a reciprocal and controllable manner, but in an anonymous and satisfying form.

Is this concept outdated? Did it not render itself obsolete as a value cherished by traditional societies when these were replaced by modern societies? Is it at all compatible with the fundamental principle according to which modern society is organized, i.e., individual self-determination and liberty? Is it possible that this concept is not only old-fashioned but even undemocratic, insofar as it may restrict the individual's right to act as he or she sees fit?

The new element in the ideology of generosity as opposed to the traditional solidarity of community and generations is inherent above all in the fact that it is a conscious attitude rather than an unconscious emotion. It is in harmony with the right to self-realization, which represents one of the most important premises of life in a democracy, whereas in traditional societies, the claims of the community prevailed absolutely over any individual needs.

The ideology of generosity does not deny the priority of the individual's right to self-realization, but it acknowledges that self-realization happens in the community and to the individual as one in a chain of generations. The generous person gives voluntarily so that a community may develop that is suited for him or her to live in. This process differs from the egotism coined by monetary concerns in that this person does not demand but expects, does not calculate but enjoys, does not sever but connects, does not foster cool but warm relations.

There are two phenomena in Western societies pointing to the need for a reorientation in the direction just outlined. For one, only a society living in affluence can afford such an attitude. This condition is met today even if the members of the developed Western societies continue to act as though they cannot get enough. This can be traced back less to traditional behavior than to the advertising industry, which continuously stimulates consumers to buy. Yet, we often have a tormentingly clear feeling of being surrounded by and drowned in things both superfluous and burdensome, and that material wealth impoverishes life. Deep inside we are revolted by affluence and are ready to renounce it. This emotion is diffuse and cannot articulate itself; it is constantly subject to confusion, feels helpless in a hostile environment—but it exists. It needs to be confirmed.

The second aspect is the growing recognition that Western societies are living beyond their means. Even using monetary categories, we are coming to realize that we are expecting coming generations and third world countries to pay for our generation's environmental pollution and exploitation. We are beginning to doubt the infallibility of the monetary ideology once praised as the ultimate wisdom. At least now and then, the monumental proportion of our sins against the coming generations takes our breath away, and we would like to change our mode of behavior. This feeling is no more than an indication, not a promise to change our minds, but a beginning on which a new social ethics could be constructed. The once sound world of monetary thinking proves brittle. An ideology in which everyone receives back exactly what he or she has expended looks highly questionable in light of the ruinous destruction it has wreaked on everything our lives are founded upon.

There are many indications that Americans are ready to redirect their lives. The great psychoanalyst Erik Erikson coined the term *generativity*, which has at its core a similar demand as the idea of generosity we just discussed.[13] Erikson defines generativity as the care one generation imparts to another. This behavior need not be forced upon humans. It already exists as a completely natural concern in the way families provide for the well-being of their children. Erikson would like to expand this inherited human virtue to where it would apply to all persons and objects in our trust, e.g., it should include concern for the society which we hand down to our children, concern for the environment and the political order.

Erikson is not alone in holding these ideas. With his design for new ways in which the liberal society assesses itself, the philosopher Richard Rorty moves in a similar direction. Bellah et al., taking Erikson's ideas as a point of departure, developed concrete suggestions for a politics of generativity.[14] This ideology would have two main pillars: a reliable "social net" for all members of society and a chance to be active not only in political but also in economic decision-making. Based on its nature, a politics of generativity cannot leave social developments to arbitrary forces. It would, rather, submit to a regulatory apparatus; it "sets limits beyond which the market and money alone have no say."

Bellah et al. are aware that such a politics of generativity cannot be enforced, that such a "Good Society," as they call their plan in reference to Walter Lippmann's vision, cannot be created by an administrative act. What would be needed to carry this out in America are fundamental changes in the national mentality, above all a shift away from the emphasis on the individual's rights within society. The individual tradition in American political philosophy, which goes back to Locke, manifested itself excessively in the eighties, as it has several times before in American history. Even though the yuppie euphoria has died down somewhat, this tradition still influences the American political climate.

Yet the ideas about an alternative social direction we devised here have certain chances to see the light of day. As American history proves, this society does not evolve in a constant linear fashion but is subject to wild swings of the pendulum from one extreme to the other. The notions introduced by Lippmann, Erikson, Bellah, and others are not alien to the American self-understanding. Even if Locke's ideology essentially influenced America's development, there always were—parallel and in opposition to it—forceful countercurrents that had a moderating and limiting impact upon the predominant social direction. There is, for instance, Henry David Thoreau's vision that situates the chances of individual self-realization not in acquisitions but in frugality. There is, on the other hand, the arch-American "community spirit," the awareness of the need to become involved in the community and that it is in the community where human life finds its ultimate fulfillment.

Bellah et al. point to the impressive list of intellectual fathers and political forerunners of their ideas.[15] There is the Protestant social gospel movement, which originated in the last decades of the past century when a similar epidemic of individualistic and capitalistic arbitrariness broke out. They regard it in its intellectual teleology as a model and as a ray of hope in its political effects.

The so-called Golden Era of a capitalism that had run amok simultaneously gave birth to a massive reform movement and even revolution. It was personified by the populists whose symbolic figure was William Jennings Bryan. Even though it did not fully succeed, the populist movement essentially triggered the passing of a wave of legislation that decisively limited and slowed the arbitrary nature of American capitalism. Bellah et al. point out that the concept of capitalism's social responsibility was adopted even in capitalist circles by the turn of the century. They quote Henry Lee Higginson, a leading member of Boston's industrialist circles, who wrote in 1911:

> I do not believe that, because a man owns property, it belongs to him to do with as he pleases. The property belongs to the community, and he has charge of it, and can dispose of it, if it is well done and not with the sole regard to himself or to his stockholders.[16]

The climax of the populist reform movement coincided with the introduction of a progressive income tax.[17] Income tax may appear to us as the most self-evident and fundamental premise of a modern state today. But the constitutional amendment in 1913, which paved the way for income tax legislation, signaled a social revolution of immense proportions. It demonstrated the force of the powerful countercurrent aimed at an unbridled extension of American capitalism.

In his book *The Present Age,* sociologist Robert Nisbet points out that in the years immediately preceding World War I, the socialist movement was in the process of establishing a toehold in America and would probably have succeeded if America had not entered the war.[18]

The war was more than an interruption; it took the political wind out of the alternative traditions in America. In the years after World War I, Americans regressed to social ideas that they had long surpassed. It was America's self-proclaimed isolation that successfully blocked the nation from intellectual movements evolving in other parts of the world. But just as in the Golden Era, intellectual and political countermovements were not arrested during the Roaring Twenties. The progressive movement laid the groundwork for Franklin Roosevelt's later social legislation. The intellectual confrontation with the myth of American individualism, which culminated in Lippmann's grandiose sociopolitical designs, also continued.

The parallels between the twenties and the eighties are obvious. There has not been a big crash yet, and there may not be one. History does not repeat itself verbatim. The consequences of the uncurbed orientation toward money, however, not only in America, but this time globally, are the same.

At the end of the roaring drunkenness of the twenties, capitalism had not only exhibited its evil side, but also its inability to cope with the economic and social havoc it had wreaked. Now President Roosevelt received an overwhelming mandate for his New Deal programs. The word *deal* is ambiguous, and this was most probably intended. One can interpret "new deal" in pragmatic terms as a new political method or in visionary terms as a sort of new social contract. The New Deal, indeed, introduced a series of radically new, socially flexible economic policies, but Roosevelt's New Deal did not see itself as a dialogue with the fundamental concepts of capitalist ideology as Hamilton had devised the official version of the American dream—where acting on one's natural egotism not only yields the individual's happiness, but is also the foundation for a flourishing community. This dream remained alive and only needed to be conjured up with a few magical words by Ronald Reagan. In our times an intellectual new deal, a reevaluation of American ideas and ideals, is needed to free the American society from the morass into which it is being driven deeper and deeper by the overwhelming egotism of its members.

Egotism, competition, growth are social values that have made America great. When they are overvalued or taken to an extreme, they threaten this society and its achievements. The new deal has to take place in the minds and hearts of Americans. The new values needed now—social conscience, moderation, generosity—are not alien to the American mind. The alternatives to American society's money-based structures are as old as the nation's history.

In the initial years of the republic, two contrasting concepts for the development of the state faced each other—the capitalist pursued by Alexander Hamilton and the pastoral divined by Thomas Jefferson. Hamilton's concept proved to be so pervasive and controlling that it has become identified with America, and America fully consents to this identification. The alternate idea of a life of moderation instead of ruthless competition is dormant for the moment but not dead. Now that Hamilton's concept that made this nation great has obviously reached its limits, perhaps the time is ripe for the opposite idea.

Notes

1. Aristotle, *"Nichomachean Ethics"* II.6.1106b36. Compare also with the third chapter—"Pursuit of Happiness."
2. Georg Simmel, *The Philosophy of Money,* p. 403.
3. Ibid., p. 404.
4. Ibid.
5. Ibid.
6. Compare with William Greider, *Who Will Tell the People?* p. 90; and Barlett and Steele, *America: What Went Wrong?* especially chapter 3—"Shifting Taxes from Them to You."
7. Walter Lippmann, *The Essential Lippmann,* p. 188.
8. Ibid., p. 192.
9. Ibid., p. 190, where he quotes Blackstone.
10. Barlett and Steele, *America: What Went Wrong?* especially pp. 12, 20, 32, 144.
Barlett and Steele show that the loss of work did not only affect the workers who became unemployed and their families, but it was also responsible for the economic depression of entire communities and regions.
11. Thomas Paine, "Agrarian Justice," *The Thomas Paine Reader,* p. 476. Compare with Blackstone quoted by Lippmann, *The Essential Lippmann,* p. 189.
12. The legitimation of the inheritance of power and its explosive effect for society had already been recognized as a serious problem by philosophers at the end of the eighteenth century. Jefferson came across this question due to his thesis that the earth belongs to the living. Jefferson to Madison, June 9, 1789, *The Portable Jefferson,* p. 450; compare also with Blackstone as quoted by Lippmann, *The Essential Lippmann,* p. 189.
13. Introduction of Erikson's expression by Robert N. Bellah et al., *The Good Society,* p. 273.
14. Bellah et al., *The Good Society,* p. 276.
15. Ibid., *Habits of the Heart,* p. 257; *The Good Society,* pp. 279, 295.
Compare also with Richard Hofstadter, *Social Darwinism in American Thought,* p. 105, chapter VI—"The Dissenters"; and *The American Political Tradition,* p. 186, chapter VIII—"William Jennings Bryan: The Democrat as Revivalist."
16. Bellah et al., *Habits of the Heart,* p. 260.
17. Barlett and Steele show that the tax legislation of the eighties and the involved social changes have practically abrogated the progressive income tax.
18. Robert Nisbet, *The Present Age,* p. 9.

The

Existential

Runner

One of the most conspicuous sights on the streets of America is the swarm of people jogging. You can see them at any time of the day, doing laps in the parks, running on the sidewalks, or even in the streets. Lately, this sport has also found a following in Europe and other parts of the world; people of all age groups have taken it up as exercise and as a measure complementing an occasional diet. In America, however, jogging seems to be more than just a pastime or a health program. Rather, it appears to be the expression of a kind of national philosophy. Even if not every member of society subscribes to it, it is predominant within those classes that determine the overall character of a nation's culture. The orientation toward physical well-being—jogging is just the most prominent of such activities as aerobics, body-building, weight-watching (organized dieting)—is not just some kind of craze. Rather, it is an important social phenomenon comparable to the vital cultural role of sports in classical Greece.

Primordial Instincts

Jogging actually seems to be the expression of a kind of primordial, all-American instinct: "To run" does not imply escape, but to charge ahead. Think of jogging as the last remnant, the ritualized repetition, a virtual version of the great American Western movement, the continuous drive toward the Western frontier. The conquest of the West may have reached its physical limitations at the Pacific shore. But this has not placated the American soul, which is perpetually searching for ever new frontiers.

Alexis de Tocqueville was of like opinion. To him restlessness was part of the American character. In his travel account he quotes the words of the well-educated Joel Poinsett, a former American ambassador to Mexico:

The land never stays in the hands of the one who clears it. When it begins to yield a crop, the pioneer sells it and plunges again into the forest. It would seem that the habit of changing place, of turning things upside down, of cutting, of destroying, has become a necessity of his existence.[1]

Commenting upon these thoughts in his analysis of democracy in America, Tocqueville writes:

America is a land of wonders, in which everything is in constant motion and every change seems an improvement. The idea of novelty is there indissolubly connected with the idea of amelioration. No natural boundary seems to be set to the efforts of man; and in his eyes what is not yet done is only what he has not yet attempted to do.

This perpetual change which goes on in the United States, these frequent vicissitudes of fortune, these unforeseen fluctuations in private and public wealth, serve to keep the minds of the people in a perpetual feverish agitation, which admirably invigorates their exertions and keeps them, so to speak, above the ordinary level of humanity. The whole life of an American is passed like a game of chance, a revolutionary crisis, or a battle.[2]

Democracy Makes People Move

Everywhere during his travels and in society Tocqueville saw America in movement, and he considered this to be further guarantee for the stability of democracy:

Agitation and mutability are inherent in the nature of democratic republics, just as stagnation and sleepiness are the law of absolute monarchies.[3]

Agitation and mutability are American national virtues. No other people professes them so clearly and proudly as positive values. Tocqueville explains:

The American has no time to attach himself to anything, he is only accustomed to change and ends by looking on it as the natural state of man. Much more, he feels the need of it, he loves it, for instability instead of causing disasters for him, seems only to bring forth wonders around him. (The idea of a possible improvement, of a successive and continuous betterment of the social condition, that idea is ever before him in all its facets.)[4]

The founding fathers also thought that steady movement in a society was an effective guarantee for the conservation of democratic structures. For James Madison, the possibility of continuous physical expansion gave rise to the hope that the new political order created by the authors of the Constitution would persist in the future. In *The Federalist Papers*, No. 10, which deals with the causes of party strife and conflict of interests in a body politic, Madison devises the following strategy to avoid the dangerous consequences:

Extend the sphere and you take in a greater variety of parties and interests; you make it less probable that a majority of the whole will have a common motive to invade the rights of other citizens; or if such a common motive exists, it will be more difficult for all who feel it to discover their own strength and to act in unison with each other.[5]

Madison's expectations were justified. The extension of territory, the possibility of unconfined movement, has reduced or prevented tensions. The migratory movement did not cease even after the country's territorial borders were reached. In the heart of Americans, the frontier is still wide open. However, the dream of the open frontier and the land of unlimited opportunities stretching out beyond is now in danger of falling short of reality.

The great migration of Southern blacks to find employment in the industrial centers of the North in the 1920s and the decades after World War II were an expression of such a dream. Many ended up leading desperate lives in the ghetto, although for others resettlement did bring the desired breakthrough to the middle class. Also, moving out of the isolation of the rural South to the urban centers of the North gave blacks the chance to develop a political representation of their own. The civil rights movement and the political progress that came with it would otherwise have been inconceivable.

A further historic migration is the movement from the city to the suburbs. It has altered America's outward appearance but also changed its social structure, its system of values, and its way of life. Even after the closing of the Western frontier, the American people are still on the move. The exodus into the suburbs was motivated by the old American dream of having a house of your own. This migration is still going on. Even if the emigration is not always voluntary, often forced by harsh economic pressures, this doesn't affect the basically positive attitude of the Americans toward mobility.[6]

The latest relocation is from the cold of the Northern states to the Southern sun, from the Northeast and Middle West, burdened with the infrastructure of the first and second phases of industrialization, to the economically promising South with its high-tech industries.

The states of the South, and especially of the Southwest—Texas, California, Arizona, and New Mexico—are the new allurements for Americans' venturesome spirit and their perpetual quest for a better life: May it this time not only be richer, but also a bit more sunny.

Movement for Mobility's Sake

Even aside from these great historical migrations, the nation remains in motion. It is not unusual to pull up stakes to find a more demanding job or more beautiful surroundings, or a better school all the way across the continent or on the other end of town. At the center of every American dream stands a house of one's own—although it doesn't have to be the same house for an entire lifetime.

Building a home may be important—climbing the social ladder is even more so. Year after year, millions of Americans take up residence in some other part of the country. The invention of the mobile home mounted on a tractor trailer is the epitome of this kind of thinking.

> *"I couldn't wait to move on. I knew here could never be as sweet as there; going was a question, staying was an answer. Questions were better."*
>
> Linda Ellerbee, Move On. Adventures in the Real World

It is important to keep in mind the words of Tocqueville's American interview partner Joel Poinsett: "Mobility does not need to be legitimized by a goal, it is an end in its own right." Motion is always better than stagnation. The road reaching all the way to the horizon is frequently romanticized and commercialized in advertisements. Or, think of all the movies singing the praise of life on the road. Usually they are stories without plot but with overwhelming shots of the American landscape.

Thomas Jefferson, too, was convinced that mobility was an essential ingredient for the success of American democracy. But he was thinking of a mobility of a different kind than practical Madison. Jefferson called for intellectual mobility in which there would be a periodical overturn of the status quo. He wanted people to relinquish all traditions, even those most dear to them.

Proceeding from the principle that "the Earth belongs to the living—the dead shall have no power over them,"[7] Jefferson called on each new generation to extricate itself from the ideas and laws that once served to organize the societies of their parents and grandparents. His intention was not that each generation indiscriminately discard all its laws, but that each generation reappraise the laws passed down to them and confirm or reject them, or make new ones, in order to adapt to new structures of quickly changing times.[8]

Jefferson's ideas have become increasingly significant. His words about the world being the estate of the living also imply that no generation was entitled to lay any claim on the resources of the following ones. Otherwise the world would belong to the dead. The significance of these thoughts for the ecological discussion of today are evident. Proceeding from these conclusions, Jefferson developed even more radical ideas in regard to the economy and political order in general.

Intellectual Mobility Lets Democracy Rule

Jefferson recognized the incredibly dynamic force lying behind the progress of time. Time means flux. There is no other way but to change with it. You cannot just mount the Constitution on a tractor trailer. It is the human intellect that has the potential to adapt societies to changing circumstances. Jefferson's call for a "revolution" is just an emphatic appeal for the citizens to be mentally flexible.

Jefferson's concept of a periodic renewal of society was not merely an abstraction; he offered concrete and detailed plans. They might well have been implemented back then. His ideas were neither impractical nor utopian. The fact is that there was no support for this kind of radical democracy. Manufacturing and commercial interests deemed the safe and secure possession of private property vital to the stability of society, and they had already prevailed. Jefferson was far ahead of his time. His theory described a problem that has become a question of the survival of this planet. May the stipulation not to let ourselves be ruled by the dead finally be grasped in all its dire consequences.

Jefferson's idea of movement as intrinsic to democracy has always remained alive in America, not always in politics, but certainly in the history of American thought. The poets of American democracy, Ralph Waldo Emerson and Walt Whitman, have harped on this notion while John Dewey put it in philosophical terms: Question yourself, go a step further, to create something even better. Henry David Thoreau, who among the American philosophers of the nineteenth century has probably been most influenced by Jefferson, has strongly emphasized the idea of the permanent renewal and has poeticized it in the image of the morning.[9] It is one of the fundamental tenets of American political philosophy that democracy gets its ultimate legitimacy from the idea of constant progress toward a better society.

A watered-down version of this idea can be found, as Wolf von Lojewski in his book on America has pointed out, in the promises of every presidential candidate to rebuild America if he is elected.[10] Especially in the election year 1992, and even more radically in 1994, we witnessed an incredible upsurge of energy to start over again—the willingness to reshape the entire political environment. It is somewhat troubling, however, if one looks at both elections in perspective, that this longing for change seems to have no clear direction, but is almost swinging back and forth. But there is no doubt that change is still the center of the agenda and that the American people are willing to take risks. How strong this impulse will turn out to be, how long it will last, and where it will lead, developments will show. American politics is definitely in motion again.

In comparison, what a sorry sight are German politics in the time of accession of the Eastern German territories. In opting for the principle of the return of all disowned assets instead of monetary retribution, the men at the top have given away a onetime chance of making a new start. Not only have they managed to paralyze Eastern Germany with unprecedented administrative chaos, but they have also failed in the moral sense by opting for the dead instead of the living and future generations.

The idea of a cyclical reform of the Constitution, admittedly not in the radical Jeffersonian sense, has been incorporated into American constitutional practice. Jefferson feared that any detailed constitution would be too rigid to adjust to changing times, would no longer fit, and would become a straitjacket for the living. The American Constitution, however, has the admirable ability to adapt to the change of times. The American Constitution is in many respects something of a masterpiece of mankind, like an opera by Mozart, the Parthenon in Athens, or a painting by Raphael, or Tocqueville's book. They are more than just products of craftsmanship. A constitution, however, is subject to use; unlike aesthetic masterpieces, it is part of practical life. The American Constitution has proven to be sturdy and resilient. Its genius lies in the fact that many important aspects of the political order are defined in a way that is open to interpretation and adaptation.

The whole area of competing legislation between the states and the federal government receives detailed treatment only to be drawn in doubt by a general clause. Of course, you could maintain that the authors of the Constitution were incapable of making up their minds; as a consequence, they arrived at this awkward compromise between state and federal rights. But the concept of compromise in itself is actually quite ingenious because it manages to make opposites compatible.

Public Life Is Restless

Public life and especially political life in America is outwardly marked by an incredible amount of activity. Tocqueville remarked that something you really notice upon coming to America is the kind of perpetual emotional turmoil in which politics seems to occur.

> There is nothing more striking to a person newly arrived in the United States than the kind of tumultuous agitation in which he finds political society.[11]

Tocqueville's observation holds true today, maybe even to a greater extent because the areas of political responsibility have grown. The life of a member of Congress is a rat race. Many times a day a bell rings and lawmakers dash from their offices to cast their vote in the House a half mile away. Having cast their ballot, they rush back to meet with constituents, lobbyists, colleagues and to hold hearings, meet in committees, etc. To save time and energy in this considerable turmoil, a trolley has been installed, which is also available to tourists when Congress is not on a roll-call vote.

> *"And government programs aren't necessarily designed to go anywhere. Like the joggers beneath my window, who are the people who run those programs, they just go. The results—sweat, ruined knees, America as a second-rate world power—don't matter. It's the effort that makes the action worthy."*
>
> P.J.O'Rourke, Parliament of Whores

The legislative process itself is the prime example of this intense political activity. Every member of Congress has the right to introduce bills. They certainly make use of this prerogative. As soon as the media report on some scandal, or a new political problem is discovered or a citizens' group starts exerting pressure on an issue, you can be sure that in no time a number of legislators will claim that they are either preparing a bill, or have already introduced it, in order to solve the problem. Every year about twenty thousand bills are submitted. Most of these are so-called "private bills," which only pertain to a single person or organization. Most of these are subsequently axed somewhere in the dark alleys of Congress, but the introduction itself was at least worth a mention in the local newspaper or maybe even in the national media.

That movement is an end to itself generally holds true in American politics. A lot of it is just a kind of activism, political showbiz. But before being overly critical, one should remember Tocqueville's words about restlessness and movement being essential characteristics of democracy, unlike Europe, where movement is usually directed toward a purpose. This often has had a stifling effect on European politics.

Running for Office

Language gives us another clue to how close mobility and politics are in the United States. When an American aspires for political office, he says: "I'm running for office." Even the highest office, the presidency, is pursued with this kind of allusion to the physical. Is this just a case of American boastfulness, does it reflect a liberal use of language, or does "running" express a certain attitude toward politics?

In the early times of the nation, you could not have fairly described this process as running for president. Since the demise of the electoral college, however, the actual campaign between the presidential candidates of the two parties is a tour of the entire country. Due to the advent of modern transportation and the growing population, it has developed into a frantic marathon.

During his 1948 campaign, Harry S. Truman toured the United States for weeks in a chartered train. He stopped at every little place and talked directly to the people. What has become known as the whistle-stop tour is considered the main reason for the very surprising outcome of an election that months before had been considered the sure booty of Truman's Republican opponent. In his campaign against John F. Kennedy, Richard M. Nixon tried the same tactic but was less successful. He unwittingly promised to visit every single state. The weekend prior to the election, you could see him, totally fatigued, getting on a plane to Alaska.

Today, even the procedures for determining party candidates have turned into public contests before the votes. Once it was more like the European way of being selected for leadership by a relatively small circle of party bosses. With more and more states opting for primaries as the mode for selecting party nominees, the candidates have to run the marathon twice. Although the greatest part of the campaign budget is invested in nationwide television ads, the greatest physical effort still goes into local electioneering. The nomination of Jimmy Carter, less than twenty years ago, would not have happened if it had not been for the run to the voter. Carter, incidentally, was an avid jogger who introduced this national pastime to the White House.

Despite this considerable increase of activity and mobility it is obvious that the element of movement, as an essential part of politics and election campaigns, is diminishing, and regardless of the activity, momentum, and frantic movement, the body politic itself has given in to stagnation.

Election campaigns increasingly depend upon the television screen. They have turned into a kind of shoot-out between candidates by means of mudslinging and backstabbing television ads. Look at it from any angle: This "running" on radio waves, the direct appeal to the voter, has only produced running pictures, not a truly personal rapport with politicians.

This is a fundamental departure from the past. Instead of change, this kind of television campaign induces stagnation. In traditional campaigning, candidates appealed directly to the people, getting in close contact with them. This gave them a feeling for the problems of real live people, even if it was not a wholly genuine dialogue between voter and politician.

Television campaigning is sterile and artificial. In most of the television ads, the candidate is not actually the real person, but a contrivance concocted by marketing experts. So it is no coincidence that television ads are turning out increasingly negative—but successful. Inevitably, these products will boomerang on the politicians. They are damaging to ethics in politics—hardly noticed in the political arena itself. But they are also contributing to the rapid transformation of politics into artificial fakery and of politicians into spiritless puppets. Sacrifice movement in the campaign process, even if you still call it "running for office," and you destroy the fundamentals of democracy.

The last campaign gives reason for hope again. Not only were the voters offered a candidate who made the promise of political change and forward movement the central topic of his candidacy, but Bill Clinton also reintroduced mobility and movement into campaigning. For the first time, a seemingly unavoidable trend has been reversed, the trend toward more and more artificial campaigning over the airwaves, a one-sided electioneering via messages whereby voters are served political fast food from the screen. By going back to a style of politics in decline, since Truman's times, Clinton demonstrated to the voters that campaigning is movement. He was constantly seen running—either jogging himself or moving around with his buses on a whirlwind tour to the people, moving into the crowds, carrying politics personally into small villages and towns as well as big-city neighborhoods. There is no question that Clinton's bus tour through the country contributed significantly to his victory.

Notes

1. Alexis de Tocqueville, *Journey to America*, p. 89.
2. Ibid., *Democracy in America I*, pp. 425–26.
3. Ibid., p. 311.
4. Ibid., p. 183.
5. *The Federalist Papers*, No 10, James Madison, p. 83.
6. That doesn't mean that the constant movement of American society—as it is mirrored in the individual lifestyle of its members—does not have its dark sides. Some are extensively described in this book, like the cancerous energy of money, the race for ever more consumer goods and ever new entertainment, the inability to be silent and to cope with silence. The constant change of jobs is not always connected with career progress. It is often just an expression of the "hire and fire" mentality of business executives. The run for money is often a rush to earn enough for keeping up with the bills or even to run away from the debts.

The belief in progress forces the society to be permanently optimistic which in turn causes psychic disorders. It is no coincidence that in America—the land without melancholy—psychoanalysts have more patients than anywhere else. But even in treating the patients, America hasn't lost its mobility. The traditional couch of the psychiatrist has become obsolete. It is already possible to take part in group therapies via conference call—even from the car via mobile phone.

Mobility is without doubt an ambivalent phenomenon. In its exaggeration it becomes total rootlessness. Bellah et al. have dealt mainly with the negative aspects of the American restlessness. It is for them the main reason for the political fragmentation of the nation. They agree with Lewis Mumford, who wrote: "No civilization can exist on such an unstable and nomadic basis: it requires a settled life, based on the possibility of continuously cultivating the environment, replacing in one form what one takes away in another" (Donald L. Miller, *The Lewis Mumford Reader*, p. 213; compare with Bellah et al., *The Good Society*, p. 265).

There is an interesting remark by Paul Hollander that this inconstancy may be one of the reason for the anti-Americanism in the world: "The United States have exported—besides the well-known clichés like fast food, blue jeans and TV series—other threatening products of modernisation: insecurity—caused by social and geographical mobility, increase of individualism, loss of community, mindless acceptance of facts, adoration of change. This American unconditional openness can hardly be understood by other peoples and causes hostility." Paul Hollander, "Anti-Americanism: Opposing Trends," *International Herald Tribune*, July 4, 1992.

7. Jefferson to James Madison, June 9, 1789, *The Portable Jefferson*, p. 445.
8. Ibid., p. 449. Jefferson never abandoned this revolutionary idea in his life. He repeated it two years before he died in a letter to John Cartwright, June 15, 1824, *Writings*, p. 1493.
9. Henry David Thoreau, *Walden*, p. 58.
10. Wolf von Lojewski, *Amerika*, p. 11 (German edition).
11. Tocqueville, *Democracy in America I*, p. 419.

The

Oral

Society

Could it be that American society is still or is again in its oral phase?

First Impression

The chain of the Grand Tetons in the Rocky Mountains, arising abruptly out of the wide valley of the Snake River, is an impressive sight even to nature-spoiled Americans. In the Grand Teton National Park, the park rangers regularly organize raft trips of about three hours in length for the tourists. The snow-covered mountains rise majestically in the distance beyond the long, winding Snake River. The splendor and beauty of nature are absolutely breathtaking.

Not so for the ranger on the raft, who does not for one moment during the three-hour trip interrupt his flow of speech. This is apparently also true for the American tourists. Patiently, almost eagerly, they listen to the torrent of words that, in the truest sense, jumps from one topic to another: from the origin of the mountain range to the population of Wyoming, to the preferred food of bark beetles, to the mating habits of elks, to the varieties of fish living in the Snake River, to fir tree types in North America and on and on.

Second Experience

Whenever there is a forecast of a big snowfall, which might temporarily impede traffic, people in Washington, D.C., rush to the supermarkets to buy loads of food to stock their refrigerators. One sees overflowing parking lots in front of the food stores, inside long lines of customers waiting up to an hour at the checkout counters. This frantic buying spree for food is a major news event that is documented by numerous television crews and broadcast over and over again. Looking at these pictures, we must get the impression that Washington is on the eve of a famine or one is reminded of the situation in the former communist countries with their permanent food scarcity. Why is it that Americans, whose refrigerators are usually well stocked, are so obsessed with food that they panic at the very thought that the supermarket, rarely more than two miles away and usually open twenty-four hours a day, may for a while be difficult to reach.

America is obviously in love with the mouth in its two functions: talking or eating and drinking.

Americans love to talk—in their private lives, in society, and in public. Any visitor to the United States can make this observation in his first encounter with an American. At the passport control booth, the immigration official is not, as is the case in Germany, satisfied with a curt "Hello" or even with a bored nod of his head; the stranger is first greeted with "How are you doing today?" and then sent on his way with "Have a nice day" or "Have a nice stay in the United States." In the time span between these remarks there is ample opportunity for a short chat. Such observations are frequent wherever one encounters people in America. A surprising yet pleasant atmosphere of natural friendliness toward strangers persists. This friendly characteristic seems to me to originate from the easy flow of speech. It has been said that Americans are more open and friendly than most other people. This openness is conveyed by means of the spoken word.

Americans may not have invented small talk, but they are without a doubt the world-champion practitioners. The extremely active social life—community bazaars, office parties, club gatherings, and social contacts of all sorts—can only be mastered if one keeps talking. It may seem superficial by European standards, but the small talk fulfills a priceless social function in that it creates the possibility for such social gatherings.

> *"It's the secret of social ease in this country [America]. They talk entirely for their own pleasure. Nothing they say is designed to be heard."*
> *Evelyn Waugh,* The Loved One, *quoted by Paul Fussell,* BAD

This talk culture has a long tradition in America and is preserved in many variations and in all sectors of society. All small and large festivities and events in the private as well as the public spheres are marked and embellished by speeches.

In American history and national folklore, speeches play a significant role. Some prime examples are the farewell address of George Washington with his warning of the emergence of political parties, Thomas Jefferson's inaugural speech with its call for political tolerance, the Gettysburg Address during the Civil War by President Abraham Lincoln, Martin Luther King's speech ("I have a dream"), John F. Kennedy's inaugural address in 1961 ("Ask not what your

country can do for you, ask what you can do for your country"), and the famous "Checkers" speech by Richard Nixon during his first candidacy for vice president in 1952 with its tearful appeal to the American people.

Robert Bellah, who in his book *The Broken Covenant* documents the religious basis of American national and cultural self-understanding, emphasizes that the extraordinary meaningfulness of the spoken word in American society found its strongest manifestation in the sermon. According to Bellah, only one nationally recognized art form, the sermon, existed during the first phase of cultural development in America. From this form political speech informally developed. Bellah reminds his readers that:

> Ralph Waldo Emerson, the fountainhead of the American Renaissance, began as a minister and continued to use as his main form a lecture, a transparently secularized version of the sermon. Even in writers such as Thoreau, Melville and Whitman the influence of the spoken word, the chief idiom of cultivated American literature, is still very strong.[1]

The nineteenth century was not only a period of charismatic and sophisticated speeches, but also a time when the public was willing and inspired to intently follow often hourlong speeches. Neil Postman in his book *Amusing Ourselves to Death* depicts the famous debates between Lincoln and his rival Stephen A. Douglas, which often went on for hours on end. Postman presents these debates as an argument for a highly developed culture of speech both on the side of the speakers and the audience.[2]

The significance of the spoken word in politics is evident even in the case of the filibuster, a practice of the U.S. Senate. This practice was originally intended as a protection of the minority, as it can prolong or even prevent a vote through continuous talk. The filibuster is, in effect, so perverted that senators sometimes prolong their speaking time—often 10, 12 hours long—by reading aloud from the Bible or the telephone book.

> *"Democracy is about speech."*
> *Max Kampelmann*, Entering New Worlds

But there are more positive traces of a culture of speech. In American politics, from time to time, there are still genuine debates characterized by passionate language. Before controversial decisions—as was the case with the authorization to enter war against Iraq—supporters and opponents organize themselves in groups and take turns presenting their speeches as contributions to the cause.

The journalist Peggy Noonan has written a notable book, *What I Saw at the Revolution*, about her work as a speech-writer for President Ronald Reagan. She points out the importance of the spoken word in politics in spite of the dominance of television with its visible picture. She says quite correctly that speech, in contrast to the picture that shows the naked truth, has the ability, with the right words, to stir the imagination of the listener.[3]

Speeches also play an important role in religious life. In Protestant churches, services traditionally are centered not so much around liturgical events as around the word of God. Likewise, the Sunday sermon is the central focus of congregational life. The prestige of the pastor as well as the financial support of the parish—which is dependent upon voluntary contributions—is to a great measure contingent upon the competence of the pastor as a preacher. Most churches announce the topic of the following Sunday's sermon on a large board in front of the church or even in newspaper ads.

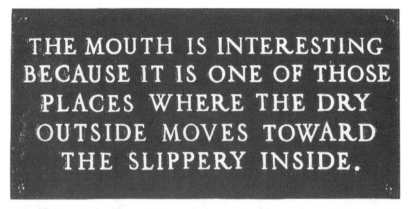

THE MOUTH IS INTERESTING BECAUSE IT IS ONE OF THOSE PLACES WHERE THE DRY OUTSIDE MOVES TOWARD THE SLIPPERY INSIDE.

Especially among black ministers, one can find great rhetorical talent. These preachers are able to hold their congregation in a religious trance every Sunday. In its extreme form, this religious rhetoric exists as television evangelism. The success of television preachers, who have built up empires of wealth on the financial profit of their appeal, is only partially explained by religious demand—it is also explained by the American love of the art of rhetoric. Despite his worldwide success, the phenomenon of Billy Graham is a social product that could only arise in America.

Already in the early nineteenth century, precursers to these television evangelists existed at enormous camp meetings, where rebirth in Christ was preached and allegedly experienced. Such meetings now take place in large convention centers or sports arenas; endless sermons and testimonials, eagerly received by the public, are the main attraction. Many of the testimonials are made by the once forlorn, now happily reborn sinners who describe their experiences of salvation through Christ.

Talk Shows as Speech Therapy

It is necessary to note the most recent speech-related phenomenon: the talk show. Although talk shows have become a widespread phenomenon, they are without a doubt an American invention that could only originate in this culture. The spread of talk shows to other societies—usually met with a degree of hesitancy and against strong opposition—again demonstrates the dynamic aspect of America's cultural conquest of the world. The talk show could only develop in a society that, as the example of the "born-again" organizations shows, is readily accustomed to personal exhibitionism and whose members wear their hearts on their tongues.

*"This was a kind of Game Show from Hell, where three women com-
peted to see who had the most miserable life. We are not making this
show up. Contestant Number One would say something like, 'Well, I
have terminal cancer, of course, and little Billy's iron lung was destroyed in the fire, and . . . ' so on. Everybody in the audience would
be weeping, and then Contestant Number Two would tell a story that
was even worse. And then Contestant Number Three would make the
other two sound like Mary Poppins. After which Jack Bailey would
have the members of the audience clap to show which woman they
thought was the most wretched, and she would receive some very nice
gifts including (always) an Amana freezer."*

                              Dave Barry, Dave Barry Slept Here

American talk shows always compete for higher viewer ratings by presenting
ever more intimate and ever more abnormal themes. Yet, they have a thoroughly
liberating, almost cathartic effect for the participants. If one listens to the participants from such talk shows as "Mistreated Wives" or "Married to Thirty-Years-
Older/Younger Partners" or "Transsexuals," it becomes clear that for many of
them, talk shows are a substitute for a visit to the psychotherapist, which the
average citizen cannot afford. There was even a talk show called "Couples," in
which therapy was practiced and presented in front of the television camera.

At any rate, talk shows demonstrate America's passion for talk. This society
can no longer keep silent. The mouth must constantly be in motion, no matter
what comes out in the process. Americans seem almost physically incapable of
enduring silence. One of the reasons for this obsession with talking is probably a
"horror vacui," a fear of emptiness that is apparent everywhere in America.

Umberto Eco detailed this American characteristic with two portrayals: the almost pathological decorating and stuffing of luxury homes, as with the Hearst Castle, and the perfecting of every last thoroughly planned detail of Disneyland's Magic Kingdom.[4] The "horror vacui" does not permit silence. The newscasters on television, the moderators of talk and game shows do not allow for any interruption in their flow of speech.

Inflation of Words

Television is an interesting proof of the weight that words carry in American culture. Although television is, as the name declares, a vision or a picture, this is never enough. Instead, the image is constantly interrupted by commentary, often boring and useless. This is especially noticeable with sportscasters who say everything on their minds about the game and the players. If the game is not particularly active or there is a timeout or pause of some sort, they pour forth endless statistics.

> *"A voice is always butting in to comment, explain, relate, and certify—the play-by-play commentator must certify each play before we are presumed to understand what's going on. 'It's a high fly to left field and Ryan is chasing it—back to the wall, back, back,' etc., when we can see it perfectly well. The assumption is clear: nothing is real unless validated by commentary and interpretation."*
>
> *Paul Fussell,* BAD

Even the cable channel CNN, which has quickly risen to prominence, is captive to this syndrome. Actually, the channel characterizes the institutionalization of endless talk. Although it is television, the majority of the broadcast is made up of speeches, commentary, and interviews behind which pictures play a secondary role. The idea of CNN, which was first ridiculed and declared impossible, is simple and for all intents and appearances suitable for American society in this day and age: There is not only plenty of information to provide material for reports around the clock; there is also enough interest on the part of viewers, a need for this endless pouring forth of words and information.

The result of such a 24-hour news program is that all of the news becomes leveled out in significance. This effect is strengthened by the effort to give all of the news the same level of importance with the help of a meaningful mode of expression. The dramatic speech style of the reporter does not distinguish relative importance of the information. Everything is presented with equal weight to the television viewer. The result is naturally not a particularly enthusiastic attentiveness or interest, rather apathy and indifference. When all things are presented as equally important, nothing seems to be important anymore.

Above and beyond this, the exaggerated rhetoric has led to a detachment of words from their original meanings. The word has become a product, as other consumer products, that can be used at pleasure. Whoever has the power over the means of communication decides and changes the meaning of words. In this way, the word *fresh* has been taken by the advertising industry and been beaten flat for so long that it has taken on the taste of a menthol cigarette. Through a dictum of saying "Operation Just Cause," the word *just* is used to explain why America invades a small neighboring country, whose government it does not favor. The stealth bomber "preserves life," as is stated in an advertisement by the Northrop Company. "War" in "Pentagonese," that is, the language of the Department of Defense, is likewise masked as an "armed situation."

The office of the president of the United States, no matter who has held it during recent decades, is obviously an inspiration for the art form of conjuring up new worlds with language. Kennedy opened up "new frontiers" for the American

nation, Lyndon Johnson wanted to create the "great society"—whatever that may be—and a "war against poverty" was declared and later one against drugs.

Self-Irony as Protection

American political rhetoric is more and more confusing reality with a more pleasant artificial reality, coming dangerously close to George Orwell's "Newspeak." Because Orwell's background for the invention and use of "Newspeak" is an utterly totalitarian state, such as the fascist and Stalinist regimes, it would seem impossible that the political perfidy of "Newspeak" could be achieved anywhere else but in a totalitarian state. Democratically organized states are, however, not immune to it. Even without the sinister intentions of the ruler in Orwell's state, politicians tend to substitute the unpleasant reality with a more attractive one in their speeches.

In America, love of words combined with the exuberance of rhetoric permits exaggeration to become the accepted norm. Peggy Noonan has described the mode of operation and the power of political rhetoric in detail in her book about the Reagan presidency, although she views it exclusively as a positive and inspiring force. As most Americans, she does not see the danger of words used as an instrument of imagination. The words are completely separate from the objects they claim to describe, creating an imaginary world of their own, which in turn influences and determines the political events.

> *"You know with the big buildup this address has had, I wanted to make sure it would be a big hit, but I couldn't convince Barbara to deliver it for me. I see the Speaker and the Vice President are laughing. They saw what I did in Japan. They're just happy they're sitting behind me."*
>
> President Bush in his State of the Union address on January 28, 1992, referring to the fact that during a state visit to Japan his wife Barbara had to make a speech because he had vomited on his neighbor's lap due to a sudden wave of nausea

Americans are protected from taking the overwhelming rhetoric too earnestly by their special talent for self-irony.[5] They have a highly developed talent to look beyond the facade in a flippant way. Even in formal situations and on serious issues, American speeches are seldom without humor, usually in the form of self-deprecation.

This lack of respect in relation to oneself leaves Americans enough distance when confronted with exaggerated statements or claims by others. Although on the surface they seem to be influenced by tirades and rhetorical ostentation to a degree that is inconceivable to a European, it does not mean that they are in the least bit emotionally involved. On the contrary, the use of excessive rhetoric is a game that everyone can play.[6]

Of course the danger of self-deception is never far away. The danger of getting carried away by rhetoric and the temptation to really believe that something that sounds so good is real is a permanent aspect of the American society. The life of illusion as a game common to all requires a high degree of practical experience and maturity of consciousness. Otherwise, the trivial game of illusion becomes a serious and crazy game of reality.

Temporary High Point of the Culture of Rhetoric: The Sound Bite

The television phenomenon of the sound bite is another aspect of American rhetoric, although at first glance it seems to contradict the usual definition of rhetoric. A sound bite is an opinion minimalized to the format of a television unit of 10 to 20 seconds.[7] The contrast to the traditional characteristics of rhetoric is remarkable: Rhetoric is rather long-winded and descriptive, while the sound bite, due to its brutal time constraints, apppears to be free from rhetorical fatty tissue. The sound bite, however, is only one other form of rhetoric that has become a primary channel of political communication, although everybody attests them as completely empty. Nevertheless, both sides, speaker and public, have grown accustomed to produce and receive information in this form.

The origin of sound bites in the advertising world is not to be overlooked. Just as in advertising, all of the energy goes into perfecting the form because the necessary brevity limits the significance of the content. A well-made sound bite requires a resonant voice, a firm tone, a self-confident performance, arresting word choice, flowing sentences, and a clear climax. Sound bites must be packaged compactly and agreeably. They are like frozen dinners prepared for instant consumption.

> *"Cheap, plentiful food is the precondition for human advancement. When there isn't enough food, everybody has to spend all his time getting fed and nobody has a minute to invent law, architecture or big clubs to hit cave bears on the head with."*
>
> *P.J. O'Rourke,* Parliament of Whores

Between the devotion to words and the constant occupation with food, there are other relationships besides the rather obvious fact that they both have to do with the same medium, the mouth. Another noticeable parallel is the pathological, hybrid aspect of both habits in America.

Humans must eat and drink or they will die, and speaking is necessary for establishing and keeping together a society. The handling of food beyond the simple act of feeding and sustaining oneself is a civilizing advancement, which not only separates humans from animals, but also from a level of development at which constant concern about nourishment completely absorbs humans and leaves no room for the fulfillment of higher needs. In the same way, the progress of language from being the vehicle of minimal understanding to an instrument that permits the exchange of ideas and emotions is instrumental in creating a state of abundance beyond sheer necessity that is the foundation of every human culture.

The refinement of the simple acts of eating and speaking is a necessary aspect of human culture. The expansions that both cultural activities have experienced in our day in America is progress only in a quantitative sense; in quality one can speak of a regression.

The first triumph of our century—at least for the industrialized nations—freeing human beings from the lash of hunger, the final relief from the nagging worry for nourishment for the next days, the next week, the next year, has seemingly not changed the attitude of humans toward food and drink. On the contrary, apparently the concern about food, the "daily bread," seems to be an ever more important aspect of human existence. It seems as though the tyrant of hundreds of thousands of years of human history does not want to let go of its slaves. Food and drink, in the broadest sense, are once again becoming the central concern of a developed society.

Food Is Big Business

Naturally, the tyrant appears in another form. The industrialization of the food industry—from production to consumption—does not allow for overproduction to result in the freedom from necessity but, rather, in a pressure to consume. A development that started as a blessing becomes the opposite through excess. Although the change of agriculture to a mechanical industry and the industrialization of the consumer market have created a society that feels itself well nourished, "big business" is so involved with providing the population with food and drinks that it cannot leave the questions of how and in what quantities the people consume up to fate or free will.

The members of this advanced society, who are fittingly called the consumers, are subjected to unavoidable pressure to consume more and more foodstuffs. Because quantity of consumption has limits—although these are unusually stretched in America—the variety of the food basket is inventively expanded. However, abundance of quantity does not necessarily mean improvement in quality.[8]

It is also important to note the tremendous waste that occurs along the food chain. The high meat consumption in America is an example of highly uneconomical nourishment: There is a great loss in nutritional value because food

products high in vegetable nutrients, for example soy beans and grains, are used as feed for animals. It takes seven times as much energy for the generation of animal products as for vegetable products, so it is not surprising and somewhat irritating to discover that approximately 70 percent of American grains are used in the raising of livestock.

The food industry, with all its different branches, is a major factor in the American economy; a marked decline in food consumption would have economic consequences. If Americans were only to consume what they needed—by no means a subsistence minimum but a comfortable average diet with plenty of variety—the American economy would most probably suffer. Whereas this is presumably also true in many other areas of the American consumer goods industry, in no area—with the possible exception of energy consumption—is

excessive production of such importance to the flow of the economy as in oral consumerism.

Eating and Drinking: An Overweight Aspect

The consequences of the excessive role of oral consumer goods are: too much buying and too much eating. Both have a marked influence on American society.

They lead to the unnecessary waste of financial resources and to physical obesity and fatty degeneration. The overwhelming advertisement of foodstuffs—if one includes Coke, crackers, cereal, beer, chewing gum, and dog food in this category—creates artificial needs that put a disproportionate demand on the family budget. Opportunities for social advancement and a life free from worry about the "daily bread" are diminished as demand for overabundant food increases.

Response to the advertisement for food and drink has serious results for the physical look of Americans. There is no other Western society in which there are as many grossly obese people as in the United States. The number of obviously overfed children also seems to the foreign visitor to be higher than in other countries.

Aside from the extreme of obesity, there is, as in other developed countries, the problem of extra weight at all levels. Approximately half of all Americans—children, adults, elderly people—according to respective studies, are overweight. Another statistic determines that on a random day, approximately one-third of all American adults are on a diet.[9] Apparently, Americans are aware of the fact that they consume too much and they are trying to do something about it. However, instead of changing their lifestyle and drastically revising their devotion to food and drink, they try to buy slenderness by taking diet classes at which they get good advice and buy prepackaged low-calorie meals.

At the current time, the aspiration to achieve slenderness has permitted a veritable industry to develop that grosses $60 billion a year, according to recent figures. Americans spend billions of dollars on excess goods that have harmful effects on their bodies and go on to spend billions more to rid themselves of this weighty burden. It is apparent that most of the diets on the market only have short-term results—if any at all. Without a change in attitude toward eating and drinking, without a willingness to change lifestyle, without turning away from excesses, these diets are nothing more than another form of consumerism—just the other way round.

The everpresent advertising has long been successful at depicting slenderness and health as products of the consumer goods industry that one simply can buy. "Big business" has long seen to it that the diet sources, e.g., diet pills, self-help books, classes, etc., do not result in consumer sacrifice.

Hunger in the Land of Excess

At the same time, real hunger and poverty still exist in America. The number of people who depend on food stamps is currently at about 25 million or 10 percent of the population. Hunger and overeating not only exist side by side within the same society, but they are also doubtlessly related. If people are slaves to artificially induced needs, they become so absorbed by them that they have neither time nor energy to devote to the needs of other members of the society. Food is certainly an elementary necessity. The desire for a refrigerator well filled by

American standards is an insignificant one. This difference escapes middle-class Americans, who are constantly bombarded by advertisements for more food. The insignificant concern for filling the cupboards has taken on the dimensions and weight of real hunger. The middle class does not consider itself free from the concern about putting food on the table. It does not see its situation fundamentally different from that of the hungry portion of the population.

"Affluent America" is becoming more sensitive to the issue of living side by side with "poor America." It has become politically correct to no longer throw away your leftovers, but to give them to homeless people (who are presumably hungry). This holds true from school food drives, where children turn in their leftover lunch sandwiches and drinks so that they can be handed on to the needy, to all-inclusive offers by catering companies to not just deliver party buffets but to subsequently pass on the plentiful leftovers to homeless shelters and soup kitchens.

Many restaurants have also begun offering their food supplies to soup kitchens when they no longer want to serve them to their customers. In San Francisco, the gourmet capital of America, this leads to the ironic situation of people in soup kitchens dining at the same level as the upper class. In high-class restaurants, everything that is not consumed on the same day, be it exotic vegetables, fruit, bread, meat, or fish, is disposed of or handed on when it no longer meets the requirement of a gourmet cuisine.

Grocery store chains, whose efforts are constantly geared toward pushing the consumers to buy much more than they actually need, nevertheless promote charity benefits to which the shoppers donate a portion of their surplus. Obviously, they are not concerned that such campaigns could increase consumer awareness about how many unnecessary and excessive purchases are made at the supermarket.

Food: The Boast of the Nouveaux Riches

The exaggerated interest in food by the rich in America is a relatively new phenomenon. In the fifties and sixties, affluent America measured its wealth with oversized homes, gardens, automobiles, the newest household appliances, and a huge collection of games and hobbies. Food was certainly present in abundance, but the dishes were simple and generally limited to American style.

There has been a dramatic change in the past 20 years in America. Today, America is a mecca for gourmands. The whole world is now represented on the supermarket shelves or in fancy gourmet shops that are sprouting up even in middle-sized and small towns. Through this, American food production has grown manyfold both in quality and in variety.

Yet, this gourmet dining is often not accompanied by real enjoyment of good food but, rather, with the satisfying feeling of participating in a new trend. People often dine expensively and exotically because it is trendy and because they can afford it. It is a part of the luxury with which people surround themselves, a status symbol that is no longer attained through wealth alone, but also through high class.

Parallels to the Roman Empire are unavoidable: the trend of making food the central aspect not only of nourishment but also of social status. It is no coincidence that in ancient Rome this development was led not by the patricians but the nouveaux riches, who came to power with the establishment of the empire, the exploitation of the colonies, and the founding of a financial market.

Talk Becomes Meaningless and Food Becomes Tasteless

The characterization of America as an "oral society" is more than simple wordplay. At the start of the chapter, it was left undecided whether the society is still or is again in its oral phase. After the presentation of the above arguments, it is clear that America is in a cultural regression because the mouth and everything that goes in it or comes out of it plays a disproportionate and unsuitable role. The leading role of rhetoric in public life—in economics, advertisement, media, and politics—shifts the society to a playful atmosphere. It is, however, no longer an innocent feeling, as in childhood, but dangerous because it prevents the nation from a confrontation with its real structure and its real problems.[10] The American rhetoric, highly developed in the technique of public relations, the sound bite, and the dream factory of television and Hollywood, creates an imaginary world for the American people in which they can live an undisturbed life as long as they do not question the founding elements of this illusion—the words.

It is an America in which justice, democracy, wealth, and equality rule, in which the opportunities of achieving something with hard work and ambition are freely available. It is the America of a childhood dream from which one does not wish to awaken. To break out from this dreamworld, to tear apart the cocoon of illusion, to expose the words, is an act of maturity and a sign of adulthood.

The obsession with nutrition, too, is an indication of a relapse to an infantile phase. The constant concern for food is the first concern of a human being. But when this concern has been satisfied, it should be set aside and room be made for higher needs. The fact that a well-to-do society continues to give such a central and weighty role to the topic of food—and simultaneously cold-bloodedly permits hunger in its own ranks—instead of putting its energies into more important tasks is a sign of cultural immaturity or of a relapse to a long surpassed level of development.

Notes

1. Robert N. Bellah, *The Broken Covenant,* pp. 55, 57.
2. Neil Postman, *Amusing Ourselves to Death,* p. 48.
3. Peggy Noonan, *What I Saw at the Revolution,* p. 69 in the typically entitled chapter "Speech!"

4. Umberto Eco, *Über Gott und die Welt,* p. 87 (German edition).

5. The importance of self-irony in the American political life is very well character-ized by Noonan: "Humor allows us to step out of the moment, look at it, and sum it up with no great reverence. It is a gift nature gives the mature intellect. (If a presidential candidate is lacking in humor then forget him. He lacks the presidential sensibility; he'll never succeed with Congress or rally the will of the people.)" *What I Saw at the Revolution,* p. 179.

6. In this context fits an interesting remark by Geoffrey Gorer in his "ethno-psycho-logical" study on Americans: "Again a function of the mouth—speech—becomes of the greatest psychological importance. When the child starts to tell of its exploits and tri-umphs it is very small and weak, and its parents are, by comparison, very big and strong. To hold their interest, to extort their admiration and approval, the child inevitably starts to speak over-emphatically, to exaggerate, to boast. The parents are so used to this (they did it themselves) that they allow it to go unchecked, mentally making the calculations which will separate the kernel of true achievement from the husk of infantile self-glorification and self-dramatization. Although as they grow up the disparity between the size and power of the speaker and the audience disappears, Americans tend to continue to talk about themselves and their accomplishments in the same manner as they did as little children; American audiences interpret this with ease; but non-Americans generally fail to, and consider it as excessive boasting and self-glorification—which it would be if they, with their quite different upbringing, spoke about themselves in the same terms and tone of voice." Geoffrey Gorer, *The Americans,* pp. 64, 65.

7. As Americans explore everything, it is already known that the statistical average length of sound bites is 7.3 seconds. Richard L. Berke, "CBS's Sound Bite Ban Catches Pols Breathless," *International Herald Tribune,* July 4/5, 1992.

However, due to the extreme shortness of the sound bites, the dynamic of sound bites seems to be broken, the climax of "soundbiteology" already surpassed (Noonan, *What I Saw at the Revolution,* p. 20); a more than just verbal revolt is growing against this political "non-culture." CBS has declared that they are no longer willing to air statements of politicians that are shorter than 30 seconds (Ibid.).

8. "Getting food—whether baked goods or breakfast cereals—to 'perform' turns out to be one of the great ambitions of America's mass-market food giants such as Nabisco, General Foods Corp. and Campbell Soup Co. Instead of bread and circuses to keep the masses happy, why not turn the bread into circuses?" Michael Schrage, "Multimedia Foods: New Products Designed to Entertain America," *Washington Post,* August 31, 1990, p. F3.

9. "Sixty-five million Americans are on a diet this evening." Dan Rather opened with this remark his new television talk show on CBS. " '48 Hours', Weighing in on Dieting," *Washington Post,* May 10, 1990, pp. D1, D10.

10. "Instead of a politics that leads the society sooner or later to confront its problems, American politics has developed new ways to hide from them." William Greider, *Who Will Tell The People?* p. 15.

Pragmatism

and

Fundamentalism

Two important currents of mainstream American history are pragmatism and fundamentalism. It would be a mistake to think of them as separate phenomena; they may occur concurrently in the same person or group. They are even found entwined in the same policy, especially in the area of foreign affairs.[1]

The term *American fundamentalism* does not refer to the fundamental theology of various Protestant churches, resurgent Islam (black Muslims, for instance), or Jewish orthodoxy. Instead, it is a kind of secular fundamentalism that upholds national values with a sort of religious zeal. The American attitude toward religion, on the other hand, can more aptly be described as pragmatic.

A Chosen People

Nevertheless, there is a connection between religious and secular fundamentalism. National fundamentalism harkens back to religious fundamentalism. Even today they interact. Early America was modeled according to the creed of the Puritans who thought of themselves as "God's chosen people." In their preaching, America was the "promised land"[2] with biblical reference to a "new Jerusalem" or "a shining city on a hill."

A comparison between American settlers and the Jewish people of the Bible who saw themselves as the chosen people is a recurring theme in the early accounts of American colonial history and also later during the nineteenth century when the conquest of the continent with the destruction of the native population needed an ideological justification. According to these accounts, God led the settlers to the Promised Land, just as he had led the Jews. Even rational-minded Thomas Jefferson, usually inclined to more sober language, chose the following comparison in his second inaugural address:

> I need, too, the favor of that Being in whose hands we are, who led our forefathers, as Israel of old, from their native land, and planted them in a country flowing with all the necessaries and comforts of life.[3]

Many thousands of sermons and political speeches contain allusions to the fate of the Jews. It is a manifestation of the belief that America's fate is decreed by divine providence and affirms the unique American experience. It is a land holding a promise not only for its inhabitants, but also for the world.

> *"By the grace of God, America won the Cold War."*
> *President George Bush, State of the Union Address 1992*

In his 1965 inaugural address, Lyndon B. Johnson deifies America when he speaks about the country's first settlers:

> They came here—the exile and the stranger, brave but frightened—to find a place where a man could be his own man. They made a covenant with this land. Conceived in justice, written in liberty, bound in union, it was meant one day to inspire the hopes of mankind.[4]

Here both aspects of American national fundamentalism are clearly stated: America is not just a geographical place or a political state, not just any place where a man can make a living. America is above all an idea. It is the result of a "covenant" with God that the citizen will gladly embrace because this idea includes three of the greatest social concepts of mankind: justice, freedom, and community.

The Civil Religion

The belief in America's calling, which once served to unify the nation, has been referred to as a "civil religion."[5] This expression harkens back to Jean Jacques Rousseau's concept of the *contrat social.* He argues for the necessity of a moral code that all citizens hold in common, not to give heed to transcendental religious concerns, but because such a code is vital for society's survival.

The American civil religion goes far beyond this basic moral consensus. It describes a creed that idolizes both the ideas and values upon which the nation was built—principles of freedom and justice—as well as the nation itself, which became the unique embodiment of these ideas. In his essay "American Civil Religion," Will Herberg describes this phenomenon:

> It is an organic structure of ideas, values, and beliefs that constitutes a faith common to Americans as Americans, and is genuinely operative in their lives.

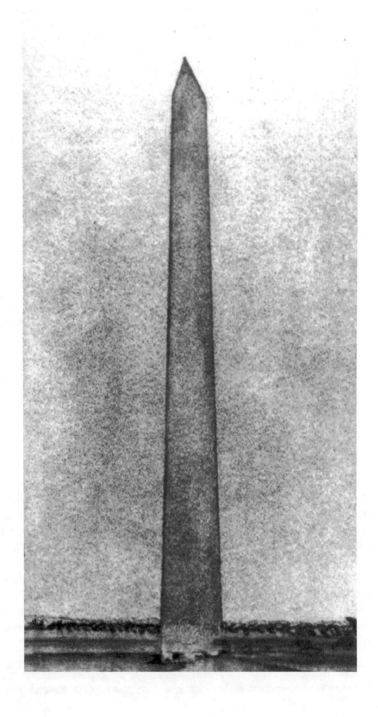

... Sociologically, anthropologically, it is *the* American religion, undergirding American national life and overarching American society. ... And it is a civil religion in the strictest sense of the term, for, in it, national life is apotheosized, national values are religionized, national heroes are divinized, national history is experienced as a *Heilsgeschichte*, as a redemptive history.[6]

The basic belief in the legitimacy and uniqueness of the American experiment and the American way of life becomes a reason for American intervention in the world. In the two world wars and the cold war, this was the prevalent argument for overcoming the ingrained reluctance to get involved in European affairs.

Nationalism as a Substitute Religion

These aspects of "civil religion," the notion of American "manifest destiny," and missionary zeal all recall the kind of extreme nationalism prevalent in Europe at the end of the nineteenth and the beginning of the twentieth century that led to the two world wars. No doubt, they are part of the same historical process that in Western Europe happily seems to have come to an end, but then the American kind of "national identification" is different from primitive chauvinism. It has deeper roots and more far-reaching consequences, not only for international relations, but also for domestic affairs.

America is not only of large geographical dimensions, but it also is a richly varied country. The states banded into the Union only reluctantly—out of necessity, not out of love for constituting the more perfect body of one people. The individuality of its separate parts remains strong.

The deep-rooted antagonism between the Northern and Southern states exploded into a vicious civil war, and resentments still run strong to this day. The citizens of the original thirteen colonies assumed cultural superiority over Western frontiersmen. On the other hand, the inhabitants of the West thought of themselves as the true Americans. Their relationship to the Eastern states was always distant. States like California continue to develop their own identity different from the rest of America.

America was a country without a national center, without natural cohesion, without unifying similarities. America does not hold a single religion nor a single culture in common. No same style of music was heard throughout the country until the event of pop music. There are no national sports teams, in the European sense, although the general enthusiasm for such all-American sports as baseball, football, basketball, and hockey may more than make up for this deficit.

The void created by the lack of national similarities has been filled by a sentiment that lets the inhabitants of the United States think of themselves not only as New Yorkers, Californians, or Texans but also as Americans because they share the same political and social values. The American "civil religion" has its own beliefs, relics, and saints in the shape of its institutions, symbols, and figureheads incarnating the body social named America: "The Star-Spangled Banner," the Constitution, the founding fathers, the former presidents, as well as the nation's current officeholders.

Just as adoration of saints and symbols is part of any religion, the congregation also needs a bible containing the truths to which everyone subscribes: liberty, justice, and equality. But the Bible, as we know from Sunday's sermons, is interpreted in many different ways.

The national cohesion of a civil religion is nothing specifically American. European history illustrates the role of vigorous nationalism as a driving force behind unification of such states as Germany and Italy. The rise of nationalism in Europe, Japan, and other nations compensated for necessary radical changes accompanying the development of the modern industrial state. The question is rather: Why does America's emotional attachment to ideas of nationhood seem undiminished or even enhanced? Is America working on a different schedule or again setting the pace?

The unique role that religion plays in American society may help to explain this special American development. It was not a coincidence that nationalism first emerged in Europe along with final secularism. Friedrich Nietzsche's dictum "God is dead" marks the decline of attempts to make metaphysical sense of the world. In the resulting void the nation as community seemed to promise a source of identity. European nationalism of the late nineteenth century and more grotesquely the fascism of the early twentieth century share pronounced religious traits. Here the state is transformed into a being with its own substance. Its qualities were not only superior to those of the individual citizen, but they were also holy.

People worshiped this new god fervently; they found a sense of purpose and self-esteem. Fundamentalist belief seductively promised to remove life's uncertainties—no more responsibility for shaping your own life. Ultimate goals were clearly spelled out—no necessity to search for one's own purpose in life. People surrendered to the idea of nation and immersed themselves in an all-encompassing movement.

The fascists took this aspect of nationalism as pseudo-religion to the furthest limit. They certainly were not the first to do so. Nationalism has an inherent religious character that may achieve social relevance when traditional modes of identification, by religion for instance, no longer seem to hold true or become superfluous.

America and Religion

> *"So it was harsh, all right, but nevertheless more and more persecuted religious minorities—Protestants, Catholics, Jews, Scientologists, Cub fans—were flocking to freedom and establishing religious colonies such as Maryland and Heritage Village, USA, site of the New World's first known Christian water slide."*
>
> Dave Barry, Dave Barry Slept Here

Unlike in Europe, American nationalism as a civil religion did not arise from a general rejection of religious dogma or traditional attitudes founded on religious beliefs. It coexisted peacefully with the religious element in society that was more pragmatic than religious in character. This pragmatic religiosity, generally left untouched by theological dispute, continues in common practice.

For most Americans, Sunday church services serving both civic and personal purposes are just an integral part of life. Surveys show that an overwhelming percentage of Americans consider themselves religious and maintain that they believe in a personal God. There are always signs of lapses, but the decline is considerably slower than in Europe and is diverted by the birth of new religious movements.

All early witnesses of American history, foreign visitors, and native commentators agree on the importance of religion in the development of the American state while nevertheless affirming the principle of the separation of church and state.

Alexis de Tocqueville, a devout man himself judging from his writings, was deeply concerned with the role religion might have in a democratic society erected on the principles of freedom. He discovered an American paradox that continues to this day: Although institutions of religion and of state are absolutely separate, at the same time religious values underlie the fundamental moral values that define and determine the political consensus. According to Tocqueville, this consensus has a strong religious bias: Americans, however, share the same moral convictions, not because of theological fiat, but because they feel that the basic moral consensus has been advantageous for the country and its social order.

The Constitution of the United States contains the same moral principles as those propagated by Christian churches. The result is a concert of understanding for mutual advantage. The state respects the role of religion. The different denominations can practice their belief in a fertile civic surrounding as long as they don't interfere with affairs of government. Tocqueville comments:

> They all attributed the peaceful dominion of religion in their country mainly to the separation of church and state.[7]

Joel Poinsett, one of Tocqueville's conversation partners, describes the relationship of religion and politics from the vantage point of the politician:

> I think that the state of religion in America is one of the things that most powerfully helps us to maintain our republican institutions. The religious spirit exercises a direct power over political passions, and also an indirect power by sustaining morals.[8]

This remark exemplifies American society's pragmatic attitude toward religion. Let religion take care of salvation, may it edify and enlighten, but its ramifications are essentially political. Religion serves as "the safeguard of morality, and morality as the best security of law and the surest pledge of the duration of freedom."[9]

Religious Skepticism, the American Kind

Another person Tocqueville talked to, the owner of a plantation and an attorney
of law from Louisiana, aptly describes this ambivalent American attitude to
religion:

> I think ... that for the majority religion is something respectful and useful
> rather than a proved truth. I think that in the depths of their souls they have a
> pretty decided indifference about dogma. One never talks about that in the
> churches; it is morality with which they are concerned.[10]

Considering these circumstances, it is easily understood why the "death of
God" philosophy did not impact on the status of religion in America as it did in
Europe. A long time ago skeptical Americans detached religion's social function
from its spiritual contents.

The harmony between religious morality and secular ethics does not mean
that political decision-making is dictated by religious belief or relies on divine
inspiration. Rather, it is the case of an agreement on general principles.

Americans take no special interest in religious disputes. Foremost, religion
does not directly serve the needs of everyday life, nor lay down the rules for
practical decision-making. Americans confine religious matters to Sundays without feeling the least bit hypocritical. They know if you want to solve problems in
this world, religion supplies only the most general principles. As a result, the
approach to daily practical problems in business or politics is pragmatic, undefined by transcendental truth.

Nevertheless, there is awareness of higher truths and deeper emotions beyond
a world of everyday business and politics. There is a genuine and deeply felt
desire to partake in this experience and to seek out spiritual fulfillment.

Church-going is a social and emotional event. The church member experiences true human community. Each Sunday people emerge from isolation and
enter into a community, where they experience a kind of weekly catharsis—one
of the most important functions of religion—without necessarily prompting them
to change their ways during the working days.

American Pragmatism

The American penchant to experience deep piety, true religion, honest love of
God on one day and to indulge in the world on the other days represents American pragmatism. It includes the ability to hold concurrent and even contradictory
opinions and aspirations within the same person.

In his book *The Americans,* published in 1947 and still considered one of the
best analyses of American mentality, Geoffrey Gorer supplies the following
description of this American trait:

This custom of looking at facts discretely, as though each were separate and each of equal validity, has important political repercussions. What members of other societies often consider to be the contradictions of American policies are quite honestly not so perceived by the Americans, because the different aspects are not considered to be connected. The most obvious instance is the frequent discrepancy between American political and economic demands or actions. For peoples whose way of looking at the world, is—for want of a better word holistic, the atomicism of the American view of the world is incomprehensible, and very often cynical and immoral intentions are imputed because the observers supply connections between different statements or acts of which the Americans were completely unconscious. In some ways the American view of the world is the furthest removed from that of many primitive tribes, from what can perhaps be called the primitive view of the world. Although there are some notable exceptions, most primitive peoples view the varied phenomena of the universe they know as deeply and intricately interconnected, so that actions in one sphere will influence or be influenced by actions in a completely different sphere—a view of the world typified by various systems of magic and taboo. In Western Europe many of these connections are rejected, but the universe is still conceived as composed of multiple and intricate interconnections. In America there is a growing tendency to regard each aspect of the universe separately and discretely, as though each existed independently of the other. The predominant American philosophy, pragmatism, is less a system of the universe than an attitude toward the universe.[11]

Nothing needs to be added to this perceptive description of American pragmatism except maybe that this American worldview, which Gorer describes, is now referred to as postmodernism and permeates the entire Western world. Gorer says the American worldview is the one "furthest from primitivism." He simply means it is the most modern way of looking at things. If you have such an attitude toward the world at large, the news that the world has lost all cohesive meaning will not shock you. So what?—We knew that a long time ago, and we are getting along fine.

Fifty years after Gorer's lucid observations, this kind of disjointed thinking still prevails, looking at parts instead of the way they hold together. The symbol of this thinking is the sound bite—an isolated but autonomous morsel of information. Gorer, who wrote prior to the invention of the sound bite, deals with the prototype of this kind of communication—the wisecrack:

> Although the atomic aspect of communication is most marked in the mass media, it is also a noticeable component of face-to-face conversation. The "wise crack" normally stands alone, self-sufficient and without context. A marked feature of the conversation of American men consists in the interchange of assorted facts, especially such as can be expressed in numbers.[12]

Gorer demonstrates his clairvoyance when he speaks about the atomizing effect of mass communication. He describes how mass media fragments productions into ever shorter sequences. They then can be more easily moved around. Even during the days of radio, programs were riddled with commercials. The novelty of our times is the remote control, which has finally hammered information to pieces. By zapping channels, viewers destroy a last remnant of cohesive meaning. Mankind has started to think in "bits" and "bytes" assuming the logic of the computer.

Pitfalls of Pragmatism

Pragmatism is not only a passive onlooker in a disparate world, it also has had its share in turning the world into conceptual piecemeal, into ever smaller fragments, easily consumed, each promising instant understanding of the world.

Taken to its extreme, pragmatism leads to total indifference: things become meaningless, equally valid and invalid. Taken by itself pragmatism is a reasonable and brave response to the world's incoherence, but taken too far it makes for the kind of nihilism it seeks to avoid.

Tocqueville saw these dangerous tendencies in the American mentality without calling them pragmatic. For him, religion was protection against this form of extreme pragmatism:

> Nature and circumstances have made the inhabitants of the United States bold, as is sufficiently attested by the enterprising spirit with which they seek for fortune. If the mind of the Americans were free from all hindrances, they would shortly become the most daring innovators and the most persistent disputants in the world. But the revolutionists of America are obliged to profess an ostensible respect for Christian morality and equity, which does not permit them to violate wantonly the laws that oppose their designs. . . . Hitherto no one in the United States has dared to advance the maxim that everything is permissible for the interests of society.[13]

Tocqueville recognized a tempering element in religion. It prevents man's curious and shiftless mind from upturning every stone and creating the world only in his own image. But religion itself has become part of the pragmatic arrangement within American society. The churches have turned into a sort of service providing moral standards within the political system. Religion for itself neither carries sufficient weight nor has the resources to get away from the Sunday alibi role and to oppose cynical and permissive pragmatism.

This is the negative side of the generally good rapport between weekdays and Sundays, their mutual noninterference: Religion has no social mandate. Don't expect help to be forthcoming.

Transcendental Desires

A danger always exists that fundamentalist currents of the civil religion might move into the spiritual void left by religious pragmatism. Civil religion, equipped with a tangible arsenal of liturgical paraphernalia, is a serious rival to the traditional religions, offering ever more convincing promises of spiritual gratification. So far, this kind of religion only needs a bigger organization. There are not enough places of worship, priests, and holy scriptures, but the "infrastructure" necessary for the practice of civil religion is currently being developed.

This kind of religion may actually stop the radicalization of the pragmatic worldview—but what price will be paid? The skeptical repudiation of absolute truths is now challenged by a desire to identify with something "larger than life" that is emotionally satisfying.

One of the sources of American national fundamentalism is certainly revulsion to this type of pragmatism, which has permeated the entire fabric of social life, including religion and clearly defining and restricting its role in society. It's no accident that from time to time religion rises up against all-American pragmatism, turning into a strong fundamental current that then grows into a true mass movement. The desire for transcendental experience, identification with the supreme being, absolute certainty, and the intoxicating feeling of community cannot be replaced by civil religion—not yet, anyway.

Joining Forces

It is alarming when, as could be observed in the past decade, national and Christian fundamentalism converge and join into a political coalition. The eighties brought a wave of religious fundamentalism, which made itself heard as a political force. The politicization of religious movements is nothing new in America. Recall the especially notorious drive toward prohibition, which had its origins in a kind of religious rigor, or abolitionism, a markedly religious movement to rid America of slavery. What is novel in our times is the coalition of religious fundamentalism with the national fundamentalism in civil religion.

The religious fundamentalists have come together in organizations such as the Moral Majority or the Christian Coalition. Calling for a return to traditional American values, they demand a strict moral code enforced by government. The style and tone of their propaganda is not much different than that of Islamic fundamentalism so abhorrent to most Americans.

But this whole development is by no means inevitable; there are alternative currents that run counter to national fundamentalism. A cultural phenomenon has emerged in American society, which deals with the tensions of modern society in a totally different manner and equally gives answers to the call for deliverance from frosty pragmatism. It raises the prospect that mankind will not forever be caught between these two extremist alternatives: fundamentalism or pragmatism. It finds expression in pop culture, especially pop music.

In the history of mankind, music has always had an important cathartic influence. The revolutionary change today is the fact that music is no longer just the province of the cultural elite. The people themselves have created their own cultural realm in music. If anything could make for the hope of the continuing existence and development of democracy, it is the fact that with pop music (and in the furthest sense pop culture) the people (the *demos*) have created a way of artistic expression with their own cultural identity.

The fragmentation of modern society and the consequent alienation is bearable only if modern man can establish himself in relationship to his surroundings. Popular culture gives people a possibility to go beyond the limitations of everyday life and to reach out. They may identify with higher values and experience community without being formally connected to an institution and taking the vows. Prerequisites of education become superfluous and so does aggressive behavior.

The Power of Pop

For the elite, culture always offered a middle road between the emptiness of pragmatism and the fever of fundamentalism. The development of pop culture has made this a grace available to everyone. The great pop songs are poetry and music seeking perfection. Authentic pop music—and this holds true for pop culture in general—is really art in the sense of having immediate access to the listener, spectator, touching that person at his or her inner core, putting in form and expressing something he or she has felt as his or her own thoughts and emotions.

An interesting current example is the emergence of rap music. Through spoken lyrics, the youth of black ghettos express their perspective on the world: their life situation, feelings, experiences, demands, relationship to society—everything which had been left in the dark—into a fascinating staccato of words, words hurled at an audience of many millions all over the globe.

Further evidence of the impact of cultural power is the fact that the democratic movements throughout Eastern Europe, which managed to break up the old institutions, were first exposed to the gradual penetration of Western ideas through American pop culture.

Freedom is threatened by the petrification of democratic institutions that need the kind of revitalization of pop culture. We are so used to the prevalence of pop culture and its social effects that we fail to recognize the extent to which it already has reshaped and liberated our society.

Pop music has also unshackled the mind from compulsions of intellectualism. Pop is successfully dismantling the painful barriers between body and soul that have existed for thousands of years, the incompatability between physical and mental life in the Western world. Nobody knows where it is going or where it will end.

Pop culture certainly has made people more aware of what is going on around them. They may not always be able to put it in their own words, but they know that they can trust their feelings to decide whether a politician speaks the truth and is acting responsibly or is just going through the motions. People have realized that a great part of political and social life is hollow pretense. Unfortunately, their first response is to retreat into their private lives instead of putting their strength into the revitalization of the democratic ideals.

But there have been direct and successful interventions of pop culture into the political life. This was especially noticeable in the opposition against the Vietnam War in America and again on the occasion of huge benefit concerts for people in need, in areas such as natural catastrophes or famine relief. Cynics call these engagements only weakly disguised public-relation stunts, or many so-called realists shrug them off as unimportant events on the political sidelines.

Personally, I am convinced that a change of values, a change of paradigms—to use the modern expression—has taken place. Undoubtedly, categories other than the established ones have slowly been introduced into the political world. To name but a few: compassion, warmth, brotherhood, spontaneity, sympathy, and humanity, (versus loyalty, distance, reciprocity, and national interest). In the long run, not even the politician has remained unaffected. The emergence of a system of so-called "soft" values in politics associated with the style of the presidency of Bill Clinton is one strong indication of this development.

The momentum of political involvement of pop culture has without doubt slowed since its apex during the sixties. The reason for this is the prevalent commercialization and marketing of pop culture. Pop culture has always been oriented toward the market. It was a child of a mammon society. But this preoccupation has been carried too far and is threatening to alter the true character of pop culture. Money used to be pragmatism's medium of measurement. Now pop culture is worshiping the golden calf while quickly eroding the potential to offer a choice between pragmatism and fundamentalism.

Notes

1. "The American character is filled with contradiction and paradox. So in consequence is American foreign policy. The conduct of policy is subject to cyclical fluctuations of withdrawal and return. . . . The conflict . . . expresses the schism in the American soul between a commitment to experiment and a susceptibility to dogma." Arthur M. Schlesinger, Jr., *The Cycles of American History*, p. 51.

2. This myth does not correspond with historical reality. John Steinbeck showed impressively the difference between this legend and reality. Actually, America was enormously malevolent toward the first newcomers (This may partly be the reason for the violent trait in American society—see the chapter "Wild at Heart" in this book.) However, the difference between the reality and myth does not change its effect. John Steinbeck, *America and Americans*, p. 12.

3. Thomas Jefferson, *Writings*, p. 523.

4. *The Public Papers of the Presidents of the United States*, Lyndon B. Johnson 1965, Book I, p. 72.

5. Robert Bellah's *The Broken Covenant* is still the most important book in this field.

6. Will Herberg, "America's Civil Religion," p. 281.
7. Alexis de Tocqueville, *Democracy in America I,* p. 308.
8. Ibid., *Journey to America,* p. 114.
9. Ibid., *Democracy in America I,* p. 44.
10. Ibid., *Journey to America,* p. 71.
11. Geoffrey Gorer, *The Americans,* p. 115.
12. Ibid., p. 114.
13. Tocqueville, *Democracy in America I,* p. 305.

Elections

and

Parties

Elections are both the motor and the gears of democracy. As with a vehicle, their quality is the key factor in the overall performance of the system. Even so, elections are not an original element of democracy but, rather, a necessary innovation when it was no longer feasible to debate and to make decisions directly in public meetings. The political philosophers of the eighteenth century called this type of direct rule democracy in its truest form; while the form of government with elected representatives was described as a republic. In the well-known tenth article of *The Federalist Papers,* James Madison refers to the advantage of an indirect and representative form of government. He goes beyond describing the difference between direct and representative democracy—a subject long decided by history—to give an impressive description of the ideals and hopes that the Enlightenment of the eighteenth century had for the instrument of elections and the role of elected representatives. These ideals remain the yardstick by which today's practice should be judged.

> The effect of the first difference is, on the one hand, to refine and enlarge the public views by passing them through the medium of a chosen body of citizens, whose wisdom may best discern the true interest of their country and whose patriotism and love of justice will be least likely to sacrifice it to temporary or partial considerations. Under such a regulation it may well happen that the public voice, pronounced by the representatives of the people, will be more consonant to the public good than if pronounced by the people themselves, convened for the purpose.[1]

There must not be too few representatives, Madison continues, as this would allow for cabals and intrigues. On the other hand, there should also not be too many representatives, no matter how large a state may be, because otherwise chaos would reign in the mass gathering. The United States, with its two legislative bodies of 100 senators and 435 representatives for a population of 250 million people, seems to be perfectly in accordance with these principles. Madison goes on to say, in his trademark pessimistic, realistic style, that the number of qualified candidates in small and large states is *relatively* equal, by which he concludes that the larger states offer a larger selection of good candidates.

> *"You can fool some of the people all the time, you can fool all the people some of the time, but you can't fool all of the people all of the time."*
> *American political proverb that is generally attributed to President Abraham Lincoln but presumably goes even further back.*

The assumption is that voters will ultimately be guided by the highest standards in the choice of representatives. In this respect, Madison is carelessly optimistic. Even though he does not directly state that the voters always elect the best candidates—indeed, he pointedly allows for the possibility of the opposite scenario—he does say that a large number of voters provides a sufficient obstacle to political manipulation and provides quality of selection:

> In the next place, as each representative will be chosen by a greater number of citizens in the large than in the small republic, it will be more difficult for unworthy candidates to practise with success the vicious arts by which elections are too often carried; and the suffrages of the people being more free, will be more likely to center on men who possess the most attractive merit and the most diffusive and established characters.[2]

In the following passage, Madison formulates his thesis concretely and refers to the influence that the size of an electoral district has on the politics and the characters of the delegates:

> It must be confessed that in this, as in most other cases, there is a mean, on both sides of which inconveniencies will be found to lie. By enlarging too much the number of electors, you render the representative too little acquainted with all their local circumstances and lesser interests; as by reducing it too much, you render him unduly attached to these, and too little fit to comprehend and pursue great and national objects. The federal Constitution forms a happy combination in this respect; the great and aggregate interests being referred to the national, the local and particular to the State legislatures.[3]

Members of Congress Are Primarily District-Oriented

For the First Congress, the size of an electoral district of a representative was established in the Constitution at 30,000 inhabitants. Today, it is more than 500,000. According to Madison's theory, the members of Congress should be less locally oriented and more focused on larger issues.

Madison's hopes for a truly nationally oriented Congress have not been fulfilled. The members, especially in the House of Representatives, are to a large degree, many even exclusively, locally oriented and are mainly concerned with the particular interests of their home states. This is because the division of powers between the federal government and the states has clearly deteriorated. Through numerous laws and regulatory agencies, but primarily through financial subsidies, the federal government has intruded upon nearly all of the areas of control that were formerly left to the states. The federal government is omnipresent. Because of this, members of the federal legislature must deal with all of the daily trivialities of the constituents in their districts, whether they want to or not.

> *"Thus we Americans have struck a remarkable bargain. We pay $566,220 a year—less than a dollar apiece—for a congressman and his staff, and in return they listen to us carp and moan and fume and gripe and ask to be given things for free. Because this is, in the end, what legislators do. They listen to us. Not an enviable task."*
>
> *P.J. O'Rourke,* Parliament of Whores

Nevertheless, this is not totally bad, even though it does not attain Madison's high goals. It reminds members that they are not only the representatives of the general public and the national interest, but that they also specifically represent individual persons in the district or state. The representatives' preoccupation with local problems is a matter of political survival because they depend wholly on the support of the voters in their districts. The constituents, in turn, base their decisions on their particular and, often, exclusively local interests: whether a military air base is being closed, whether a bridge is being built with federal funding, whether a school receives special funding from the federal government, or whether the representative has helped out with a complicated Social Security problem.

The weakness of Madison's argument is that the constituents themselves do not necessarily cast their vote for persons because of their general public service or their competence in national politics but, rather, more often in exchange for their service to special interests. In Alexis de Tocqueville's day this trend toward representation of the interests of the electoral districts was already evident. This can be deduced from Tocqueville's observations:

> Independently of his position as a legislator of the state, electors also regard their representatives as the natural patron of the constituency in the legislature ... and they flatter themselves that he will not be less zealous in defense of their private interests than of those of the country.[4]

Winner Takes All

For a foreign observer, and most Americans as well, the American electoral system is an indecipherable and complex system of changing rules and old traditions that differs from state to state. Yet there are some fundamental principles that underlie the system and have given it a certain character. The maxim "winner takes all" stands as a general principle. This attitude has led to the rigorous enforcement of the right of majority vote at all levels and in all political institutions.

The well-known consequences of the majority voting system, in which minorities of considerable size are often damned to political powerlessness, are clearly evident in America. For example, the principle of majority rule determines the presidential election in such a way that the winner of the majority of the votes in one state garners all the electoral votes of that state. This has led to distortions in recent presidential elections, with winners receiving 95 percent of the electoral votes even though they actually received at most 60 percent of the popular votes. In a very close election (by popular votes), a clear lead in the official results (electoral votes) gives the candidate added legitimacy; it psychologically strengthens the mandate won by his election victory.

Majority Rule

A particularly crude example of the principle of majority rule is the organization of Congress. It is fair and insightful that the Speaker of the House of Representatives be a member of the majority party, but less understandable and politically decisive is the fact that members of the majority party hold all of the committee chair positions, and, beyond that, the majority party claims the chairs of all subcommittees and special committees for itself. While more than every third Democrat of the 250 Democrats in the House of Representatives chaired a committee or subcommittee prior to the 1992 election, not a single one of the almost 200 Republicans held such an influential position. (This has been completely reversed now that the Republicans are in the majority, but to the same effect that the sizable minority party is excluded from chairing any legislative committee.) The same situation is true for the Senate. If the majority party changes, as was the case some years ago in the Senate after the first election of President Reagan and a short while later in the reverse direction, then the other party organizes the Congress. This means that entire committees rearrange their chair positions.

The chairperson of such a committee has considerable power over the procedure and the legislative agenda of the committee. In the American parliamentary system, the chairperson may use this power to manipulate the process of deliberating and drafting laws on personal whim or simply to let them die. In earlier times—approximately until the end of the sixties—this power was practically unlimited, but in recent decades Congress has made democratic and administrative reforms. Even so, the "winner takes all" principle in the leadership of Congress remains untouched.

Stable Conditions—Little Change in Personnel

Political stability is routinely praised as the main advantage of this type of electoral system, as it essentially guarantees clear majorities and with that the functioning of the political system. Political stability is only a blessing when it does not lead to a gridlock in power but is accompanied by an organized, regular, and quite frequent change of power. Otherwise, a basic element of democracy is lost—the opportunity to take over from those already in power. The stabilizing function credited to majority rule is very pronounced in the American system and strengthens the conservative character of American politics in a negative fashion. This extreme "stability" is without a doubt the main reason why America has trouble coping with its enormous domestic political problems.

To be sure, much has been set in motion in this area. Triggered by exposure of relatively minor irregularities and administrative failures, a much deeper frustration over the immobility of the political system and the incapability of established politicians to deal with the monumental problems in America has been unearthed.

It is possible that we are experiencing the beginning of a radical reform movement, such as has occurred periodically since the founding of the United States. The political scientist James Reichley predicts a cycle of seventy years in which the party system in the United States will gradually change. After a revolutionary turnaround, the new political order will establish itself and reach its climax after approximately thirty years, at which point it—still in power— will lose more and more power until it is replaced by the next "revolution."

Reichley sees occurrences such as Thomas Jefferson's election in 1800, which ended the leadership of the Federalists and brought in a populist era with the election of Andrew Jackson, as the cycle's high point. The next great event is the electoral victory of the newly founded Republican party with its candidate

Abraham Lincoln in the year 1860. The end of the Republican era is marked by the election of Franklin Delano Roosevelt in 1932. The Democratic era that Roosevelt brought about experienced its high point with Lyndon B. Johnson's social laws at the same time that it experienced its downfall. According to this theory, the cycle is again at the point of a revolutionary turnaround, which, as Reichley claims, could be set off by the rise of a new party as was the case in 1860 with the Republicans.

Likewise, Kevin Phillips has developed a cyclical theory of the American party system with shorter swings of the pendulum of approximately twenty to twenty-four years. However, both agree with the thesis that the decade of the nineties will again bring a radical change in the direction of American politics.

The Two-Party System as a Result of the Majority Rule

> *"So what if I don't agree with the Democrats? What's to disagree with? They believe everything. And what they don't believe, the Republicans do. Neither of them stands for anything they believe in, anyway. And from this, we've built a great nation."*
>
> P.J. O'Rourke, Parliament of Whores

A direct result of majority rule is the creation and consolidation of the two-party system in America. An explanation of the American two-party system in its structure and in its effects on the entire political culture of the country requires some basic information on the fundamental structures of American parties.

First, one must free oneself from the conception of parties that is prevalent in Europe. There is no membership with formal admission, party book, or membership fee. One becomes a member of a party when one votes for a particular party at election. One must be registered in order to vote, but it is not necessary to register for a party; one may also register as an independent without party affiliation.

With the registration for a party, one has the same fundamental rights as a dues-paying party member in Germany: The right to take part in party events, to vote for party leaders, to send delegates to district, state, and national conventions, to vote on policy statements, and to nominate candidates for public office.

The organization of parties in the United States is basically a matter of the individual states. The parties themselves are independent within each state, and the national party primarily exists for the purpose of the presidential nomination. Because the states have legislative authority over election and party matters, there are basically fifty different rules for the procedure of nominating candidates.

The System of Candidate Nominations

Party candidates for elective office are nominated by a caucus of party members or by primary elections conducted by states. The system of public primaries exists at all levels and for all offices—not only for the presidential election—although it is dealt with differently from state to state. American voters are involved in the choosing of persons for political offices to a much greater degree than in any other democracy in the world. In closed party systems, common outside of the United States, voters do not have the opportunity to directly select candidates to represent them. This is an exclusive right of the party members. In America, theoretically and in practice, the voters choose the party nominees for the general elections.

Such a system influences the personality, the character, and the behavior of the politicians who live by its rules. The system frees the politician from party decisions and party discipline. He or she is basically independent—except of course from the will of his or her constituents—and precisely as a result of this is focused on their interests.

Any eligible voter can run for any office open to election at whatever level of government. Even without the blessing of a party organization, he or she can become the official candidate of that party. Thus, it is possible that even for the highest office persons with different political backgrounds, inside and outside of the political structure, may announce their presidential candidacy for one of the two major parties. In addition, there are numerous presidential candidates of smaller parties and even candidates who are independent of any party.

The Disadvantages of the Primary System

The independence of the politicians from their parties also carries a price, quite literally. Because the nomination of candidates takes place in public, they must make themselves known to voters. For major offices (governor, representative, or mayor of a city), building name recognition can cost millions of dollars: The result is that these offices usually fall to persons with large personal fortunes or to candidates who can attract large financial contributors who will certainly expect appreciation after the election.

Another price of this system is the exclusion of persons who lack personal charisma and a talent for communication. These talents do not necessarily reflect superior intelligence or greater integrity. The primary system therefore encourages the trend toward media-politicians.

In addition, the system favors incumbent officials who are well-known and can use the resources of their office for the special benefit of their constituents.

The representatives trade the independence from the party for a loss of independence in their own political positions because they are subject to the unabating pressure of the special interests and the particular interests of their constituents. The greatest threat to their independence and integrity is created by the influence of money and the corruption of politics. The contributions do not only come from the electoral district but also from organizations and individuals whose interests may be influenced by the representative's position on a particular committee or as head of a party faction.

Influence of the Political System on Voting Behavior

In addition to the party and electoral system, the political system promotes the independence of American politicians. Unlike in a parliamentary system, American voters do not have to combine their votes for the legislative body with their votes for the administration. They have two separate votes for their representative and for the president, separate votes for their state senator and for the governor, as well as for their state representative and mayor. This makes them free to vote across party lines and to choose the person who appeals to them.

It would be wrong to give the impression that party identification plays no role whatever in the voting decision. There is a basic party affiliation that is created and based on social class, on individual and social value judgments, and also, but less every year, on historical traditions. Districts with affluent populations are generally Republican-oriented, and working-class districts are Democratic-oriented, not so much for ideological reasons, but because as a general principle they do not trust a Democrat or a Republican, depending on the case, to represent their social and economic interests.

In spite of this limitation, it is generally true that in an election of representatives—and this is valid both at the state and local levels—the personality of the candidate and his program, as far as voters realize, are deciding factors in casting their votes. The results of the elections every four years speak for themselves when a presidential election coincides with a congressional election. In many congressional districts in which a Democrat was voted into the House of Representatives by a large majority, the Republican presidential candidate received the majority of the votes from the same constituents.

Political Maturity of the American Voter

The split ticket is the result of a continuously developing ability and readiness of constituents to play with the opportunities and possibilities of the political system. This development presupposes the same qualities of the citizen that are necessary factors in the business world: experience, initiative, an eye for opportunities, readiness for innovation, and courage.

The electoral system itself influences and forms the political culture of the voters and the elected. It does not on its own, however, create political engagement and political finesse. A certain political talent, an interest in political "business" must be present as a basic precondition, otherwise the best offers of the system remain untouched and useless. Americans have, as Tocqueville has said, a natural political talent:

> But the political activity that pervades the United States must be seen in order to be understood. No sooner do you set foot upon American ground than you are stunned by a kind of tumult . . . a thousand simultaneous voices demand the satisfaction of their social wants. Everything is in motion around you; here the people of one quarter of a town are met to decide upon the building of a church; there the election of a representative is going on; a little farther, the delegates of a district are hastening to the town in order to consult upon some local improvements. . . . The great political agitation of American legislative bodies which is the only one that attracts the attention of foreigners, is a mere episode, or a sort of continuation, of that universal movement which originates in the lowest classes of the people and extends successively to all the ranks of society.[5]

The American electoral system eases the transformation of the political activity of the citizen into parliamentary action. The voting of personalities makes the representative visible and directly approachable. Rather than an anonymous party organization, a human of flesh and blood is responsible for political action. Because the representatives are solely dependent upon the vote of their electoral district, they make the effort to remain close to their constituents and responsive to their suggestions. The relationship between representatives and their constituents does not end with the election but remains open and alive throughout the term in Congress.

Personal contact between the individual citizen and representatives is incomparably more intense than in Germany and other developed democracies.

Americans write, telephone, and fax their representatives with their opinions and even visit them when they happen to be in Washington. Members of Congress often go out of their way to personally greet their visitors from the district. "Come in" is written on the doors of many congressional offices, and it is meant seriously.

American Parties: Organizations for Acquisition of Power

It is apparent that the independence of politicians has prevented the formation of tight, unified parties and with that has adversely affected the emergence of political ideologies. The parties themselves are prime examples of pluralism.

"Vocabulary Lesson for an Election Year"

The existence of the traditional parties of the Democrats and the Republicans provides people with the opportunity to politically join together on a nationwide level, at least in sharing a common name and in politically identifying themselves with a symbol.

> *"The Democratic party is, to be polite about it, broad based. It's the Cat-Canary Love Association, Dogs and Mailmen United. Some people say the only reason Lloyd Bentson is a Democrat is to keep Republicans from being embarrassed by his ties to big business. And Jesse Jackson—if you listen to what he says rather than how he says it—*

sounds like Fidel Castro's Jimminy Cricket. Jackson told the 1988 Atlanta convention that the Democratic party 'needs both its left wing and its right wing to fly.' But putting Bentsen out on the tip of one primary feather and Jackson way over on the other makes for a bird the size of the Chicago Merchandise Mart. Don't stand out in the yard when it flys overhead."

P.J. O'Rourke, Parliament of Whores

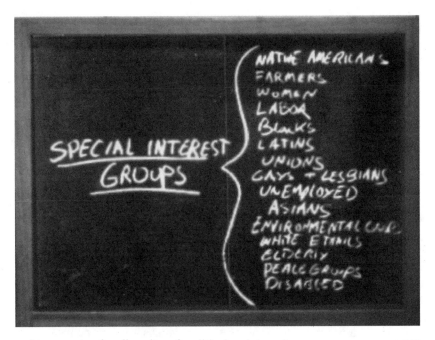

At any rate, the diversity of political opinions is so enormous, especially among Democrats, one must again cite the American rhetoric in order to find an explanation for the fact that people of such differing political views can come together in a political party that reaches from arch-conservative senators or representatives, governors, mayors, council members, especially of the Southern regions of the United States, to radical representatives of minority, ethnic, racial, feminist, and sexual-orientation groups, who all have quite progressive viewpoints on social politics and civil rights.

American political parties can only achieve identification and integration of the population of the entire country, at least at a surface level, because the substance of their programs is general and vague. The party program—in an exaggerated sense—is created by each candidate, either alone or in agreement with colleagues. A national program is only developed for the one person who holds a truly national office—and this is renewed every four years.

The Exclusion of Minority Groups

The danger of the two-party system lies in the fact that minority groups are excluded from the political process. As positive as it is on the one hand that the candidates lean toward the center of the spectrum and stay away from radical positions because they have to obtain majorities, it means on the other hand that progressive ideas can only very slowly, if at all, find a foothold in the system.

Often enough, the parties have achieved their reform efforts through the development of independent third or even fourth parties, whose programs responded to the needs of the time and were so attractive to voters that, in spite of the institutional and legal hindrances that protect the two-party system, they posed a serious challenge to one or even both of the established parties.

> *"In the American political system, you're only allowed to have real ideas if it's absolutely guaranteed that you can't win an election. Thus the only substantive political platforms belong to candidates such as Norman Thomas, Henry Wallace and Eugene McCarthy, and—as you can see by that list—saying a candidate has real ideas is no compliment."*
>
> P.J. O'Rourke, Parliament of Whores

The Democrats, for example, owe their transition to a social democratic party to the progressive movement of Robert La Follette and his sons—ironically a split from the Republican party. The presidential candidacy of George Wallace, the conservative populist who surprisingly found great success outside of his home base in the Southern states with the white working class in the urban areas, was one important impulse for the strategic planning of the Reagan Republicans. They focused on specifically addressing this logically and traditionally democratic social group that was apparently breaking from its ranks.

In a two-party system, the votes of minority groups have less political impact than in a proportional system because the chances for political power lie in the middle of the political spectrum. The success of a political party such as the German F.D.P. (Free German Party), which quite consciously is geared toward the representation of the interests of a minority group, is unthinkable in America. One does not need someone to procure a majority in parliament. Either one has the majority or one does not.

In any case, even in the two-party system there is opportunity for minority groups to receive not only a proportional representation but even an unfair advantage in the parliamentary realm. If none of the parties has a solid majority in the electoral district, well-organized minorities tip the scale with a significance that is not representative of their numbers. This is dependent not so much on their strength in numbers but on whether they actually go to the voting booths and whether they are united on specific issues. The American Jewish community has recognized and made use of this opportunity for many years. There are now quite a few other racial, ethnic, and ideological groups who play their political cards in embattled electoral districts.

The Financing of Election Campaigns

Election campaigns for political offices have always been very expensive undertakings. The situation is intensified by the primary system because the candidate practically conducts two public election campaigns. For several decades, public campaign financing has existed in the presidential election, extending to the primaries as well. Quite sensibly, this public financing is balanced by an obligation to limit the costs of the election campaign, and quite unreasonably it is not, as is the case in Germany, tied to the election results but, rather, to the candidate's own campaign funds as so-called "matching funds." Yet these spending limits can be disregarded if one does not apply for public co-financing. Frequently there have been candidates who afforded themselves the luxury of depending solely on private funding in order to bring more ammunition into the election campaign.

There are efforts to introduce public funding for other election campaigns besides the presidential election. Yet these efforts are blocked by resistance of a public that vehemently rejects the funding of politics at the cost of the taxpayer. This is a schizophrenic and hypocritical attitude because they also loudly denounce the low moral standard of their politicians being corrupted by their need to lobby interest groups for campaign funds. A similar schizophrenia on the part of the politicians lets them give preference to the status quo, which on the one hand makes them subject to the influence and immense pressure of the interest groups but on the other hand allows them to draw on their advantageous position of elected officials over challenging candidates.

> *"When buying and selling are controlled by legislation, the first thing to be bought and sold are legislators."*
>
> P.J. O'Rourke, Parliament of Whores

Money comes from many different groups within the society, especially from business groups, corporate organizations, and labor unions as well as wealthy individuals. One must label this practice as the "financing of politics," as these contributions are raised and spent not only during the campaign period, but also year round. This "financing" is accomplished chiefly through political action committees (PACs), which any club, any company, any organization, and any group of persons can form in order to collect money that is then given to politicians or to the party itself. Not just economic groups, but also ideological groups and so-called "single-issue groups" make use of this practice to promote particular political goals. With money one can achieve access to the decision-making bodies.

In his book about America, Peter Lösche correctly points out that the rise of PACs strengthens the already existing tendency of fragmentation within the decision-making process in the American political system because representatives now focus their attention not only on their districts, but also on regional and ideological interest groups as well. The significance of PACs for American political life has grown immensely in the past decades.[6] Between 1974 and 1988, their number has grown from 608 to 4,268, a sevenfold increase. Within the same period, the contributions to the candidates increased from $12.5 million to $150 million for each election period.

A senator's campaign costs on average $4 to $5 million. Therefore, during his or her six years in office, a senator must collect from $15,000 to $20,000 each week. During the last senate campaign in Texas, both candidates together spent $25 million. The candidate for the office of mayor of New York, with the world famous name Lauder, invested more than $10 million of his cosmetic fortune in a losing primary campaign for the Republican nomination. The independent candidate for president, billionaire H. Ross Perot, offered to spend $100 million of his personal fortune on the campaign.[7]

It is no coincidence that a large number of politicians, particularly in high positions, are wealthy persons, some of whom already were wealthy before they got into politics and others who made their fortunes during their time in office. It is surprising that people without personal fortunes can play the game of politics at all. These politicians must depend upon the generosity of their supporters, which is usually not without a price tag.

The "Financing" of the Politicians

The salaries of politicians are not lavish even in comparison to the incomes of middle-ranking business people, especially considering the cost of living in Washington, D.C., and maintenance of a household in their home states. If a member of Congress has a family with college-age children, an annual income of $125,000 does not support an exorbitant lifestyle.

One positive aspect to this mixing of money and politics in the United States is the requirement of public disclosure of the sources of income and contributions. The press considers itself as a fourth branch of government in the United States. Not only are obvious misdeeds covered in great detail and with persistence, but the media also offer information about legal financial transactions of interest to the public. The *Washington Post* published regularly, for example, a list of the honoraria that representatives and senators had received from various groups during the time period covered by the report.[8] Similarly, a list of contributions from PAC's for members of Congress are from time to time published in the media.

Under the Freedom of Information Act, the public and the media have access to much of the government information that is often treated as a private and state secret in Europe. Notable are the public reports of tax returns released by elected officials in the United States including those of the president. Every year after the April 15 deadline for the remittance of tax returns, detailed reports on the size and sources of the income of the president and the first lady are published in the American press. Occasionally, surprising insights into the private lives of politicians, and also into the structures and laws of American society, are revealed with these reports. An example would be the disclosure that for her book about Millie, the dog who was in the White House at the time, Barbara Bush "earned" more than the salary paid to her husband in the most important office in the nation.

Notes

1. *The Federalist Papers,* No. 10, James Madison, p. 82.
2. Ibid., pp. 82–83.

3. Ibid., p. 83.
4. Alexis de Tocqueville, *Democracy in America II*, p. 91.
5. Ibid., *Democracy in America I*, pp. 249–50.
6. "Campaign Financing in Federal Elections: A Guide to the Law and Its Operations."
7. Alexander Cockburn, "The Perot Program," p. 810.
8. House members were only allowed to keep part of the honoraria. The rest had to be given to nonprofit organizations.

Plebiscite

and

Participation

In the United States, many more public offices than in any other democracy are filled not by appointment but by public election. It is a surprise to Europeans that even some members of the judicial branch are elected by the people. This is also true for leading administrative and even law-enforcement positions. The practice varies from state to state. The Western states tend to fill most official positions by public elections. In many of these states, almost all cabinet positions, for example lieutenant governor, secretary of state, and secretary of the treasury, are not appointed by the governor but filled by public elections. Judges of the appellate courts and state attorneys are elected. The tradition, which we all know from Western movies, in which the sheriff is elected by the people remains the practice today.

Plebiscite Elements: Proposition, Recall, Write-in

In addition to the overwhelming number of direct elections that crowd the ballot, there are several other instruments of direct democracy. In the states and in the communities—although not at the federal level—the people have the right to call a referendum. As a "proposition," a political issue is taken from the jurisdiction of the legislature and presented directly to the people for a decision. There is even a tendency to submit highly controversial questions, such as tax increases or bond issues directly to the people. Americans have more readily accepted the idea and practice of direct democracy than Europeans. It stems from a fundamental concept of American democracy—the right of the voters to have the final decision over matters affecting their lives.

Decisions of the people also serve as a barometer of political trends among the populace. The successful initiative in California in the seventies to reduce property taxes signified the beginning of a reversal in the political attitudes of the middle class. The vote in favor of a reduction in state welfare programs and the lowering of taxes was especially well received and understood by the Republicans in Ronald Reagan's circle dominated by Californians. It forecast a successful appeal to this group of voters in the presidential election of 1980.

Another plebiscite element is the write-in candidacy, which means one can write in a different name than those already listed on the ballot. Unfortunately, this procedure is not allowed in the official presidential election. On the contrary, the election rules in many states are so restrictive that even declared presidential candidates, if they run as independents, have difficulties entering their names on the official ballot. In the primary elections, however, write-in candidacies are permitted in most states.

Another instrument of direct democracy is the recall. The possibility to legally vote out an elected representative exists mainly in the Western states where it has been put to use again and again over the years, at times successfully. The governor of Arizona was unseated by recall some years ago.

Considering all these marvelous possibilities for active participation in elections, it is remarkable that participation, even in presidential elections, is constantly decreasing and is currently at 50 percent. Can it be that the voters have too many possibilities and that they feel overwhelmed? Or do they sense that in spite of this diversity in electoral opportunities, they have no influence on the political scene in the end? Do they feel that the change of people or parties in reality makes no fundamental difference, that above all their personal fate is not affected by the results of elections?

The Origin of Election Fatigue

The numbers on voter turnout in the United States cannot be compared out of context to the election participation rate in Germany. In the American governmental system, a citizen does not automatically have the right to vote when he or she reaches the minimum age of eighteen. The citizen must specifically register as a voter. It is a bothersome requirement to many Americans who fail to register out of apathy or forgetfulness. Because Americans change their place of residence frequently, a change of registration is frequently put off. In some states, a registration automatically also expires if the citizen fails to vote for several elections in a row. At the time of registration, the voter can also declare party affiliation. In most states, it is necessary to declare a party affiliation in order to be permitted to take part in the primaries for this party. But one can always reregister one's party affiliation at any time.

Thus, many Americans have the right to vote in theory but not in practice. It is nevertheless fair to assume that even with an automatic registration system, as exists in Germany, a great part of the population still would not vote.

In addition to this, the act of voting is a time-consuming and lengthy process. In the presidential election year, citizens also vote for the House representatives, often times for senators, at times for the governor of the particular state, and also for representatives at the regional and local levels. Sometimes a vote on citizen initiatives is added to the ballot. An election ballot in the United States can be a form the size of a newspaper on which dozens of elections are listed. The paper ballot has been largely replaced by voting machines on which the voter simply has to punch a hole or pull a lever.

In addition, elections are not held on a Sunday, as is the case in Germany, but on a workday, invariably a Tuesday. If one considers all these obstacles, the election participation rates are surprisingly high, but the consistently downward trend in citizen interest and participation in politics is cause for concern.

The nonvoters primarily include the unemployed, the underclass, and the uneducated who barely comprehend the voting system. Nevertheless, they sense instinctively that their participation in the democratic process would (from their point of view) not change anything.

Other members of society have extended their consumer behavior to all parts of their lifestyle, so that active participation in public life is not even a consideration. The consumer lets the system work for him or her but does not engage in political activity.

For the remainder of the nonvoters, elections seem an empty ritual that is supposed to give the impression that democracy is being practiced. The vague feeling of the members of the underclass that elections change nothing is for them a sure and established fact and reason enough not to participate. This group rationalizes that from their point of view elections change nothing and therefore participation is fruitless.

Decreasing Voter Participation—A Danger for Democracy

Election fatigue is not an American phenomenon, although in this country it has taken on dramatic dimensions. The real cause becomes clear when one examines the three motives just mentioned. For half of the citizens of the United States, democracy does not function as it should: It cannot guarantee a decent living standard and minimal education to a large segment of society. It allows citizens to look at politics as a consumer product that they can enjoy or not, but it does not inspire participation. It produces in their view politicians who do not represent voters but act, rather, as representatives of special interests and create politics that do not deal with the realities of society.

Low voter turnout is symptomatic and dangerous, dangerous not for those already in office or for the stability of the nation, but it is a threat to the vitality of a democracy that depends at the very least upon the silent approval of the majority.

In his book *Who Will Tell the People?*, William Greider poses the rhetorical question:

> If the people no longer believe in elections, will they continue to believe in the power of the elected to govern their lives?[1]

Even more dramatically, Paul Weyrich, director of a conservative think tank declares:

> Nonvoters are voting against the system and, if we get a bit more of that, the system won't work.[2]

These phenomena are not new in the United States. Groups on the margins of society have always been excluded from the political process, and corruption and mediocrity among politicians have been common. Yet, failure to vote was always a temporary problem that concerned primarily the newcomers to the society who in a generation or two were integrated into the so-called "mainstream." Integration, a singular phenomenon of social development of the United States, no longer functions as it once did. Hunger, unemployment, homelessness, and illiteracy have become a permanent part of life for certain population groups in recent decades. They see no prospects of improvement and no social solidarity from the rest of society.

Political corruption in the past was surely more severe and more widespread, but it was always reprehensible. Today the immense and still growing influence of money in politics is legalized. Buying political influence has become public and accepted as an integral part of politics.

Another new phenomenon is the "mediazation" of politics and of the politicians. Rather than taking part in the actual political events, an arduous and complicated process, one can now have it predigested on television, which is not only short and precise but also entertaining.

The Meaning of Democratic Customs and Practices

It would be a mistake, however, to judge the vitality and prospect of democracy in the United States only by its official structures.[3] The traditional institutions—parties, elections, legislatures—may all be caught in a dangerous process of disintegration, yet beside them and as kind of an undercurrent there are new forms of participation and involvement. It is possible that these new or renewed forms of democratic life will slowly and eventually replace the antiquated and corrupted institutions of today. Of course, the other extreme development is also imaginable, that the power structures are ever more gridlocked in their state of isolation from political reality, and under the weight of their lifeless mass they slowly bury and suffocate the vitality of democracy.

Taking the optimistic view, it is quite possible that the functioning of today's democratic institutions is not all that relevant for democracy. In many parts of his book, Tocqueville points out that the success of the American experiment in democracy is based not so much on the institutions and the laws themselves, but primarily on the democratic customs and practices from which all else (laws, institutions, and political content) get their democratic quality to begin with. Democratic customs and practices are not natural talents but, rather, ways of life that are acquired and cultivated through social custom. In his portrayal of the municipal organization, which he quite rightly sees as the origin and life blood of the American democracy, Tocqueville remarks:

> The American system, which divides the local authority among so many citizens, does not scruple to multiply the functions of the town officers. For in the United States it is believed, and with truth, that patriotism is a kind of devotion which is strengthened by ritual observance. In this manner the activity of the township is continually perceptible; it is daily manifested in the fulfillment of a duty or the exercise of a right; and a constant though gentle motion is thus kept up in society, which animates without disturbing it.[4]

At another point he writes:

> Democracy has gradually penetrated into their customs, their opinions, and their forms of social intercourse; it is to be found in all the details of daily life as well as in the laws.[5]

So the strengthening and restoring of established democratic institutions and mechanisms are not the most urgent assignments. The ongoing political reform discussion, concentrating on low election turnout, neglects the topic of actual importance because it reduces the role of the citizen of a democracy to his or her function as a voter. To achieve real reform, it is more important to strengthen possibilities for self-initiative and personal responsibility. Democratic institutions are only alive in democratic spirit and democratic customs. To develop and sustain these habits takes more than the occasional trot to the ballot box.

Thomas Jefferson's Model of the Citizen's Permanent Participation in the Political Process

For Thomas Jefferson, the great theorist and master of American democracy, the need to constantly practice democracy was at the center of his political thought. He called upon the American people to continually test and reform the entire structure of the state. This challenge is only one aspect of a broad and established concept of maintaining the awareness of the people of their democratic rights and their ability to use them to their advantage. At the center of this theory, for which Jefferson also designed a detailed model for practical realization, stands the concept of "ward republics" in which, as in the city-states of ancient Greece, the citizens would directly and daily discuss and decide upon their matters. This was not a utopian model born of nostalgic yearning for the ideal of Greek civilization; there were indeed practical examples in the townships of New England of at least an approach to this concept. Jefferson wanted to preserve and improve upon the political esprit of these communities and eventually make them the general rule.

In the "wards," Jefferson saw the lowest of four levels of a state pyramid; they were the lowest, however, only in the local sense. In the qualitative sense they were the highest level because in them democracy was being played out and could be further developed. In a letter to Joseph Cabell in 1816, he explained his concept:

> The elementary republics of the wards, the county republics, the States republics, and the republic of the Union, would form a gradation of authorities, standing each on the basis of law, holding every one its delegated share of powers, and constituting truly a system of fundamental balances and checks for the government. Where every man is a sharer in the direction of his ward-republic, or of some of the higher ones, and feels that he is a participator in the government of affairs, not merely at an election one day in the year, but every day; when there shall not be a man in the State who will not be a member of some one of its councils, great or small, he will let the heart be torn out of his body sooner than his power be wrested from him by a Caesar or a Bonaparte.[6]

Jefferson's idea of a permanent state of involvement in the political process is the means toward qualification of the voters as well as of the political leaders. Only with constant practice can the citizens learn about compromise as a civil virtue, respect for the opinions of others, the ability to bring together seemingly incompatible goals, tolerance, and modesty. The ward-republics in which "every citizen is a member of the government," are the most important part of Jefferson's state structure because they are the place in which the inhabitants or voters become fully responsible citizens. For Jefferson, politics are obviously not the work of the elite but, rather, an honorable duty of all citizens.

Political Involvement in Voluntary Associations

In the United States, such a democratic esprit is still or is again alive in the hundreds and thousands of voluntary associations that are the working units of social and—in the broadest sense—all political life in America. The phenomenon of voluntary association is wide-ranging, it includes self-help groups, neighborhood associations, spontaneous action committees, hobby groups, and also business associations and political interest groups.

Tocqueville gave an extensive description of this phenomenon in his portrayal of democracy in the United States:

> Besides the permanent associations which are established by law under the names of townships, cities, and counties, a vast number of others are formed and maintained by the agency of private individuals.

The citizen of the United States is taught from infancy to rely upon his own exertions in order to resist the evils and the difficulties of life; he looks upon the social authority with an eye of mistrust and anxiety, and he claims its assistance only when he is unable to do without it. This habit may be traced even in the schools, where the children in their games are wont to submit to rules which they have themselves established, and to punish misdemeanors which they have themselves defined. The same spirit pervades every act of social life. If a stoppage occurs in a thoroughfare and the circulation of vehicles is hindered, the neighbors immediately form themselves into a deliberative body; and this extemporaneous assembly gives rise to an executive power which remedies the inconvenience before anybody has thought of recurring to a pre-existing authority superior to that of the persons immediately concerned. If some public pleasure is concerned, an association is formed to give more splendor and regularity to the entertainment. Societies are formed to resist evils that are exclusively of a moral nature, as to diminish the vice of intemperance.

In the United States associations are established to promote the public safety, commerce, industry, morality, and religion. There is no end which the human will despairs of attaining through the combined power of individuals united into a society.[7]

The American Principle: Self-Initiative before State Welfare

Two things in this description are especially worth noting: first, the preference that an American gives to self-help over the interference of the state. This is a fundamental difference in the political attitude between Americans and Europeans (perhaps with the exception of the British). This difference is valid even today when the Europeans have experienced democracy for many decades and the Americans reluctantly accepted increasing government interference.

The second decisive difference with the European tradition lies in the fact that the United States never knew anything other than freedom of assembly. This right is by no means self-evident; in most countries it was only wrested by the people from the state after a long struggle. Tocqueville remarks:

> The right of association was imported from England, and it has always existed in America; the exercise of this privilege is now incorporated with the manners and customs of the people.[8]

The absolute state has carefully followed the development of associations and societies—well aware of their threat. In the German edition of Tocqueville's *Democracy in America,* interesting examples from history are quoted in a footnote from the publisher.

> In Rome under the rule of the emperors it was specifically prohibited to form associations (a *lex Julia* by emperor Augustus). As hostile toward private associations as the Roman empire was the emerging police-state of the European Absolutism. In the police-state there was room only for such associations which were approved by the authorities. To obtain legal capacity a club or society had to be approved by the sovereign.[9]

The measures that Metternich took against the German athletic clubs, in which he justifiably saw the beginnings of a democratic movement, should be remembered. The hostility of totalitarian states toward associations of any kind is well known. In order to satisfy the need of human beings for association, these regimes founded their own clubs that they could easily control.

The preference given to associations and self-initiatives for solving society's problems is based in the United States not only on a distrust for government but also on a strong self-confidence that developed through experience and practice. The opposite to this is the fearful call for government intervention in the European nations, as a result of a lack of self-confidence. This in turn is the result of the fact that the Europeans have not much experience with associations and clubs as instruments of political participation and therefore do not feel comfortable using them.

The Different Forms of Voluntary Associations

Besides the formally organized associations, there are a greater number of loosely formed organizations, both short-term active and long-standing organizations that are formed primarily to provide social services or to serve as self-help groups for people who are affected by a special problem.

This social development has a long-standing tradition in the United States. In 1935 Alcoholics Anonymous was founded and spread throughout the world. Self-help groups are nothing short of the ultimate example of the American version of a "voluntary subsidiarity": the will to care for oneself together with the awareness that this occurs most effectively in association with other people of the same set. If it were possible to carry over this concept from the close private sphere into the social sphere, the underlying concept of self-help could form the origin for the revival of the democratic idea and its structural enhancement.

Social involvement is more deeply rooted in the United States than in Europe. This may seem surprising, because the United States has suffered the reputation of having an especially rough and unfriendly social atmosphere. Yet the contradiction is only in appearance. Precisely because of political apathy toward social concerns, in comparison to Europe, the citizen feels directly addressed. The voluntary organizations substitute in many areas for the lack of involvement of the administrative bodies. The community steps in where the authorities pass by.

Galas and goodwill fairs also belong in this category. These types of events are organized not only by the members of high society but also by the middle class to collect money for social services. The promotion of culture and the financing of universities through private donations are part of this social culture of voluntarism. Even the way the election campaigns are financed is an aspect of the American "voluntary spirit." Finally, the churches are voluntary associations that live mainly off the generosity of their members.

**The Political Lobby Is a Part of the Spectrum
of Voluntary Associations**

> *"We usually think of 'special interests' as being something out of a
> Thomas Nast cartoon—big men with cigars conspiring over a biscuit
> trust. But in fact, a special interest is any person or group that wants
> to be treated differently from the rest of us by the government. Every
> charity is a special interest. So is the League of Women Voters, the
> Episcopalian church,* Consumer Reports *magazine and anybody who
> threatens to write to his congressman. A special interest may be
> humble. It may be (this happens) worthy. It may even be morally
> correct about its need for special treatment. . . .*
>
> *Traditionally American special interests have been frank about
> their political goals: They want money and privileges that other
> Americans don't get. . . . . But recently special interest groups have
> begun dressing themselves in the clothes of altruism. And some of
> these groups have become so well costumed that it's hard to tell what
> their special interest is, let alone what's so special about it."*
>
> P.J. O'Rourke, Parliament of Whores

To the "voluntary associations" also belong, by definition, the trade associations
and professional organizations whose goal it is to influence legislation to their benefit. This may be a legitimate goal in the American view, but this type of involvement
in the political process was apparently not what Jefferson meant when he demanded
that "every man feels that he is a participator in the government of affairs."

The role of associations and their lobbyists in the American political system is completely ambivalent and should be judged without bias. The term
lobbyist, now also common in Germany, has a sinister tone to it for Germans.
Forbidden entrance to the legislative chambers, interest groups waylaid members in the entrance hall or lobby. In the United States this is a constitutional
right of citizens to petition their government. It is also a service to legislators
hard-pressed to distinguish government propaganda from public opinion in
the effort to study the minute details of complex legislative programs.

This type of service has been corrupted into a struggle for influence with all
legal and also illegal means available. The trade associations and their lobbyists

are not always interested in working together in the political process in Jefferson's sense. They are interested in completely controlling the process to the extent of eliminating all the other players. Of course, the representatives of a particular interest are challenged and offset by other interest groups. According to the optimistic American theory of checks and balances, these different interest groups balance themselves out. This balance is tenuous when political power is unevenly exercised as sheer force without the ameliorating effects of democratic compromise. Compromise is possible only if the "citizen," in the emphatic sense that Jefferson gave the term, understands that personal interests are only partial aspects of a whole—the enlightened citizen continues the democratic struggle fully aware that his or her personal well-being is also dependent upon the success of the whole.[10]

The Political Significance of the Charitable Voluntary Associations

Charitable voluntary associations exercise great political influence at every level in the United States. They are highly successful in those areas where they can apply pressure directly on regional issues and thereby include the public in their efforts. At the federal level, there are also numerous well-organized associations that have effectively helped form American politics and continue to influence it. An especially noteworthy example is the Ralph Nader Consumer Protection Organization, formed more than thirty years ago by the efforts of one man, the former provincial attorney, Ralph Nader, to promote product safety in the American automobile industry.

Nader contended that the superficial competition within the American automobile industry demanded government regulation to enforce standards of safety, energy conservation, and environmental pollution.

Nader's organization was originally supported chiefly by the co-operative work of thousands of volunteers across the country—Nader's Raiders. In time, their efforts expanded to include basic research on many aspects of consumer protection and public policy generally supported by active and effective lobbying.

There is no doubt that Nader and his movement have helped to promote and secure the passage of numerous consumer-protection and environmental-protection laws and, on the whole, have established the necessity of regulatory state control and intervention in the free market.

The successes of the public interest lobby, considered annoyingly left-wing (a common charge against socially conscious movements), roused political movements on the right. There are now numerous conservative-oriented lobbies that espouse the revival of traditional American moral values. Their concrete goals are, for example, the reintroduction of school prayers, prison sentences for the desecration of the American flag, and the prohibition of pornography and of abortion (of course, there are also well-organized pro-abortion lobbies).

Finally, voluntarism plays a significant role in American election campaign organizations. With the trend toward television election campaigns, the professionalization of the campaign efforts, especially at the state level and for the presidency, is highly developed. Yet, even at this level, the strength and efficiency of grassroots organizations are decidedly important for many candidates, particularly in the primaries. The last time a grassroots organization decisively influenced an election, even at the federal level, was the candidacy of Senator Eugene McCarthy for the Democratic presidential nomination in 1968. Although it failed in the end, it had a mighty effect in forcing the withdrawal of one of the most powerful presidents of this century, Lyndon B. Johnson, and in starting the process of ending the Vietnam War. It also initiated a reform movement within the Democratic party still in evidence today.

The brief candidacy of H. Ross Perot as an independent candidate for president carried strong strains of a grassroots movement. Perot emphatically declared that he would run for election only if enough followers organized support in all of the states. Shortly after the public announcement, corresponding committees sprang up spontaneously across the country. When Perot first withdrew his candidacy (he later stepped back in), his followers had already qualified him by petition in almost forty states. Even though Perot strained the patience of his followers by his in-and-out spectacle, his candidacy brought new life to political participation in the United States.

Notes

1. William Greider, *Who Will Tell the People?* p. 21.
2. Ibid., p. 22.
3. Ibid., p. 30.
4. Alexis de Tocqueville, *Democracy in America I,* pp. 67–68.
5. Ibid., pp. 321–22.
6. Jefferson to Joseph Cabell, February 2, 1816, *Writings,* p. 1380; compare also with Jefferson to Samuel Kercheval, July 12, 1816, *Writings,* p. 1399, and *The Portable Thomas Jefferson,* p. 556.
7. Tocqueville, *Democracy in America I,* pp. 191–92.
8. Ibid., p. 194.
9. Rudolph Solm, *Institutionen: Geschichte und System des römischen Privatrechts,* pp. 231–32 (German edition), quoted by the German publisher in Tocqueville's *Democracy in America I,* p. 280 (German edition).
10. Bellah et al. point out that not only Jefferson, but also "the hard-headed advocate of the political machinery of checks and balances, James Madison, was of the opinion that the public good is the supreme object to be pursued; and that no form of government whatever has any other value as it may be fitted for the attainment of this object." Robert N. Bellah et al., *Habits of the Heart,* p. 253.

"Astrocracy"

and

Bureaucracy

The American democratic spirit is threatened by the easy comfort of the evolving television democracy, which reduces citizens to passive onlookers and consumers of politics. The final and total submission of politics to the culture of television was completed in the eighties. Television appropriated political information and communication not only quantitatively by supplanting other media; above all, it changed its quality by forcing onto politics a mode of communication commensurate with the medium.

This development, which comprises the whole spectrum of political activity, is especially advanced in the area of campaign strategies. The share of television ads in an election campaign has steadily grown since the advent of television. Public appearances by the candidates, of course, continue to be unavoidable, but they are often considered a bothersome necessity, except when press and television turn these stagings into media events.

Because stations have been added everywhere on the local and regional level, television ads dominate campaigns on the community level as well. There may still be posters for small town or suburban political candidates on trees and street lamps and on the front lawns of private houses but the colorful variety of party posters that is still the norm in Europe during election campaigns is seldom to be found in the United States. The election campaign is carried out almost exclusively in the living room.

Politics as Consumer Goods

But it is not only the quantity of television advertisement that has grown exponentially; what has changed most significantly in political television ads is their content. Political ads no longer differ from those for consumer products, and this is intentional. By adapting the general style of commercial advertisements, campaign strategists can best expect political ads to be accepted by an audience that is conditioned to perceive commercial ads as an integral part of any program.

The style, however, often dictates the content of the political message. Formerly, a candidate introduced his political program, or parts thereof, in a rational form, spoken directly into the eye of the camera. Even if his "message" had to be short due to financial considerations, the gist was to convince the audience with arguments. Formerly, ads were based on argumentation; today they are based on drama. Just as in commercial advertisements, a sketch unfolds visually and dramatically, documenting the central idea that one wants to get across to the voter. A voice in the background supplies the comment instructing the audience on how to interpret the mini-drama displayed on the screen. The powerful visual and acoustical images carry the political message, which is then summarized and encapsulated in an easily remembered slogan.

This change of political advertisements into ever shorter forms has already shown its impact on politics. The attention span of the American television audience has been completely attuned to the ten, twenty, or thirty seconds of a usual commercial spot. As a consequence, political statements are uttered more and more frequently in the form of highly stylized sound bites.[1]

An American politician, or anyone who regularly discusses politics in public, becomes used to speaking in sound bites. While this procedure is still for many in public life a difficult task, for others it has already become second nature. As a further result of abbreviating political argument to a twenty- or thirty-second format (and frequently to an even shorter one), political spots, just as commercial ads, have become increasingly shrill in tone. This development climaxed with the so-called negative campaigning practiced with growing tendency since the late eighties, the main reason for this being the fact that one's own political positions—if indeed there are any—are much too complicated to be compressed into such a short time. Furthermore, these positions could displease certain target groups, and their depiction might not be dramatic enough. Consequently, what remains as a focus for election spots are the real or imagined failures of the opponent, which are totally distorted to evoke fear and hatred.

In the election of 1988, George Bush used this tactic masterfully. In order to attack the liberal policies of his opponent Michael Dukakis, then governor of Massachusetts, a television spot used the case of a black convict, Willie Horton, who had raped a white woman while on leave from a Massachusetts prison. Here, sex, criminal behavior, and racism were all mixed together to create a campaign spot whose subtext read: "Vote (you whites out there!) for a man who keeps criminals (especially black ones!) behind lock and key so they cannot rape your wives." Do not forget that we are not talking about the election for a local sheriff but for the president of the United States.

Because this kind of election campaign has been successful, many politicians today conduct similar mud fights and smear each other's reputation with the most hair-raising allegations.

The Replacement of the Democratic Spirit
by Consumer Mentality

But these excesses are only the beginning of a decline that has its fundamental roots in the usurpation of politics by television. Tocqueville, who could not foresee anything even remotely like television politics in his days, nevertheless points out the danger of abdicating the participatory rights that only democracy offers to its people. He praises the Americans for their activism and mobility in politics, which he considers an absolute requirement for the safeguarding of democracy:

> In some countries the inhabitants seem unwilling to avail themselves of the political privileges which the law gives them; it would seem that they set too high a value upon their time to spend it on the interests of the community; and they shut themselves up in a narrow selfishness, marked out by four sunk fences and a quickset hedge. But if an American were condemned to confine his activity to his own affairs; he would be robbed of one half of his existence; he would feel an immense void in the life which he is accustomed to lead, and his wretchedness would be unbearable. I am persuaded that if ever a despotism should be established in America, it will be more difficult to overcome the habits that freedom has formed than to conquer the love of freedom itself.[2]

Doubtlessly, Tocqueville was thinking of a despotism that wields authoritarian power. This is an unlikely danger in the United States. Customary freedoms

could be slowly eroded by a subtle despotism of a consumer orientation, and this process could be all the more dangerous because it offers an incredible variety of choices on the surface while simultaneously undermining the only freedom that counts—the freedom to say "no" to consumerism.

Movement, the essential element of democracy, stops when consumerism holds individuals and society totally in its thrall. Democracy becomes as static on the inside as authoritarian regimes, which, also, keep up a front of external activism. Democracy has to be shaped and lived out in participatory fashion; it cannot simply be "lapped up" like a television movie.

In a television democracy, politicians become manipulators and the governed receive happiness. Three-quarters of a century ago, Aldous Huxley developed the vision of just such a consumer society in which citizens voluntarily and happily accept a despotic regime that they do not perceive as such because it fulfills all their wishes. In his book *Amusing Ourselves to Death*, Neil Postman proffers the thesis that conditions in the United States already approach those of Huxley's utopia.[3] Contemporary circumstances in America do not support this theory. They seem to announce an eruption of social tensions rather than a gradual decline into a state of satisfied stupefaction. But Postman is right with his warning that freedom could, so to speak, be checked at the door to the living room because people tend to assume that the mere consumption of politics is sufficient involvement in democratic practices.

"Couple considering suicide because TV Broadcasting is halted by limited nuclear warfare raging outside window"

Modern Corruptions of Democracy: "Astrocracy" and Bureaucracy

Democracy cannot be taken for granted; it must be nurtured and virtually reborn again and again. The dangers threatening democracy are not despotism or violent overthrow but a creeping erosion of its substance by indifference, laziness, and carelessness, while the exterior facade remains untouched and is decorated and polished like a monument.

According to classical theory, anarchy and despotism are the two bastardized and deteriorated forms of democracy, neither of which will likely occur in today's peaceful, modern mass society. However, two new forms have evolved that—unlike anarchy and despotism—are not mutually exclusive but can be found in conjunction: bureaucracy and "astrocracy."

By astrocracy, derived from the Greek *aster* (star), I mean the reign of experts and the adulation of stars in politics. There even exist combinations that could be called supernovas. Some, like the former Secretary of State Henry Kissinger, establish themselves as fixed stars and maintain a lasting role. Others, like the military celebrity General Norman Schwarzkopf, dominate the stage for a short period of time. The light intensity of political stars is not being measured in lux but by the number of megadollars paid for their book contracts or honoraria.

Astrocracy can establish itself in the place of democracy when the *demos*, the people, give up their political aspirations and their political will in favor of a new aristocracy made up of politicians, political experts, aides and handlers, gray eminences, star journalists, think-tank experts, lobbyists, and functionaries. These experts and stars are in loose but constant contact; they occasionally exchange positions, they feud and fight with each other, but on the whole they form a sort of club that dictates public opinion on all political matters. It is by no means a unified opinion, but a broad spectrum of miscellaneous positions which is then presented to the rest of the nation via the media, which in turn are governed by this club. There may be a multiplicity of opinions, but it is limited to established views. There are no fundamental deviations in the circle of stars because they would not be admitted to this clique.

"Astrocracy"—The American Version of Nomenclature

What we call astrocracy here is the same phenomenon dissidents in the Eastern European countries were dealing with when they talked about the governing party elite in communism as nomenclatura—a closed circle of politicians, intellectuals, and functionaries that gives the nation's social and political life its spiritual and factual imprint quite independently of the people.

The American nomenclature is, of course, open to anyone admitted by the club members after thorough examination. But that was also true for the Soviet nomenclatura that, after all, had to regenerate over time. The initial premises are different: The requirement in the United States is to have moderate political views that may range from slightly to the left to sharply to the right. It is almost of utmost importance for members of the astrocracy that they are able to present their opinions in an entertaining fashion because political views can be digested by the public only in the form of sound bites.[4]

Most of the members of the astrocracy are not elected but appointed or self-appointed, adopted and co-opted, called or chosen, but the creme de la creme of the elected politicians is among its members as well. The dividing line in astrocracy does not run—as in democracy—between the elected officials and the voters, between those governed and the governing body. Instead, the dividing line is between a) those who form opinions and in doing so impart influence; this includes people who—although they may have no opinion—still exert genuine political power, and b) the mass of all others who have only one voice, perhaps even an office, but certainly no influence, and who are permitted to choose an opinion out of the potpourri presented to them.

Astrocracy is neither capable nor willing to get involved in the details of how politics is actually conducted. In this respect, bureaucracy is the ideal complementary force to astrocracy, which would run the risk of sliding into anarchy without it. As it stands, astrocracy is constantly doing a delicate balancing act to stay aloft while also flirting with disaster.

It is bureaucracy's task to make sure that the state at least does not fall apart and occasionally even moves forward incrementally. Bureaucracy is an institution of the modern mass state and is independent of the form of government. Just

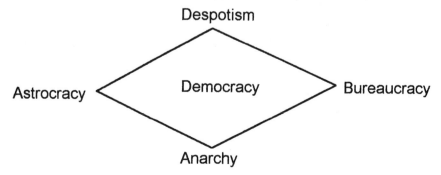

as astrocracy tends to be closer to anarchy, bureaucracy is closer to despotism. With its merciless tendency to administer everything, bureaucracy threatens not only the citizen's personal freedom, but it also limits the freedom of social restructuring.

Americans' Tense Relationship with the Civil Service

In terms of its structure, the American bureaucracy is no different from that of any other modern state, of an industrial complex, or any other large organization. While the bureaucracies of other nations are remarkable in their arrogance and authoritarianism, the trademarks of American bureaucracy are above all ineffi- ciency and bloatedness, which has historical reasons. All of the federal bureau- cracy used to be a personal domain of the president. Upon his election, he could fire all officials and hire new ones. This is exactly what most presidents did. After all, the president had to reward the friends who had supported his election.

This is not the only reason why federal officials rank at the bottom of the social ladder. Added to this is the opposition to government power and apparatus born out of a republican mistrust and a spirit of voluntarism. As little govern- ment as possible means as much freedom as possible. Even today, Americans adhere to this principle with fanatical loyalty. About 100 years ago, the first attempts were made to form a cadre of civil servants in the United States.[5] The majority of federal employees can no longer be fired each time the government changes. Nonetheless, every time the other party takes over, all personnel in the three political ranks below the secretarial level are changed.

> *"The bureaucracy must dispose of government proposals by dumping them on us."*
>
> P.J. O'Rourke, Parliament of Whores

Americans are to this day not convinced of the necessity of a well-functioning bureaucracy. Because they perceive their administration as inefficient and bloated, they would hasten to dissolve all bureaucracy or at least reduce it drasti- cally. This is a promise each new president makes. And just as happened under Ronald Reagan, who had made the reduction of the bureaucracy one of his major election goals, the number of federal employees has increased with each new president. The first president who not only promised a reduction in the federal work-force but who also has been successful in this endeavor is President Bill Clinton, but he does not even get credit for it because Americans in their impati- ence want even bigger and faster results.

The nation has never come to terms with the tremendous growth of American bureaucracy as a consequence of the Great Depression. Until the Crash of 1929, America had conceived of itself as the land of unlimited opportunities in which everyone could make it on his or her own. In this scheme, there was no role for the state in the organization of internal matters and no need for a competent federal administration. Then came the social legislation of the New Deal in the thirties, which required an appropriate administrative apparatus. This bureaucratic machine not only had to be virtually produced overnight, it also was made to feel the nation's distrust from day one.

England, France, Prussia had for centuries cultivated a corps of loyal and competent state servants able to form the core of a massively expanded bureaucracy when the modern welfare state dawned. In the United States, bureaucracy lives under the curse of a self-fulfilling prophecy. Because there is little prestige in working for the federal administration, it is difficult to find competent employees; as a result, organization does not improve, administration of legislation remains unsatisfactory, the preconceived distrust of the population is confirmed, and thus the vicious cycle begins again.

Parallelism of Federal and State Administrations

Notwithstanding, or perhaps because of this, the American federal bureaucracy is a Leviathan of immense proportions and corresponding power that is augmented by the administrative apparatus on the state and local level. The tendency of American politicians to offer a law or at least an amendment to a law whenever a problem arises does not contribute to a shrinking of the administrative machinery. The often contradictory signals emitted by Congress, which writes the laws, and the executive branch, which sees to their administration, create a veritable jungle.

How administrative powers between the federal government and the states are distributed has never been decided in a clear-cut way. The creation of a federal state by the Americans was an amazing political achievement for its time 200 years ago, because there had never been a comparable precedent with two sovereign entities within the same realm. The structure devised then is now creaking and cracking in all its joints. Modern political and administrative tools simply do not exist in the American system and are politically unpopular. Such systems could include one general income tax to be divided proportionally among the federal government, the states, and the communities, a system of shared legislation—like in Germany—in the form of general laws issued on the federal level, which are to be filled in detail by the state, and a mechanism by which federal affairs would be administered by the states. The American principle is one of parallelism, which often means a duplication of bureaucratic machinery and occasionally results in the two sides working against each other. The federal government has its own administration for all its programs, and because it financially intervenes in almost all areas of its citizens' lives, this machinery has, by necessity, grown tremendously.

> *"When it's better for enthusiastic and ambitious professionals to go to work for a country's government than it is for them to go to work, the country is in trouble."*
>
> P.J. O'Rourke, Parliament of Whores

Bureaucracy is the transformation of the state according to the corporate model. Just as modern industry created the corporation as its instrument for growth and efficient use of its energy, the modern state installed bureaucracy as a tool for the efficient shaping of society.

The other counterpart to democracy, astrocracy, is a different solution to the needs and challenges of a modern mass society. It is no coincidence that it developed much later than bureaucracy. It came with the onset of the era of television, which made it possible not only to reach all members of society but also to capture them by entertaining them correctly. Astrocracy achieves power when the citizens of a democratic society not only let others act for them—as it should be in a system calling for representation—but also let them think in their stead.

In contrast to bureaucracy, which makes itself clearly and offensively felt, astrocracy is painless, nonviolent, almost unnoticeable, and, above all, entertaining. Unobtrusively, it robs the democratic citizens of their right to participate in the political process and disempowers them, though they may feel fully in control of their democratic faculties.

While bureaucracy's threat to freedom is generally recognized, the indisputable loss of freedom under astrocracy remains hidden. Citizens surrender freedom to shape politics when they accept a brief, easily digestible and piquant opinion bite from the supermarket of published opinions instead of developing their own views.

Is this process irreversible? The process whereby the citizen voluntarily surrenders power to bureaucrats and stars can at least be slowed if not stopped. The way to do this is to reduce the needs and demands one has from government and to limit one's expectations of politicians' and experts' skills. Bureaucracy not only grew along with population numbers, but it also grew exponentially with the expectations citizens have of what government should do for them. The political establishment seeks to accommodate these wishes; it does so partly out of fear of losing popularity with citizens and partly out of a drive for power because more activities in favor of the citizen also signal greater political influence over him. The more needs are satisfied, the higher future expectations grow. The price for the fulfillment of more and more citizen needs is the disempowerment of the citizen, the hollowing out of democracy as a living form of government. Only if people are willing to reduce their needs can the growth of the Leviathan be arrested.

It is similar with the experts and the stars. The citizen trusts their guidance and no longer sees through the complexity of living conditions and the political environment. They offer simple answers and safety of judgment. They show that everything is clear, simple, and transparent. They relieve the worry of finding a path; they offer the option of identifying with a single symbol.

Only if we shun this easy path, perceive problems as such, and accept some as unsolvable, then these stars can be retrieved from the sky and brought down to life-size. Not only do they not have all answers to all questions, but they are also—to quote Socrates—less wise than we are when they act as though they know what they do not.

Notes

1. There may be, however, a change of attitudes in emergence due to the relentless overstraining of this "communication instrument." Compare also with note 7 of the seventh chapter, "The Oral Society."

2. Alexis de Tocqueville, *Democracy in America I*, pp. 250–51.

Tocqueville points out in a note that the same phenomenon could be so observed in Rome under the first Caesars when the remembrance of the republic was still strong and alive. Ibid., p. 250.

3. Neil Postman, *Amusing Ourselves to Death*, especially in the foreword, p. vii, and in the last chapter, "The Huxleyan Warning," p. 155.

4. For the role of talk-show journalists in the transmission of political contents and opinions, compare also with Eric Alterman, "Pundit Power," *Washington Post Magazine*, March 18, 1990; and with Howard Kurtz, "Washington's Talking Heads: Sound Bite Superstars and the Television Expert Game," *Washington Post Magazine*, May 19, 1991.

5. In 1883, the Pendleton Civil Service Act laid the foundation for the cadre of civil servants.

The

Imperial

Presidency

The authors of the Constitution conceived the presidency as an office of limited powers. Actual political power was conferred upon Congress as the people's agent and representative of their will. The president's task is to administer and execute the laws—which are the formulated will of the people. The president is the chief executive. What is called the "government" in Europe, i.e., the president, his advisers, and his cabinet, is called the "administration" in the United States. Government in the United States is the totality of the three branches of state power within which the president is assigned by the Constitution a secondary role as executive. This division of powers actually defined America's political reality for a long time until the expansion of the federal government began in the thirties.

Power Shifting in Favor of the President

There is no provision in the Constitution for the president to provide his own political program when he assumes office. This changed fundamentally when parties were formed in the beginning of the nineteenth century. In our time, the president's leading role has not only become firmly established, but has also become absolutely necessary for the functioning of a government in a complex mass society. The demands made upon politics and politicians have grown immeasurably. Just as members of Congress who used to meet in Washington for only a few months now are busy all year round as professional politicians, the president has long become an active participant in the shaping of legislation.

It should be remembered, however, that the president was never merely an executive organ of Congress, and in that respect the term *chief executive* never sufficiently described his function. He is a direct part of the legislative process by virtue of his veto power, and he is indirectly involved through the very threat of veto.

It is misleading to talk about a separation of powers in the American system of government. It would be much more appropriate to use the term *power linking* as James Madison described it in the fifty-first article of the *Federalist Papers*. In this essay, Madison expressed the hope that in the American Constitution the influence and powers assigned to the various branches were distributed so skillfully that they would hold each other in check by necessary compromise and collaboration. The steady growth of presidential power has upset the balance. The increase of executive power is accompanied by a shift of power to the federal government from the individual states, a development which further strengthens the president's authority.

To an ever growing degree, the president participates as initiator of laws not only by exercise of his veto power, but also even more directly through the gigantic apparatus of the departments and agencies.[1] By the same token, the participatory rights of Congress in the affairs of the executive branch guaranteed by the Constitution are being limited, undermined, or simply denied.

The constitutional right of the Senate to advise as well as to consent to appointment of cabinet members and other officials has become less significant as presidents have come to rely heavily on their own personal staffs in the White House. From the chief of staff, the national security adviser, the economic adviser, legal counsel, and other experts, the members of this staff have become real centers of power. As personal assistants to the president, they are appointed without the Senate's consent according to the principle of "executive privilege."

The Senate's right to participate in the drafting of treaties with other nations is being further and further eroded by a growing number of so-called "executive agreements," which may be as binding as treaties but are not to be placed before the Senate. The question whether these executive agreements represent a breach of the Constitution is occasionally discussed in a newspaper article or a scholarly essay, but this custom has been practiced for so long and so widely that it has quietly been accepted as constitutional reality.

Presidential Arrogance

The most questionable arrogation of presidential power linked with a limitation of Congress's constitutional right to advise, participate, and decide concerns the use of military force. In the Constitution, Congress is expressly given sole right to declare war. But presidents—pointing to their function as supreme commander of the armed forces—have ordered military action without formally involving Congress. Since the end of World War II, American troops have been sent to participate in more than forty wars or military conflicts. Only in a few of these instances was Congress asked for authorization.

Occasionally, presidents have asked Congress for blanket authority "to take all measures necessary for the safety of American forces." Such a decision by the Senate, the so-called Gulf of Tonkin Resolution, although based on faulty information, was the only official authorization to conduct the war in Vietnam, which cost almost 60,000 American lives.[2] Presidential arrogance reached the height of cynicism when President George Bush used as proof for the correctness of such unconstitutional action the fact that almost all participation in military conflicts since the end of World War II has been conducted without formal congressional consent.

Beyond these public attempts to expand the president's power in foreign policy, there is increased use of secret and illegal operations. The Iran-Contra affair during Ronald Reagan's presidency is another example of a creeping usurpation of power by the president. During the Iran-Iraq war, high-ranking White House officials—it is still a mystery whether this happened with or without the president's consent—secretly sold weapons to Iran. With the profits made in these deals, they continued to finance the right-wing guerrillas in Nicaragua (the so-called Contras) whose financial support had been expressly terminated by Congress. The extent of corruption within the constitutional process is evidenced by the fact, that the "hero" of the Iran-Contra affair, Oliver North, assistant to the White House security adviser, is admired for his alleged patriotism by many members of the same Congress he betrayed. The expansion of presidential powers does not only manifest itself in military invasions or a subversion of parliamentary rights; it simply follows upon the heels of a Congress that has abdicated its rights—out of cowardice, ignorance, or demagoguery.

Erosion of the Power Held by Congress

The power of Congress vis-à-vis the president has been eroded in internal affairs as well although issues here are complex and in flux. Congress is fiercely protective of its rights on budgetary appropriations and matters of taxation. But the legislative initiative in domestic affairs granted to Congress by the Constitution has been shifting during the course of the past decades to the president's office where most of the really important acts of legislation originate. This is basically not a bad development; it advances the cooperation necessary between the administration and Congress in tackling increasingly complex problems. This procedure is largely condoned by the Constitution whose premise is a linkage of powers rather than division. What does constitute a danger is its one-sidedness. Congress is not invited in equal measure to participate in the executive branch's power structure. In a parliamentary system, a prime minister constantly must defend his or her policies and actions to Congress and has to receive that body's approval.

Independence from congressional approval certainly has advantages for the president; in the long run, however, it may turn out to be politically unwholesome that he and his personal advisers have no constitutional duty to explain and defend their policies before Congress and to get a vote of confidence for these policies. There are hearings before congressional committees that are usually public and often televised; department secretaries and officials are heard in support and defense of the administration's proposals, but the president himself is never directly questioned. The president's appearances before Congress—once a year to deliver the State of the Union address—are usually ceremonial. The members of Congress listen politely or applaud exuberantly, but they do not openly challenge the president's statement in direct debate with him.

The press conferences held by the president at irregular intervals—as he pleases—are no substitute for political discourse. They are a home game for the president in which his responses are carefully prepared and researched by his press and media advisers. Although American journalists exhibit a remarkable irreverence, persistence, and independence in dealing with their president, the press conference is not a forum for political debate. The president may answer questions evasively, or he may leave them unanswered. He alone decides when to terminate the question period.

The president is surrounded by a small circle of close personal associates who have access to him and with whom he most frequently discusses his ideas—if he does so at all. This leads to political isolation in a small protected circle into which fresh thoughts enter infrequently and with difficulty.[3] It is particularly dangerous for the president if he receives advice only from people who are dependent upon him in nearly all areas. In his book *The Twilight of the Presidency,* George E. Reedy describes the danger of the president's political isolation:

> From the president's standpoint, the greatest staff problem is that of maintaining his contact with the world's reality that lies outside the White House walls. . . . Since they are the only people a president sees on a day-to-day basis, they become to him the voice of the people. They represent the closest approximation that he has of outside contacts, and it is inevitable that he comes to regard them as humanity itself.[4]

The Presidential Election—A National Dizziness

The presidential election is something less than a public forum to explore the political will of the American population. The American primary system may well provide the citizens of the United States with a measure of participation unknown in other parts of the world, but the seemingly open procedure for the presidential election results is a distorted image of political representation. The electoral process surrounding the president's office has always been a great spectacle. In the era of the ever present television cameras, it has become part of the nation's entertainment, although for most people not as suspenseful or entertaining as popular television programs but definitely as disassociated from the viewer's own reality. The candidates reinforce this appearance of surrealism by trying, as if in a boxing match, to score points in their confrontation with the opponent instead of focusing on the nation's problems.

Back to an Indirect Presidential Election?

> *"To call our system of primaries and party caucuses a beauty contest is to slander the Miss America pageant. No Miss Texas ever had a voice as grating or diction as tangled as George Bush. No Miss Massachusetts ever plucked her eyebrows as incompetently as Michael Dukakis. And neither Mike nor George could twirl a baton."*
>
> P.J. O'Rourke, Parliament of Whores

Is it possible that dilution of the electoral college was a serious error and that the seemingly more democratic direct vote by the people has led to less rather than more representation? The popular election advances people to this office who do not meet the high standards of the Constitution, or, conversely, the process so damages them during the election campaign that they have lost considerable stature by the time they move into the White House.

In the founding fathers' philosophy, the electoral college was not merely an emergency measure utilized instead of the preferable popular election procedure. On the contrary, it was consciously employed as an instrument to prevent a direct election, which was considered dangerous. One of the main arguments against the direct election voiced during the constitutional congress was the warning that it would open the door to demagoguery. The populists rejected this claim as aristocratic and antidemocratic and have diminished the electoral college. If one looks at the development of modern presidential campaigns in the United States and especially at their results, one might attribute prophetic vision to the founding fathers. Today's presidential campaigns often are pure demagoguery, at times more perverse as in the past few years, at times more subtle or naive—but in the final analysis they are not representative dialogues.

Is it possible that it was a mistake to strip the electoral college of any political clout? There is much to be said for a return to an indirect presidential election by the voters, even if it formally reduces popular participation in the electoral decision; ultimately, it represents progress toward increased democracy because it may permit a truer and more responsible representation of the political will of the people. There is nothing inherently undemocratic about entrusting somebody else to cast one's vote in proxy. It is actually the essence of representative government. An indirect election of the head of state is to be preferred in a complex country the size of the United States and is more conducive to a political system where a president is politically not accountable to a parliamentary body. A transfer of the presidential election to an electoral college is no more an emergency measure today than it was in the time of the founding fathers; it would, rather, be the proper instrument to select the best and most capable politician as head of state.

If this body actually were to be empowered to hold elections, i.e., if it could choose the president from the number of candidates without an imperative mandate and with political independence, it is not only possible but probable that every four years the most eminent citizens of the nation would seek to serve on this body, and these candidates would be recruited not only from among professional politicians but also from all walks of life. The time dedicated to this political commitment would be limited, permitting even the busy artist, university professor, lawyer, business person to put himself or herself at the disposal of such an electoral body.

The work of an elector is such that it does not so much require political expertise and experience but common sense and sound judgment. On the other hand, the presidential election is so important that it is worthy and honorable to be a candidate for the electoral college. The office is limited in time with so little influence that financial considerations do not play a role when running for the office of an elector. The constituency for the electors would still be relatively small—about the size of a legislative district—so that a candidate for the elector's office could personally and with little expense become known to voters.

> *"The turning point in the election campaign came during the October 8 debate between Reagan and Carter, when Reagan's handlers came up with a shrewd strategy: No matter what Carter said, Reagan would respond by shaking his head in a sorrowful but personable manner and saying: 'There you go again.' This was brilliant, because (a) it required the candidate to remember only four words, and (b) he delivered them so believably that everything Carter said seemed like a lie. If Carter had stated that the Earth was round, Reagan would have shaken his head, saying, 'There you go again,' and millions of voters would have said: 'Yeah! What does Carter think we are? Stupid?'"*
>
> Dave Barry, Dave Barry Slept Here

The voters would have the option to send a person to the electoral college whom they could get to know as a person instead of voting for an artificial product styled according to the newest findings of communications technology. The decisive advantage would surely lie in the fact that higher expectations would be attached to all prospective candidates for the presidential office if these candidates had to compete with one another before a body of approximately 550 of the nation's prominent personalities, instead of being packaged by a glib media campaign directed at the lowest political instincts.

The President—A Superstar

The president does not become more powerful solely by assuming an important role in the legislative process nor by becoming the supreme commander of the mightiest armed force on earth nor by his remarkable independence in questions of foreign policies. The power the president actually accrues has its roots in the realm of the intangible, immaterial, unreal: It is the image, the aura of the presidential office that has spread in the course of this century, especially since the sixties. John F. Kennedy's entrance into the White House enhanced the luster of an image already embedded in American history. The Kennedys recognized the star quality of the presidency and conferred on him the appropriate "glamour." After that it was only a matter of time until Hollywood itself usurped the White House in the person of Ronald Reagan, who not only was a former actor, but who also changed the presidential office into a dream factory.

The point of origin of the president's "star" role lies in the fact that he also represents in his own person the state, the nation, the people. This representation is not limited to speaking and acting in the state's stead in matters of foreign policy; the president unites all of America in his person, so to speak, and Americans identify as a community with this office and its holder. The president is part of a national world of symbols, which has become a force in America as a sort of civil religion. The office undeniably endows the president with a religious aura that is expressed in the feelings connected with worship: admiration, the wish to identify, faith, hope, and love—and, of course, all the opposite emotions: hatred, vilification, defamation, the urge to destroy and annihilate.

The president as an institution and as a person is made heroic (or villainous) with all the consequences of uncritical hero worship or demonization, something sharply observed and criticized by Americans in connection with authoritarian regimes. The original concept of the president as "one of us" who is temporarily entrusted with the execution of important tasks has been given up in favor of the media-conforming "celebrity" type, someone who has "star" qualities and, of course, can afford to have "star" eccentricities. This development is the product of a media-dependent public sphere with its need for idols that can never be satisfied. One who has tried to stop this model of the president as a celebrity was Jimmy Carter, who very consciously wanted to be a citizen just like anyone else when he was president; his failed presidency can largely be attributed to this attempt. The same can be said about Bill Clinton, who has made a serious effort to tone down the aura of the presidency, to be just himself, a very normal human being, to show the American people that he is just one of them, that he is accessible as much as the office allows and that even a president is prone to make mistakes. This—as many political commentators have observed—is one of the reasons for his decline in public opinion. "The American people. . . also want majesty and dignity in the office of the presidency—and some distance."[5]

Royal Lifestyle

A position in the White House is like a post at court: the decisive step toward influence, money, and self-assurance. Political influence is created by working for the president, and financial reward is reaped after leaving office when a person's success and connections can be transformed into riches, and self-assurance comes from experiencing the "sex-appeal of power," as Henry Kissinger has said, the admiration of the masses for the small "star" who stands in the light of the big one.

But these privileges are unevenly distributed at court, and thus there is a dogged jockeying for positions, a toadying and fawning on all levels. The definitive battle is waged about the question of who has access to the president and who controls the access others have to him. External privileges become larger than life; they signal survival, e.g., whose office is closest to the Oval Office, who is permitted to accompany the president on his fishing trips or on a visit to a restaurant, and who is invited to which official reception at the White House.

Louis XIV did not call himself Sun King without reason: All light, all energy, all warmth emanates from this one person and radiates upon those who have access to him or who even control him.

"The Clothes Have No Emperor"

> *"What the president really does is get watched. . . . His slightest comment is analyzed and puzzled over. Even his tone of voice is dissected and assayed. There are three hundred or so members of the White House Press Corps who do nothing but this. . . . And there are also scores of television camera crews on hand at all times, with videotape constantly running, waiting for the president to say 'fuck' or get shot."*
>
> P.J. O'Rourke, Parliament of Whores

Next to the favorites and courtiers, it is the press that constantly reminds the president of his special significance until he finally—understandably—believes so himself. Because they are tied both to the producers of news and their consumers, the media not only play the role of intermediaries, but they also play that of amplifiers. They thus contribute to the development of weighing the importance of news no longer according to the content of the statement but according to the speaker.

Because the president inhabits the only national office and is not only political chief executive but also ceremonial head of state, the interest of the whole nation concentrates on him. The president's acts, his smallest uttering, everything around him, his wife, his children, his dog and cat, which are jokingly called "First Dog" or "First Cat," all are news. It is ironic that under totalitarian regimes, the media are obligated to constantly report on the ruler. In the United States they do it voluntarily.

A president's sickness, especially if remotely life-threatening, leads to endless detailed reports with descriptions of the diagnosis, the medications, expert opinions, public reactions, and prognosis for the future. It is like the observation of a solar eclipse by the priests of the sun god in old Egypt.

In reality, the single holder of office is relatively insignificant for the body of the state. During a transition, the routine of normal business probably continues for a good while without anyone at the helm. The positive aspect of the presidential court is that the staff and confidential advisers who have set things into motion before just continue to operate on their own.

> *"Eisenhower, buoyed by the inspirational and deeply meaningful campaign theme "I like Ike," won the election and immediately plunged into an ambitious and arduous schedule that often involved playing golf and taking a nap on the same day."*
>
> Dave Barry, Dave Barry Slept Here

The president, especially a relatively weak, politically inexperienced office-holder, can be replaced easily and without negative consequences for the nation. *The Clothes Have No Emperor* is the appropriate title of a chronicle of the Reagan presidency, but this expression fits the image of the American presidency in general. The presidency has become a myth; the president appears larger than life, outside of the norm. It is as though a sort of sanctity had been bestowed upon him at the moment of his election, a divine right recalling that which surrounded the kings of the Middle Ages and of the absolutist era. This aura of enchantment denies the fact that the usually rather mediocre politicians enthroned on the presidential chair are interchangeable.

The Dangers of the Imperial Presidency for Democracy

In politics, however, the enchantment emanating from the star can have dangerous consequences. The founding fathers quite clearly did not want a star for their chief executive. They saw keenly before their eyes the monarchical constitutions of Europe; as a result they were intent on structuring and equipping the office in such a way that it distinctly differed from the monarchy whose constitutional role it had to assume, following the theory of the three branches of government.

As late as 1830, after important figures such as George Washington, John Adams, John Quincy Adams, Thomas Jefferson, James Madison, James Monroe had held the office, and with the strong and impressive personality of Andrew Jackson installed, Alexis de Tocqueville observed the relative insignificance of the presidency:

> Hitherto no citizen has shown any disposition to expose his honour and his life in order to become the President of the United States; because the power of this office is temporary, limited and subordinate. . . . No candidate has as yet been able to arouse the dangerous enthusiasm or the passionate sympathies of the people in his favour, for the very simple reason, that when he is at the head of the Govern-

"Waiting out Reagan´s Curse - Weiter auf Reagans Kurs"

ment he has but little power, but little wealth, and but little glory to share amongst his friends; and his influence in the State is too small for the success or the ruin of a faction to depend upon the elevation of an individual to power.[6]

With equal clarity, Tocqueville recognized a possible change in the balance of power:

However the functions of the executive power may be restricted, it must always exercise a great influence upon the foreign policy of the country, for a negotiation cannot be opened or successfully carried on otherwise than by a single agent.[7]

But neither the founding fathers nor Tocqueville foresaw this as a problem:

The policy of the Americans in relation to the whole world is exceedingly simple; and it may almost be said that no country stands in need of them, nor do they require the cooperation of any other people.[8]

And thus it went until World War I and in some degree these same principles prevailed until the beginning of the cold war, which fundamentally changed America's relationship with the world and concomitantly changed the president's role and significance.

Yet foreign politics only comprises one side. Something that Tocqueville could not foresee was the development of the modern welfare state that led to economic and social policies and active intervention; it also led to an enormous expansion of the bureaucracy serving the president. Today the president can—to paraphrase Tocqueville's words—supply his friends and party cronies with lots of power, great wealth, and fabulous glory.

But while there is more power, vigilance against this office and against those who hold it has not grown accordingly. True, there is a relentless and almost grotesque scrutiny of the president's personal character and behavior including his sex life and his personal finances, but there is no call for regular political accounting. American citizens continue to consider it a sufficient degree of control if they have the chance to elect another person every four years; stronger controls over the president during his term in office is not a topic American people are interested in arguing intensively. They are willing neither to reduce the president's role, which was not conceived by the Constitution to be as powerful as it has become, nor to cut down on the imperial pomp, which—as kings, emperors, and rulers of various religions well knew—has served as a political weapon with which to intimidate subjects.

The experiences of Watergate, which so clearly demonstrated the temptations of uncontrolled power in the White House, are forgotten. Worse than that, Americans proudly point out that democratic safeguards are sufficiently well-established because the Watergate hearings forced President Richard Nixon to step down and the law saw to it that the criminal accomplices in the White House went to jail. Exactly the opposite is the case. The impeachment procedures in connection with the Watergate scandal proved to be so wearing on the American public that it is unlikely that this tool to control and limit presidential usurpation of power will ever be used or even considered again.

> *"Eventually, the nation overcame the trauma of Iran-contra and went back to reading the sports pages."*
>
> Dave Barry, Dave Barry Slept Here

Proof for this was the Iran-Contra affair, for good reason dubbed "Iran-Gate," during Ronald Reagan's presidency. When this scandal was explored, it became obvious that no one—neither politicians, press, nor public—had special interest in following the trail that could have shown the president's participation in these criminal activities. The nation wanted to spare itself an impeachment procedure against the president at all costs. And thus it is no coincidence that the immediate agents in this criminal political plot received mild sentences and were celebrated as national heroes by a voluble part of the public rather than suffered imprisonment and public contempt like the players in the Watergate scandal.

> *"We treat the president of the United States with awe. We impute to him remarkable powers. We divine things by his smallest gestures. We believe he has the capacity to destroy the very earth, and—by vigorous perusal of sound economic policy—to make the land fruitful and all our endeavors prosperous. We beseech him for aid and comfort in our every distress and believe him capable of granting any boon or favor. The type is recognizable to even a casual student of mythology. The president is not an ordinary politician trying to conduct the affairs of state as best he can. He is a divine priest-king. And we Americans worship our state avatar devoutly."*
>
> P.J. O'Rourke, Parliament of Whores

From the Republican Spirit to a New Royalism

Tocqueville had already considered the possibility of presidential power growing beyond the limits delineated by the Constitution. He observed that the balance among the branches designed by the creators of the Constitution had its origin not only in constitutional norms and institutions, but also in the state's external circumstances:

> The President of the United States possesses almost royal prerogatives, which he has no opportunity of exercising; and the privileges which he can at present use are circumscribed. The laws allow him to be strong, but circumstances keep him weak.[9]

But it is not only the external situation that has changed; the revaluation of the presidential office takes place in people's minds. The quasi-religious adoration that combines the general American desire for a star culture with the older tradition of a civil religion issues from the need to identify with an entity that reaches beyond one's own life. But the origins of religion are only part adoration: The other part is made up of fear of the powerful being who intrudes into human life with punishment and protection. The president partially owes his lofty status to the heroic image of the man who can loosen the arsenal of horror upon the world by pressing a button or by lifting the receiver of the red telephone, just like Zeus who could hurl lightning or like the Mosaic God who could send plagues and tempests and storms.

Political star culture is not at all an American phenomenon. Europe's fascist dictators perfected it to a preliminary high level. Fascist ideologies, especially National Socialism, had clearly religious overtones; they offered identification, ties, stability, and they promised redemption through a blending with the collective. America's political star culture lacks the totalitarian, dogged, and forced aspect. It is more refined, more playful, more modern, but no less dangerous.

It is lamentable that this development, which may dismantle democratic structures in the long run, is hardly being discussed in the United States. One of the reasons for this is that most of the political commentators and chieftains of think tanks have been drawn into the larger or smaller circle of the imperial court by material or immaterial incentives and rewards so that they now enjoy their roles as court astrologers and secret counselors. The economy that supports these think tanks also rejoices in the system of an overly strong presidential office, which is best held by someone who is himself not a strong personality.

The only criticism carrying with it nominal influence comes from the corner of the caricaturists, satirists, and cartoonists, who contrast the office's pomp and bombast with the incompetence and lack of character of the persons holding this office. It is especially Gary Trudeau's cartoon series "Doonesbury" that frequently attracted the ire of the White House. Perhaps the satirical comics by Trudeau and others today fill the role played by Voltaire's satires in preparing the French Revolution: by opening people's eyes to the reality hiding behind the glittering but always brittle surface.

Radical Reform: The Separation of the Representative and the Political Function of the Presidency

After the Watergate scandal and the Vietnam trauma, it appeared for a time as though the outrage about the presidential arrogance of power would inspire a broad reform movement to diminish the role of the president. The balance of power between the president and Congress was shifted in favor of the legislature by a number of laws, especially the War Powers Resolution, which clearly limited the authority to deploy troops. But this measure remained without lasting effect, and the healthy mistrust against the autocrat in the White House gave way a few years later to a wave of reforms designed both to simplify and to cater to the need for strong national leadership. The War Powers Resolution is the best example of the limited effect of the reforms initiated during that period. While the president sent one of the largest concentrations of troops since the Vietnam War to the Persian Gulf, not even a vocal minority insisted that Congress pass an act legitimizing this military action after sixty days had passed as provided by this law.

The imbalance between the president and Congress is not likely to be corrected by laws. For the reasons mentioned earlier, it will grow rather than shrink, and in the long run it will be a burden on the democratic system in America. It is quite possible that radical reforms of the Constitution are needed to provide for stricter controls on the executive branch by Congress and to limit the president's importance within the political system and within the life of the nation.

Besides the changes in the election procedures already mentioned, one might contemplate eliminating reelection in combination perhaps with a longer term in office. A more radical but more appropriate strategy would be to separate the representative from the political aspect of the presidency. Like the flag and the national hymn, the president as the nation's father would remain an object of national admiration without being part of the partisan power struggle.

Notes

1. Formally, the administration is not entitled to initiate laws as it is normally common in a parliamentary system. But most of the important bills are prepared by the president's office or the departments and then—so to say "by courtesy"—brought in to the legislation procedure by a member of Congress.

2. The Senate made the decision as a response to the outrage of the American people over an attack by North Vietnamese ships on American warships outside Vietnamese territorial waters. Meanwhile it has been established that these attacks were provoked by the American warships.

3. The assembly of the secretaries is called the cabinet. There are also regular meetings, but in contrast to the German system the cabinet has no real political power. It is not even mentioned in the Constitution. The president is the only one who makes the decisions, and he relies ever more on his personal staff than on the departments. President Franklin Roosevelt described this powerlessness exactly when he quipped during a cabinet meeting: "There are eight 'nays' and one 'aye.' The 'ayes' have it."

4. George E. Reedy, *The Twilight of the Presidency,* p. 95.

5. Elizabeth Drew,"Desperately Seeking Stature," *Washington Post,* December 11, 1994, p.C1.

6. Alexis de Tocqueville, *Democracy in America I,* p. 129.

7. Ibid., p. 131.

8. Ibid., p. 131.

9. Ibid., p. 126.

Pax Americana

Part I

Mission to Save

the World

"There was no corner of the known world where some interest was not alleged to be in danger or under actual attack. If the interests were not Roman, they were those of Rome's allies; and if Rome had no allies, then allies would be invented. When it was utterly impossible to contrive such an interest—why, then it was the national honor that had been insulted. The fight was always invested with an aura of legality. Rome was always being attacked by evil-minded neighbors, always fighting for a breathing-space. The whole world was pervaded by a host of enemies, and it was manifestly Rome's duty to guard against their indubitably aggressive designs."[1]

J.A. Schumpeter, Imperialism and Social Classes

After the war against Iraq, with its impressive display of American military power, and after the sudden collapse of the Soviet Union, its military competitor for decades, the United States sees itself as the single power in position to assert global responsibility.

The United States appears not to have a ready response to this challenge. It would indeed be greatly disturbing if such momentous changes were met with easy answers; what is required is a careful and thoughtful examination of na-

149

tional purpose and global goals. Reactions range from the euphoric concept of a Pax Americana for the whole world to a new "America-first" isolationism focused almost exclusively on domestic affairs. In between is an enormous no-man's land of insecurity and confusion demanding an active search and experimentation with both new and old and tried concepts.

> *"Maybe it's understandable what a history of failures America's foreign policy has been. We are, after all, a country full of people who came to America to get away from foreigners. Any prolonged examination of the U.S. government reveals foreign policy to be America's miniature schnauzer—a noisy but small and useless part of the national household."*
>
> P.J. O'Rourke, Parliament of Whores

The basic model of American foreign politics is not isolationism, even though it was prevalent throughout long periods of American history. Rather, it is a missionary instinct embodied in the concept of a Pax Americana.

The idea of a Pax Americana has long existed but it becomes especially fascinating in a time of dramatic change in world order. The term *Pax Americana* appeared first in the late sixties to characterize America's global engagement, but the idea has much deeper roots. It originated with the doctrine of manifest destiny, this sense of a special mission for Americans that led—after the conquest of the North American continent—to a missionary zeal to extend American values to the entire world.[2]

Parallels to Pax Romana

Pax Americana—like the Pax Britannica of the British colonial empire—is a clear reference to Pax Romana, which provided the ancient world one last period of peace before its final collapse.[3] There are surprising parallels between the American and Roman world empires.

Like Rome, the United States has mostly been called upon to enter into conflicts from other threats rather than out of imperial ambition. It has unintentionally become world referee, conquerer, and superpower. The Roman empire differed from most empires that came before and after it. It was unparalleled in its duration, expansion, sovereignty, cosmopolitanism, and civility. In spite of its enormous domestic tensions arising from social problems (another parallel to the United States), the empire lasted many centuries and created a long period of peace and cultural development that continued to affect the world long after its physical collapse.

The political and cultural development of the early Middle Ages began in the Romanized region of Franconia and in the still existing Eastern Roman empire, and Christianity built its church on the ruins of the Western Roman empire. Will achievements of a Pax Americana, should it occur, be so honored in future history?

It has already had an effect on the world. For Western Europe and Asia, the years of the so-called cold war after World War II were, in effect, a period of a Pax Americana that created a climate for prosperous development and for homogenization under the umbrella of a militarily and culturally dominating power.

The American Programmatic Awareness

American imperial politics are founded on a deeply ingrained idea of mission that cloaks the brutal and ruthless pursuit of American interests. Like the Americans, the Romans had a specific rhetoric for this attitude most pointedly expressed with the word *pacare*, by which Romans described the forceful assimilation of other peoples into the Imperium Romanum. It stems from the word *pax* (peace), and literally means to pacify. The Romans saw their imperialism as a peace mission and their military campaigns as the pacification of other peoples.

In the United States, the conviction of the moral self-evidence of its own policy and the unrestrained pursuit of its own interests exist side by side. Moral self-righteousness and naked national egotism, the proclamation of high ideals and the pursuit of self-interest, live in an innocent symbiosis almost incomprehensible to other people.

> *"I asked a group of refugees, 'Was the U.S. invasion [of Panama] right or wrong?' 'We got rid of that man,' said one of them. Then they all complained that they hadn't gotten any U.S. aid money yet."*
> P.J. O'Rourke, Parliament of Whores

One aspect of American "innocence" in the pursuit of foreign policy goals is the total identification of American interests with the highest values and best interests of humanity. It is accepted by Americans that the United States has given to the world its most prized accomplishments—democracy and market economy. In addition, there is the capacity of the American mind to hold opposing viewpoints and attitudes simultaneously. As Geoffrey Gorer writes:

> What members of other societies often consider to be the contradictions of American policies are quite honestly not so perceived by the Americans, because the different aspects are not considered to be connected.[4]

This life of plurality, this endurance of contradictions seemingly unaware to them, is a characteristic singular to the American people.

Manifest Destiny as a Justification of American Expansion

Manifest destiny, the first and essential keystone of the foreign policy of the United States, can be retraced to the early years of the nation, even to the first settlements. The invasion of the Western frontier was not prompted simply by the need for land to escape poverty and deprivation; the attitude of the pioneers toward the continent that lay before them was also inspired by the ideal of America as the promised land.

Manifest destiny dismissed other cultures; it became the justification for the expulsion or subjugation of the Native Americans. The alternative of including the Native Americans in the colonization of their own country and integrating them into the American nation was never considered. Thomas Jefferson stood almost alone against popular opinion and public policy. In his writings as well as in his policies as president of the United States, he worked toward a better understanding of the Native Americans and recognized the influence their culture could have on the development of North America. He considered and treated them as partners with equal rights.

The violent repression of the Native Americans is not the only sign of the martial birth of the United States. Florida, Texas, and the entire Southwestern region including California were annexed by wars or threats of war. Florida was purchased from the Spanish royalty under pressure of the American forces already positioned in this region.

The final stage in nation building was the war to hold the seceded Southern states in the Union. This conquest, too, was glorified as the victory of a morally superior power.

Missionary Zeal as the Export of American Values

> "THE AWAKENING OF IMPERIALISM
>   The first thing American imperialism noticed when it woke up was Cuba. At the time Cuba technically belonged to Spain, . . . the only problem being that at the time the United States did not have what international lawyers refer to, in technical legalistic terms, as a 'reason.' So things looked very bleak, indeed, until one day in 1898 when, in a surprise stroke of good fortune, the U.S. battleship 'Maine' exploded and sank in Havana harbor. . . . This inspired [President] William McKinley . . . to issue an ultimatum to Spain in which he demanded a number of concessions. Spain immediately agreed to all the demands, an act of treachery that the United States clearly could not tolerate. It was time to declare: THE SPANISH-AMERICAN WAR."
>
> Dave Barry, Dave Barry Slept Here

Manifest destiny, not content with the colonization of the promised land, became a missionary zeal to bring the blessings of America to the rest of the world. When President Woodrow Wilson declared World War I a crusade to make the world "safe for democracy," he introduced a powerful new concept with lasting consequences. It must be remembered that the American people were determined not to get embroiled in the national quarrels of far-away Europe and had just reelected Wilson, whose campaign slogan was: "He kept us out of the war."

" 'The War to End All Wars'

*President Wilson's theory at the time was that America would march
over there and help France and Britain win the war, and then the winners
would be extremely fair and decent and not take enormous sums of money
or huge chunks of land from the losers, plus the entire system of world
government would be reformed so that everybody would live in Peace
and Freedom Forevermore. Needless to say, France and Britain thought
this was the funniest theory they had ever heard, and they would beg
Wilson to tell it again and again at dinner parties. 'Hey Woody!' they'd
shriek, tears of laughter falling in their cognac (CONE-yak). 'Tell us the
part where we don't take money or land.' "*

Dave Barry, Dave Barry Slept Here

American nationalism was based on the conviction that its social order was
superior to anything in the world and envied by the world. The constant flood of
immigrants was a daily confirmation of American superiority. Why else would
these hundreds of thousands of people leave their homelands if America were

not an infinitely better place? Here was a modern democracy that was not only richer, but it was also morally superior to the depravity of Europe with its feudal structures reminiscent of the Middle Ages.

World War I was a military victory for the United States. However, the war failed to bring democracy to the world. Americans gave little thought to reconciling their motives for the war with their moral claim. Neither did they consider whether or not this moral claim justified the war. Finally, they have never really seriously come to terms with why their mission in the name of democracy was, on the whole, a failure.

The Rhetorical Moralism of American Foreign Politics

World War II was another crusade to save freedom from dictators. For all that, Franklin D. Roosevelt did not acknowledge that a chief ally was a bloodthirsty dictator not unlike Adolf Hitler in his cruelty and inhumanity. Joseph Stalin was first portrayed as likeable "Uncle Joe."

The inclusion of Stalin in the crusade for democracy and freedom set the standard for the hypocritical morality of the cold war. With it, even autocrats, oppressors, exploiters, and dictators, such as Syngman Rhee in Korea, the Shah in Iran, Diem in South Vietnam, Franco in Spain, Mobutu in Congo, Batista in Cuba, and dozens of others, became collaborators in the battle of the "good guys" against the "bad guys." For the United States, the war against communism was not a political confrontation to gain spheres of influence in the world but, rather, a moral struggle against the "evil empire," as Ronald Reagan still called it in the last years of the American-Soviet rivalry.

As though on order, a new figure entered the picture after the end of the cold war—Saddam Hussein—and in his shadow Islamic fundamentalism and terrorism again made it easy to distinguish good from evil. The military success in Kuwait again demonstrated the moral superiority of American politics. In his Memorial Day speech at Arlington Cemetery in 1991, former Vice President Dan Quayle said that the victory over Saddam Hussein was a victory of good over evil. The Manichaean view of politics has moved from the East-West confrontation to this new era of interventionism without a tear in the seam. As long as one represents the good side, everything is permitted.

Other aspects of this confrontation also bring to mind the standard pattern of American politics in foreign policy. President George Bush, in a speech in August 1992, explained U.S. intervention in Kuwait in the tradition of Presidents Wilson and Franklin Roosevelt—again, the promise of a war to end all wars and to create a new world order. Wilson used the same justification for World War I and Roosevelt for World War II.

These presidents' words were not merely empty gestures; both Wilson and Roosevelt presented concrete plans for the organization of world peace. To be sure, the realization of these plans failed their proudly stated objectives. Wilson's peace plan failed primarily because the United States did not even take part in it. The much more effective organization of the United Nations—Roosevelt's gift to the world—is usually respected by Americans only when it is an instrument of American policies.

The danger of the U.S. foreign policy is the rhetorical reduction of complex issues to simplistic slogans. It becomes a political marketing mechanism. Just as one sells orange juice with the code word "fresh" and cornflakes with the key word "crunchy," without regard to nutritional value, quality, or ingredients, American foreign policy is reduced to national security "in defense of freedom and democracy."

Security Hysteria

Even the most eccentric foreign political escapades are justified in the name of "national security." National security has become the second major cornerstone of U.S. foreign policy. The United States, the strongest and almost unassailable nation, is increasingly paranoid about its security. In this paranoia, the protection of the nation is by no means considered to be a matter of simple defense but, rather, of offensive intervention. Possible threats must be prevented—coalitions, friendship pacts, and areas of support must be built around the world to forestall any possible threats. What threatens the security of America is defined by America on its own terms.

> *"[The Monroe Doctrine]*
> *1. Other nations are not allowed to mess around with the internal affairs of nations in this hemisphere.*
> *2. But we are.*
> *3. Ha-ha-ha"*
>
> Dave Barry, Dave Barry Slept Here

The excessive preoccupation with security can be explained psychologically as a reaction to the earlier history of American isolationism. Since its founding, the United States has not had to fear any threat from the outside, with the exception of the invasion of the English in 1812, which produced quite a shock. The famous doctrine by President James Monroe, "America for the Americans," has never really been seriously challenged by foreign powers in its 170 years of existence.

Both world wars were fought far away from the home front. After World War II, when the United States alone possessed the atomic bomb, it experienced a brief period of security and absolute world power. With the advance of the Soviets in Europe and of the Communists in Asia, and the emergence of the Soviet Union as an atomic power, not only did the United States lose its position of hegemony, but it also gave way to an absurd insecurity.

The United States had not only lost its security, but as a shock-reaction to this new situation, it also worked itself into an intensified security hysteria that is still in effect today.

The Shock of Lost Invulnerability

> *"The government established a wool and mohair price-support program in 1954 . . . to encourage domestic wool production in the interest of national security. Really it says that. I guess back in the fifties there was this military school of thought that held that in the event of a Soviet attack we could confuse and disorient the enemy by throwing blankets over their heads. Then, while they were punching each other in the dark and trying to figure out who turned the lights off, we'd have time to run into our missile silos and destroy Russia with ICBMs."*
>
> P.J. O'Rourke, Parliament of Whores

Throughout their history, Europeans have lived with invasions, conquests, and destruction and have resigned themselves to limitations of security. Americans do not have this experience. They have never experienced the awful devastation of war on their homeland and, therefore, look at war, by European standards, from a more neutral and less fearful attitude. On the other hand, the thought of war threatening the homeland is so frightening that they are constantly planning and devising means to protect against it.

Armament hysteria became especially evident during the presidency of Reagan. Strategic Defense Initiative (SDI)—known as "Star Wars"—was proclaimed the ultimate safeguard against an attack; it was to be an impenetrable umbrella of thousands of satellites over the American skies that would keep out the attackers, as the oceans did for 150 years.

Feasibility of such a technique remained technically questionable, but even to imagine a project with such immense costs can only be explained by an absurd form of security hysteria. How extravagantly Reagan and Reagan's America are reasoned on the security issue becomes obvious from the famous statement by Reagan about the conflict in Nicaragua at that time. As an explanation for the American support of the anticommunist Contras, Reagan said, "It is better that we fight the Communists there [in Nicaragua] than in Harlingen, Texas"[5]—the border town, mind you, not to Nicaragua, but to Mexico, a country that has neither the intention nor the means to behave even the least bit hostile toward the United States.

The United States pumped more than $10 billion into the ten-year civil war in the tiny country of El Salvador in order to prevent the victory of a leftist movement against the existing oligarchic-feudal social structure.

Central American Politics as the Result
of Security Paranoia

U.S. Central American politics are the prime example of the exaggeration of security interests. Americans fight the emergence of leftist governments with every available overt and covert means because they consider these governments a threat to their security. What is threatened, perhaps, are the interests of major U.S. industries doing lucrative business in many of these countries but whose profits are not vital to the national well-being of the United States.

Until recently, the East-West conflict has been something of an excuse for this argument, although the North American politics of intervention in South and especially Central America long preceded the cold war. Nicaragua, Mexico, Guatemala, the Dominican Republic—the Marines were going in and out of these countries long before World War II and even before World War I.

With the opening of one front of the cold war in Cuba, in the backyard of the United States, the argument for security became substantial. But the Cuban Missile Crisis, the U.S. resistance to the transfer of Soviet atomic missiles to Cuba, convincingly proved the American ability to cope with such threats.

The United States's policies toward its South American neighbors reflect a related theory of spheres of influence not unlike the political and military control the Soviet Union held over its East European satellite states:

1. For security reasons, the United States considers it necessary to be surrounded by a circle of allied or at least friendly neighbors.

2. A state can only be allied with or befriended by the United States if it has the same ideological, political, and economic outlooks. Establishment of any socialist-communist economic systems will be politically discouraged or prevented by intervention. If a hostile system is established and cannot be stamped out (example Cuba), it is isolated and starved out.

"Sinatra" Politics

As long as the rivalry of the systems and the competition of the superpowers in their spheres of influence existed, these policies could find a certain justification on both sides. Today, such policy undermines the moral prestige of the United States in the world and, perhaps more important, among its own citizens. The double standard with which the United States declares its interventions as the export of democracy, and then seeks to undermine the self-determination of neighbor states, strains its political rhetoric.

In his day, Mikhail Gorbachev justified the demobilization of the Eastern European satellites in the security region of the Soviet Union not only with the democratic ideal of self-determination, but also with an ironic challenge to the Americans. He described this political act of strict noninvolvement in the affairs of neighboring states with a distinctive American flair. He called it "Sinatra" politics in reference to the refrain of the well-known hit song: "I did it my way." It remains to be seen whether Americans accept this challenge and also finally adopt a Sinatra policy toward their neighbors in Latin America.

After the recent experience of the triumphal victory of Western ideas over the communist and authoritarian state theories of the East, the United States should have greater self-confidence and faith in the persuasive power of its political ideas on the Latin American continent, even if it means tolerating a socialist-communist period of rule. With the changed geopolitical relationships, the dynamics of Western political ideals, and the superiority of the principles of market economy, such an interim stage would not last forty-five years as in Eastern Europe but perhaps one-tenth of this time. The peaceful change of government in Nicaragua shows that these opportunities are available and possible.

Notes

1. J.A. Schumpeter, *Imperialism and Social Classes*, p. 66.

2. This idea—which has its parallel in the notorious aberration of German nationalism—is based on the belief of Americans in the singularity and superiority of their own society and has found many expressions in American history. Robert N. Bellah documented many examples in his book on American civil religion (*The Broken Covenant*, chapter II—"America as a Chosen People," p. 36). Compare also with Gustav H. Blanke, "Das amerikanische Sendungsbewußtsein," in Klaus-M. Kodalle, *Gott und Politik in U.S.A.*, p. 186 (German edition).

3. Eugene McCarthy mentions in his book *America Revisited* that in 1965 the Army contracted with Douglas Aircraft for a study of what would be required to impose order upon the world. The name initially given to the study was "Pax Americana" (Eugene McCarthy, *America Revisited*, p. 208). The Oxford English Dictionary names a book by R. Raine, *Wreath for America*, which was published in 1967 as the earliest source for this expression and quotes: "The whole western world . . . is living under . . . a Pax Americana, just as the world once lived in peace under a Pax Britannica." In the seventies the expression became common.

4. Geoffrey Gorer, *The Americans*, p. 115.

5. "A victory for the Sandinistas would create a privileged sanctuary for terrorists and subversives just two days' driving time from Harlingen, Texas." Reagan quoted by Paul Slansky, *The Clothes Have No Emperor*, p. 156.

Pax Americana

Part II

Militarizing

the Society

The military orientation of American government that began with the cold war is a completely new development in the history of the United States. Though missionary zeal had manifested itself throughout the nation's history in countless military interventions, the military nevertheless had led a marginal existence within the society in peacetime. With the cold war, this military influence became established as a permanent and prominent part of government.

The militarizing of American society occurred on two levels, emotional and institutional. The reaction to the victory in Kuwait was a loud and clear demonstration of the importance of the military in the emotional life of the nation. The jubilation of the citizens, who spent months on end planning homecoming festivals and grand parades for the soldiers, seemed disproportionate to the military event. A combination of several emotional tendencies occurred: the general American tendency to exaggeration, a wish to ameliorate a distinct discomfort with the general condition at home, and the need to identify with a national cause.

As long as the military does not play a governing role in society—and in the United States it does not have any significance because of the country's geographic isolation—the fascination of the people with the military is relatively harmless, as Alexis de Tocqueville already observed:

> They [the Americans] have nothing to fear from a scourge which is more formidable to republics than all these evils combined: namely, military glory.[1]

Nevertheless, Tocqueville was irritated by the political success of then President Andrew Jackson, whose political advancement was only to be explained by the "recollection of a victory which he gained, twenty years ago, under the walls of New Orleans ... a very ordinary achievement and which could only be remembered in a country where battles are rare."[2]

Apparently, the jubilation and the enthusiasm about the success of Desert Storm have their tradition in American history.

The Soldier as a Hero

The hero worship accorded to American soldiers is another manifestation of the star cult so ubiquitous in this society. The nation is constantly seeking larger-than-life celebrities with whom people identify and relieve the mediocrity and boring uniformity of their own existence. The military establishment encourages hero worship and identification of the military with national myth. The Pentagon has learned the lessons of Vietnam; it has marketed the Kuwaiti expedition as a triumphal demonstration of American technology.

But America only loves its soldiers when they are successful. This is what the Vietnam War veterans discovered (and to some degree also Korean War veterans) who were unfortunate enough to be involved in a losing war. Upon their return, Vietnam veterans were something of an embarrassment to society. The nation was eager to forget a war that eroded its self-confidence.

The United States has only now begun to come to terms with this aspect of its history. As is so often the case, this process was set into motion by Hollywood. After a period of total amnesia, the Vietnam War became the subject of Rambo-type films that cloaked the trauma of defeat with a revisionist version of history. More recently films have exposed the American people to the realities of this war.

With the enhanced self-confidence inspired by the Kuwaiti expedition, the American people are able to identify with their Vietnam veterans. As a kind of public compensation, veterans from the Vietnam War and the Korean War were invited to participate in the parades for the homecoming legions from Kuwait.

The United States loves its heroes to be decorated. After all, what is a star that does not glitter? After the awkward and ridiculous invasion of the tiny island of Grenada, in which three of the four armed services (the Army, the Navy, and the Marines) were dispatched to overpower 600 Cuban guest workers, only half of whom were even armed, the "victory" was celebrated with the award of 8,000 medals.[3] The invasion of Panama called for a similarly rich blessing of medals for those involved (and also for those not involved).

> *"Nice parade—it wasn't boring."*
> *Commentary from a woman watching the [Gulf War victory] parade*
> *in Washington on June 8, 1991.*

The heroes of the Gulf War were honored with medals and the biggest military parades since the end of World War II. To be fair, it should be mentioned that American parades are not the grim military reviews that one is accustomed to from pictures of the Nazi Party rallies or the October parades on Red Square. People are very relaxed—in the parade and on the sidelines. In the United States, military parades, too, must be entertaining and festive.

While this gives reason to hope that the militarization of the minds and hearts of Americans has run up against a natural skepticism, the increasing influence of the military in government raises questions for the future.

Large areas of the economy and an even higher portion of academic research are tied either directly or indirectly to the military and are contingent upon defense contracts. The prosperity of many communities and entire regions depends on decisions of the Pentagon or of Congress to award contracts to a local company or for the construction and upkeep of a military base. The people who live and work in these communities have an immediate interest in defense research and the defense industry and oppose any cutbacks.

The Symbiosis of the Military, Big Business, and Science

Today, the term *military-industrial complex* as a characterization of the symbiosis of the military and big business is a common phrase not only in the United States but also throughout the world.[4] In his farewell address in 1960, President Dwight D. Eisenhower first warned of this rising danger. It is less well known that, in the same speech and in the same context, Eisenhower identified the scientific-technological elite as another powerful force in service of the military.

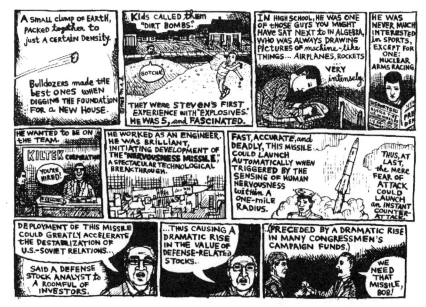

Eisenhower warned that the ties among the military, private industry, and scientific research would limit society's freedom of choice about its future. He warned that each area would nourish the others, in effect actively stimulate and encourage military growth with plans and suggestions. At the same time, the financial dependency grew, but as in a happy marriage, without being perceived as oppressive.

Eisenhower especially advised universities to hold on to their integrity and their role in society.

> The prospect of domination of the nation's scholars by federal employment, project allocations, and the power of money is ever present—and is gravely to be regarded.[5]

Eisenhower's warnings were not heeded. They were not fully understood because the developments he was speaking about went unnoticed by the public. On the other hand, the consequences of this symbiosis—the mutual dependency and the mutual advantages—had advanced to such a degree that a disentanglement would not have been impossible without painful interventions into the entire economic and social system.

The military, industry, and academia all feel very comfortable in this mutual dependency because they prosper in it. They will never voluntarily give it up. This mutual feeding on and supporting one another have to be broken up by political leaders who in the face of a changing geopolitical situation and limited financial resources radically redefine the concept of security and the role of defense. But even at the end of the cold war, this reevaluation of the concept of national security—long overdue as it is—was not seriously tackled.

Politics itself has become a part of the military-industrial complex and has made the symbiosis even tighter and longer lasting. In practically every electoral district and in every state, there are either military installations or industries and research institutes that are dependent upon the military. These military bases are strongly supported by members of Congress in representing the interests of their constituents.

By the way, Eisenhower was not the first to bemoan the militarizing of American society. More than 150 years before him, Thomas Jefferson complained about the dangerous but inevitable connection between the military and industry. After the war with Britain in 1812, he resigned himself to the idea that the United States had to build up its own industry to defend it militarily. He wrote:

> Our enemy has indeed the consolation of Satan on removing our first parents from Paradise: from a peaceable and agricultural nation, he makes us a military and manufacturing one.[6]

The dependence of politicians on the military-industrial complex has made armament production a dominating factor in foreign policy. Military aid in the form of defense goods are generously distributed all over the world, either as gifts or as loans because it means contracts for U.S. industries.

Increase in Defense Exports

The entrenchment of the military-industrial complex within the American political system shows no sign of weakening, even as the Pax Americana is appearing in outlines. The prospects of a reduction in arms production has ironically declined after the triumphal victory in the Persian Gulf. In analyzing the Gulf War, the military-industrial complex came to the conclusion that the new role of the United States requires an even larger assortment of defense weapons. The war was a reminder that political goals can be achieved by military means; it was decided by the enormous superiority of military technique and war materiel. It is natural that the United States will do everything in its power to maintain and develop this advantage.

> *"We are plunging ahead on a number of crucial multibillion-dollar defense items, including the B–2 'Stealth' bomber, which is being built by the Northrop Corp. for $865 million per plane (excluding sunroof). The B–2, which is designed to be invisible to radar, has had some minor technical glitches, such as that it is not actually invisible to radar. But it nevertheless appears to be superbly capable of carrying out its vital mission of penetrating deep into Soviet airspace and . . .*

Hold it! We just remembered that there is no longer any NEED to penetrate deep into Soviet airspace, other than to scout locations for Pizza Huts. But never mind. Even as you read this, top Pentagon strategists are thinking up a NEW vital mission for the B–2. Maybe it could penetrate deep into Elizabeth Taylor's next wedding."

Dave Barry, "The Best of Stealth"

So even after the end of the East-West conflict, there will be new and certainly more costly weapons of destruction. Not only in the United States but everywhere in the world, more money will be spent for this unproductive section of the economic system. Though the war with Iraq had the short-term effect of putting the crisis on the back burner, the resulting demand for more and better weapons will, in the long run, heighten the threat of war and the insecurity in the world.

The Growing Tendency to Military Interventions

The conviction that it was in the best interest of the United States to be militarily involved in every corner of the world where a threat was perceived was shattered with the Vietnam War. The involvement in Vietnam was not only a failed mission, which left hundreds of thousands of Americans wounded or killed, ruined the dollar, piled up enormous deficits, and deeply divided the nation, but also the war that raised for the first time a fundamental question about the real interests of the United States.

This basic new orientation of American foreign policy did not survive long, and its tenuous beginnings were undermined by the "easy" victory over Iraq. It proved again that war can be very successful—even at minimal cost.

Militarizing Society

"But the best and final argument against cutting defense spending cannot be put into words. It's visceral, hormonal. It is that excitement in the gut, that swelling of the chest, the involuntary smile that comes across the face of every male when he has a weapon to hand."

P.J. O'Rourke, Parliament of Whores

The Pax Americana will extort a high price from the American society. It will perpetuate the militarization of politics and undermine the democratic structures in the long run. Tocqueville recognized the dangers of a powerful military in a democratic state:

Not indeed that after every victory it is to be apprehended that the victorious generals will possess themselves by force of the supreme power, after the manner of Sulla and Caesar; the danger is of another kind. War does not always give over democratic communities to military government, but it must invariably and immeasurably increase the powers of civil government; it must almost compulsorily concentrate the direction of all men and the management of all things in the hands of the administration. If it does not lead to despotism by sudden violence, it prepares men for it more gently by their habits.[7]

Former Senator Eugene McCarthy, one of the most penetrating critics of the secret powers of the military establishment, sees this prophecy fulfilled with the consolidation of a national security bureaucracy composed of the civilian Central Intelligence Agency (CIA) and the various military secret services in cooperation with the national police force, the Federal Bureau of Investigation (FBI), which has become a surveillance agency in the name of national security.

In search of the public enemy, all of these secret services work together in gathering information about American citizens. They are all formally under civilian control, but the weakness of this is exposed by the example of long-time FBI Director J. Edgar Hoover. No president dared to send him into retirement—apparently for fear of exposure of a secret portfolio on his own person.

Even more serious than the lack of control is the corruption of political attitudes by the existence of a security apparatus in which established cold war techniques become standard procedures in relations with other governments or with dissident citizens. Watergate and the Iran-Contra scandal are just the tip of this iceberg.

It is not possible for a democratic society to force its political moral code on its secret service. The only healthy course for a democracy is to never allow such a security apparatus to come into existence or, if it appears necessary, to keep it as small as possible. Neither option is likely in the United States and the militarily influenced Pax Americana will probably result in further consolidation of the national security state.

The Military Is Rendered Independent through the Establishment of a Professional Army

With the end of the civilian draft after the Vietnam War and the establishment of a professional army, the United States took another step toward eroding civilian control of the military within democratic society. This is another reminder of the Roman empire. Pax Romana was also created and maintained by an army of professional soldiers after the general compulsory military service was abolished along with the republican government. The threat of a professional army to a democracy is not that it might be tempted to topple the government but, rather, that it might be too obliging to military adventurism on the part of the government. Experience during the Vietnam War when many draftees refused to fight in a politically controversial war was frustrating for the government but extraordinarily positive for democracy itself. This could never have happened with a professional army.

Tocqueville also called attention to these inherent contradictions between a democratic society and its military:

> They [enlisted soldiers] adapt themselves to their military duties but their minds are still attached to the interests and the duties that engaged them in civil life. They do not therefore imbibe the spirit of the army, or rather they infuse the spirit of the community at large into the army and retain it there.[8]

At another point he says:

> The general spirit of the nation, being infused into the spirit peculiar to the army, tempers the opinions and desires engendered by military life, or represses them by the mighty force of public opinion. Teach the citizens to be educated, orderly, firm, and free and the soldiers will be disciplined and obedient.[9]

According to Tocqueville, the best protection for the preservation of a democracy is a minimal role of the military in the government:

> After all, and in spite of all precaution, a large army in the midst of a democratic people will always be a source of great danger. The most effectual means of diminishing that danger would be to reduce the army, but this is a remedy that all nations are not able to apply.[10]

Outside Financing of the American Military Power

Obviously, the United States cannot—given the current state of the world—radically reduce its military power. It cannot suddenly shun its responsibilities as the only remaining superpower, a position that it has attained partially by its own efforts, partially by the collapse of its competitors. Yet this duty does not legitimize an excessive arms buildup or an interventionist policy. An attempt to set up and maintain a "new world order" with military power, or even with the threat of it, overstrains and corrupts the American society.

As well as confirming the superiority of the United States, the last war illuminated the distressing fact that the nation can no longer afford such wars or any war for that matter. The war in Iraq was financed completely by outside sources. Establishment of a professional army is followed by fighting wars as mercenaries.

> *"Adding up the cash contributions we are receiving from Saudi Arabia, Kuwait, the United Arab Emirates, Germany, Japan and elsewhere, I see that, if we play our cards right in the Gulf War, we might even make a profit."*
>
> P.J. O'Rourke, Parliament of Whores

The prospect of America's armed forces as mercenaries compensated by other countries concerns even such old "hawks" as Henry Kissinger. He categorically demands that this must be the last war that the United States fights with the money of others. "America cannot be the mercenary of a new world order."[11]

Correct! But where else is the money supposed to come from?

Financial Collapse as a Result of Military Expenses

For some time now, the United States has not been in the position to balance its enormous budget because of huge military outlays in peacetime even without a war like the Gulf War calculated to cost about $1 billion a day. Each year, the U.S. budget runs a deficit of roughly $300 billion, about the budget outlay for the Pentagon. The gigantic American military machine is running on borrowed money. The most urgent domestic programs, not only for the disadvantaged lower class but also for the middle class—health care, education, job creation, and housing, to name just a few—cannot be addressed for lack of the funds being consumed by the military.

> *"Giving Manuel Noriega the bum's rush cost about $2 billion. . . . Two billion dollars is two thirds of 1 percent of our 1990 defense budget. America has the money to oust 150 tin-pot dictators a year if there are that many dictators left and restore democracy and human rights to 150 countries per annum if there are that many countries that want any."*
>
> P.J. O'Rourke, Parliament of Whores

The United States cannot much longer maintain the defense posture that it considers necessary for its role of superpower, even if it continues to irresponsibly neglect its urgent domestic problems. America risks the same danger as other empires; they had long been on their last legs financially when they reached their military peak, which was followed quickly by their final downfall.[12]

In his book *The Rise* and *Fall of the Great Powers,* the historian Paul Kennedy impressively documented this syndrome from the beginning of modern times with the successive examples of Spain, France, England, and Germany. This book was greeted with great interest in the United States because of its direct references and parallels. But it was also a type of Cassandra call, whose gloomy prophecy is momentarily irritating but is actually not taken very seriously.

A Waste of National Energy

The chief cause of the downfall of the precursors of the American "empire" was, as Paul Kennedy pointed out, the simple fact that the costs of the military machine were far higher than the economic advantages. Just as the Spaniards supported a huge fleet to guarantee the supply of gold and silver from the exploited colonies to finance the boundless expenses of the royal house, so today the American military serves as a guarantor for the irresponsible lifestyle of American society.

In the debate over the necessity to "liberate" Kuwait, the Americans unreservedly pointed out the vital interest of maintaining the unfettered flow of valuable oil for the American economy and the American consumer. Because a large portion of the nation's oil resources are in the Near East, a disproportionate attention is invested in this corner of the world that would otherwise be so insignificant to the United States.

The "American way of life" consumes huge amounts of energy. An increase in the price of energy to the European level would cause an economic and eventually a social crisis in the United States. Because relatively inexpensive energy has always been readily available, there has never been a special effort to conserve energy as there has been in Europe.

On the contrary, U.S. dependence on raw oil imports from the Near East is greater today than it was during the oil crisis of the seventies.

In the seventies, there was a brief period of serious concern about the extent of dependence on energy from the Middle East. Under President Jimmy Carter, measures were taken to conserve energy, and compliance was reasonably good.[13] However, America was not ready to give up old habits easily, and many people were jubilant when newly elected President Ronald Reagan, in one of his first official acts, turned up the thermostat in the White House in front of the television cameras.

America's dependency on oil from the Near East will continue to grow as will the need to militarily dominate this region. It would certainly be interesting to calculate the true price of a barrel of oil if one includes the cost of a military presence. If this war had not been paid for by other nations, oil would, likely, have become much more expensive for Americans than even Saddam Hussein could ever have imagined.

The "Crusade" Morality Comes to Its Limits

The war in Kuwait revealed the hypocrisy of the American politics of intervention in its dual form of high moral claims to save the world on the one hand and the enforcement of its own interests on the other. This contradiction was concealed from the world and the American people with the demonization of the Iraqi dictator and the promise of a new world order.

Yet, the war in Kuwait was not limited to the reestablishment of the status quo. The tensions and inner contradictions in this part of the world, many of which can be traced back to the former colonial powers with their arbitrary boundaries, are too strong.

The intervention on behalf of the Kurds was not in the script. The allies of the status quo, Turkey and Saudi Arabia, insisted that no changes be made in the internal structure of Iraq once the expansion had been rebuffed because this would inevitably have repercussions on their own fragile power balance. President George Bush was only too happy to accept this logic.

But the logical consequence—from the standpoint of the politicians—was dismissed in favor of the inner logic of intervention. The people in the United States and other Western countries, confronted on television directly with the misery of the refugees and hyped by the rhetoric of intervention on behalf of the Kuwaitis, could not follow the fine distinctions being drawn up by their statesmen between intervention of one type and intervention of a different kind. If one intervenes in favor of a people wallowing in parasitical opulence, then why not also help out the hundreds of thousands of fleeing Kurds whose annihilation seemed imminent?

The Petty Morality of Order

In the face of the misery of the fleeing Kurds, the petty morality of maintaining the existing order came to an end. There are optimists who consider this intervention to prevent genocide as the beginning of a real new world order. In this new world order, the abstract international law of national sovereignty is superceded by a supreme law of human rights.

Pax Romana also depended heavily on a petty morality of order, the maintaining of the status quo, especially in its late phase when the fires of cultural mission had long died down. In relishing its prosperity on the exploitation of others, the empire was supposed to be a refuge of security and luxury for those who were within its confines. The barbaric have-nots were beaten back and, in the end, even kept out with high walls. In consideration of the misery of the Third World and the threatening new migration of nations, the Pax Americana should not be confining but really comprehensive, not only in a geographic sense, but in a social-political sense as well.

Pax Americana can only achieve stability if it proclaims the goal of a world society to be the global expansion of the democratic idea. To be sure, in a world society of democratic ideals with its concept of justice, equality, freedom, self-determination, and equality of opportunity, the current distribution of wealth between the developed and the undeveloped nations is no longer sustainable. Today the same relations exist on a global level between the nations as existed in the predemocratic ancien régimes within a nation-state. At that time the state, that is, the sum of all citizens with inherently different social, political, and property rights, was viewed as a system of carefully separated social classes; no one took exception to the one-sided accumulation of the national assets by the aristocracy and the poverty and exploitation of the rest of society. But when in the course of the political enlightenment and the revolution, the nation, the state, the society was experienced as a collective whole, the abomination of this system of asset distribution was revealed.

Today we have on a global level the same view of the community of nations. We see the world as an entity; we see the necessity for a world order—mainly to be protected from the repercussions of turmoil and warfare outside our borders—but we have not come to grips with the fact that the world is a collective whole in which rights can no longer be so unevenly parceled out.

But as long as the United States is not in the position to satisfactorily enforce this self-evident principle within its own society, there is no prospect that Pax Americana will develop into anything other than an instrument of imperial politics.

Notes

1. Alexis de Tocqueville, *Democracy in America I*, p. 289.
2. Ibid., p. 289.
3. Robert Nisbet, *The Present Age*, p. 12.
4. *Public Papers of the Presidents of the United States*, Dwight D. Eisenhower, p. 1038.
5. Ibid., p. 1039.
6. Jefferson to William Short, November 28, 1814, *Writings*, p. 1357.
7. Tocqueville, *Democracy in America II*, pp. 268–69.
8. Ibid., pp. 271–72.
9. Ibid., p. 270.
10. Ibid., p. 270.
11. Henry Kissinger, "What Kind of New World Order?" *Washington Post*, December 3, 1991.

12. Gore Vidal, who is one of the most incisive critics of the security state, is of a similar opinion as Paul Kennedy. Compare with Vidal, "The Day the American Empire Ran Out of Gas," in *At Home: Essays 1982–1988,* p. 105.

13. It was President Carter, however, who declared the Persian Gulf region to be a strategical security zone and laid the ground with this doctrine for the military engagement of the United States in the war with Iraq.

A State

of

Law(yers)

The active role of a constitutional court in imposing the rule of law on politics was a revolutionary step that came with the establishment of American democracy. We can only agree with Alexis de Tocqueville that the incorporation of the judiciary into the political process was the ultimate perfection of the democratic idea and a guarantee of the preservation of a democratic constitution.

The Power of Justice

In 1835, this principle established in America was new and unique and set American democracy dramatically apart from other political models in use in Europe. Tocqueville remarks:

> I am not aware that any nation of the globe has hitherto organized a judicial power in the same manner as the Americans.[1]

With this he does not refer to the nature or the function of the judiciary because these are, according to Tocqueville, the same in all societies:

> The first characteristic of judicial power ... is the duty of arbitration. ... As long ... as a law is uncontested, the judicial authority is not called upon to discuss it, and it may exist without being perceived. ...
>
> The second charactereristic ... is that it pronounces on special cases, and not upon general principles. ...
>
> The third characteristic ... is its inability to act unless it is appealed to. ... The judicial power is by its nature devoid of action. ... A judicial functionary who should open proceedings, and usurp the censureship of the laws, would in some measure do violence to the passive nature of his authority.
>
> The Americans have retained these three distinguishing characteristics of

the judicial power; an American judge can only pronounce a decision when litigation has arisen, he is only conversant with special cases, and he cannot act until the cause has been duly brought before the court.[2]

Why then, Tocqueville asks, does the judge in America possess a power that his peers in other countries do not have?

> The cause of this difference lies in the simple fact that the Americans have acknowledged the right of the judges to found their decisions on the constitution, rather than on the laws.[3]

This right comes from a provision in the Constitution by which the Constitution itself is declared to be the supreme law of the land. Tocqueville expresses it in these terms:

> In the United States the constitution governs the legislator as much as the private citizen: as it is the first of the laws, it cannot be modified by a law; and it is therefore just that the tribunals should obey the constitution in preference to any law.[4]

Every law that is approved by the legislature and every administrative act of the executive branch is conditional. Every judge has the fundamental right to refuse to apply laws if he or she considers them unconstitutional. Also, every judgment is conditional in that it may not coincide with the essential principles of the Constitution. The final authority for testing and deciding a ruling is the Supreme Court. Its decisions are final—but also only for a limited time. A new case with the same issues some years later, in different circumstances and with a different composition of the bench, can have a slightly or even very different outcome. This judgment then becomes the supreme law of the land until the next such case comes before the court.

Tocqueville points out that because of this right of recourse under the Constitution, the authority of the American judicial branch over the legislative and executive branches is very powerful. But this power is restricted by the procedures that the judiciary must follow in its interventions into politics. It is always required that the issue—in form of a singular and special case—has to be brought to the court from outside.

> If the judge had been empowered to contest the laws on the ground of theoretical generalities, ... he would have played a prominent part in the political sphere. . . .
> If the judge could only attack the legislator openly and directly, he would sometimes be afraid to oppose any resistance to his will; and at other moments party spirit might encourage him to brave it at every turn. The laws would consequently be attacked when the power from which they emanate is weak, and obeyed when it is strong. That is to say, when it would be useful to respect

them, they would be contested; and when it would be easy to convert them into
an instrument of oppression, they would be respected. But the American judge
is brought into the political arena independently of his own will.[5]

With this new definition of a vastly enlarged role of the judiciary in politics,
the United States has set an example that by now has become the standard for
democratic constitutions, that all laws are subject to a challenge on constitutional
grounds and that a Supreme Court has the final say not only over judicial decisions by lower courts but also over political decisions made by the parliament or
by the administration.

The Supreme Court as Constitutional Reformer

For the American political system, the power of the courts, in general, and of the
Supreme Court, in particular, has also had direct practical significance in the
development of the Constitution. The American Constitution had been approved
in 1787 with the urgent vote that a comprehensive catalog of fundamental rights
must immediately be appended. This occurred in 1791 with the first ten amendments, known as the Bill of Rights. If one counts these articles as part of the
original version, there have been only seventeen "real" amendments to the Constitution in more than 200 years, two of which (both pertaining to the prohibition
of alcoholic beverages) cancel each other out, so that the number is reduced to
just fifteen.[6]
   The fathers of the Constitution purposely complicated the procedure for
amending the Constitution in order to provide stability to the laboriously created
political system. A two-thirds majority in both houses of Congress is required to
approve an amendment, which then must be ratified by three-fourths of all the
states (the Women's Equal Rights Amendment, for example, ultimately failed
due to this requirement). The last amendment, which went into effect in May
1992, was first proposed more than 200 years ago and just recently received the
necessary three-fourths approval.
   The alternative method to passage of an amendment is a constitutional convention, which is even more complicated. Congress may convene a constitutional convention upon a motion of two-thirds of the states. The amendments
passed by this convention must then be ratified by three-fourths of the states. The
limited number of amendments to the Constitution is surely due to these procedural safeguards. There is no doubt that the United States would not have survived as a political system these past 200 years—during which the country
became a continent, an agrarian society became highly industrialized, and an
isolated settlement across vast oceans became a world superpower—if the Constitution had not been "amended" and adapted to new circumstances and changing times.

MARBURY v. MADISON, 1803

The doctrine of *judicial supremacy*, the most important milestone of law in our history, was established in *Marbury v. Madison*. The Supreme Court held that it had the power to consider the constitutionality of laws enacted by Congress, and to find a law invalid if, in the opinion of the Court, Congress was not authorized to enact it.

This decision, which grew out of a dispute over executive appointments made during the John Adams administration, has been fundamental in making the United States subject to "the rule of law." The power to declare a law unconstitutional is seldom given to the courts of other nations, and it is the basis for the special role which the Supreme Court plays in the government of the United States.

Changes reflecting the transformations the country has gone through have indeed been made, but not in the form of written amendments. The ability to adapt the constitutional text to an ever changing political and social environment stems from the administration of justice by the Supreme Court. Judicial review rather than amendments to the Constitution, is the mechanism most used to adapt and interpret the meaning of the Constitution in a changing political environment.[7]

The Openness of the American Constitution

> *"[Marbury v. Madison] is the case that established the Supreme Court's review powers, thus making the Supreme Court supreme. I think you more or less have to cite it when you're arguing before the Supreme Court. It's like telling your wife her dress looks pretty before you go to a party."*
>
> P.J. O'Rourke, Parliament of Whores

This unique flexibility of the Constitution to change and adapt itself to new circumstances is one prime example of American pragmatism. The text of the Constitution does not achieve doctrinaire exactitude for every aspect of political life. It has left areas unresolved and has even placed concepts beside one another that theoretically appear incompatible. Because of this openness, problems unknown when the Constitution was adopted can be dealt with in contemporary historical context.

This is true, for example, in the area of relations between the federal government and the individual states. The new and complicated concept of federalism was regulated by the authors of the Constitution with amazing foresight but certainly was not decisive in every detail and for every circumstance. As a result, there is both room and necessity for continual interpretation, which has, by degrees, allowed the Supreme Court its practical role as constitutional reformer.

In the early years, the main function of the Supreme Court was to maintain a steady balance between the individual states and the central government. In the first decades of the nineteenth century, Chief Justice John Marshall led the Court to advance a dynamic interpretation of the Constitution in support of a strong federal government. As a supporter of the Federalists (advocates of strong federal powers), he was committed to the promotion of trade and industry necessary for the economic development of the United States.

Fluctuating between a Liberal and a Conservative Interpretation of the Constitution

Throughout its history, the political philosophy of the Supreme Court, like public opinion itself, has fluctuated widely in a rhythm of pendulum swings: A period of activism was followed by a period of conservatism. Changes have not often occurred abruptly but, rather, over long periods of time due to the lengthy tenures of the judges in office (at times thirty to forty years). The justices of the Supreme Court are appointed by the president, with the confirmation of the Senate, and serve for life.

The pendulum swings do not develop coincidentally. They reflect the fact that the Supreme Court, despite its institutional independence, does not stand apart from politics and other influences in America. This can be clearly seen in the reversal of the ideological outlook that has taken place in recent years. The sixties and seventies were characterized by a pronounced liberal and progressive interpretation of the Constitution despite the growing trend toward conservatism in American society in the early seventies and on a broad scale in the eighties. When vacancies occurred, the presidents elected in this conservative wave—namely Richard Nixon, Ronald Reagan, and George Bush—appointed new justices who shared their political philosophy, eventually establishing a solid conservative majority on the Supreme Court.

Supreme Court justices, however, are not henchmen of the politicians. Justices often fundamentally change their outlooks early into or during their long tenure in office on the Supreme Court. A recent example is longtime Chief Justice Earl Warren, appointed by the conservative President Dwight D. Eisenhower, who became a vigorous voice for a liberal, reform-oriented, progressive interpretation of the Constitution and led the Court to the most revolutionary changes in American society and the American political system. It was precisely the growing opposition of public opinion to the legal philosophy of the Warren court that led succeeding presidents to change the composition of the Supreme Court.

The Controversy between President Roosevelt and the Supreme Court

A similar clash between judicial and political philosophy occurred over social welfare laws in the thirties. President Franklin Roosevelt was elected by a large majority and carried an overwhelmingly Democratic Congress ready to enact far-reaching laws to restore the economy and provide basic security for working people. A continuing economic catastrophe—the Great Depression—called for drastic new measures. The Supreme Court, however, declared entire so-called New Deal laws unconstitutional and brought Roosevelt's program to the point of failure.

In his frustration, Roosevelt seized upon a plan to increase the number of justices and fill those new positions with justices of his political philosophy. Although public opinion mostly supported the president and a landslide election victory in Congress brought him a solid majority in favor of his social programs, the Congress refused to support the president in his attempt.

The plan "to pack the court," as this maneuver was called, had to be abandoned. But what Roosevelt was unable to achieve through change in numbers occurred of its own volition. Eventually, and certainly under pressure of the political climate, the Supreme Court relaxed its conservative grip, enlarged its outlook, and broadened its interpretation of the Constitution.

The Supreme Court as the Avant-Garde of Politics

> *"Then there was a problem. Because at the time the nation was functioning under the racial doctrine of 'Separate but Equal,' which got its name from the fact that black people were required to use separate facilities that were equal to the facilities that white people kept for their domestic animals. This system had worked for many decades. "*
>
> Dave Barry, Dave Barry Slept Here

After 100 years of racial segregation and social oppression of the black minority in the United States, the activist Warren Court dramatically forced the issue to the forefront of the American consciousness. The historical opinions of the Warren Court concerning segregation in schools, in particular the pioneering verdict of *Brown v. Board of Education* of 1954, gave decisive impetus to the civil rights movement. This movement certainly would not have been as strong and would not have had such striking results without the continuous support of the Supreme Court. Congress would likely have prolonged the struggle for many years, maybe decades, and enactment of the Civil Rights Act of 1964 would not have been achieved without the pressure created by the Supreme Court.

Whereas the rulings against segregation dealt with the fundamental democratic principle of equality and gave it a new and more expanded meaning, the Warren Court also developed a new constitutional philosophy about the principle of freedom in a constitutional state by defining the limits for government actions. Important laws flowed from these decisions, including the Freedom of Information Act, which severely restricted the power of government to withhold "state secrets." The death penalty was abolished (since restored), abortion was made legal (a decision that no longer commands a safe majority in the Court), the rights of the accused in criminal cases were strengthened, and the methods of police and public prosecutors restrained (here, too, the Court is backtracking).

These decisions as well as affirmative action measures taken to remedy racial discrimination were influential in arousing a conservative "backlash" in the early seventies that is still growing in American society today.

A Pragmatic Philosophy of Justice

Tocqueville rightly pointed out that the enormous influence of the Supreme Court and courts in general cannot be explained solely by the structure mandated by the Constitution but rather by the high esteem for the concept of justice in the United States. The law by itself is powerless. The Supreme Court has no administration and no troops to enforce its decisions.

Tocqueville's admiration of American respect for law and the decrees of the court should be taken with a grain of salt. American politicians are very imaginative in cleverly undermining unpopular decisions of the courts through laws enacted by Congress.

Respect for the law is not necessarily identical with a public passion for justice. The power of the Supreme Court to effect changes in the political sphere is limited by the public's perception of justice. Tocqueville addressed this problem:

> Their [the judges of the Supreme Court] power is enormous, but it is clothed in the authority of public opinion. They are the all-powerful guardians of a people which respects law; but they would be impotent against popular neglect or popular contempt. The force of public opinion is the most intractable of agents, because its exact limits cannot be defined: and it is not less dangerous to exceed, than to remain below the boundary prescribed.
>
> The Federal judges must not only be good citizens ... but they must be statesmen,—politicians, not unread in the signs of the times, not afraid to brave the obstacles which can be subdued, nor slow to turn aside such encroaching elements as may threaten the supremacy of the Union and the obedience which is due to the laws.[8]

The political influence of the Supreme Court is limited by political circumstances. It does not act in a purely philosophical realm of truth and justice. To a great degree, public conscience, the moral values of society and the prevailing perceptions of justice all influence the decisions of the Court just as the decisions of the Court influence and change the views of society. It is a thoroughly Aristotelian view of justice: The definition of what is just is not an abstract concept but based upon a consensus of society.

This is both advantageous and dangerous. The greatest advantage is that justice conforms to public opinion and is therefore readily accepted. This is almost certainly one of the reasons why the law has such authority in the United States. It is understood, and it is a part of society in and of itself. The danger lies in the fact that this kind of justice becomes a servant of the prevailing public opinion.

The Supreme Court as the Repair Shop of Politics

Some problems prove to be too difficult for elected officials. They evade or delay hard decisions out of ignorance or cowardice. They seem to wait helplessly for the Supreme Court to force them into action. On others they almost drag the Court into the political arena, as with a constitutional amendment to balance the budget instead of cutting the deficit through sound and responsible fiscal policy.

Abortion is one issue that immobilizes politicians and occupies the courts in many countries. Euthanasia and gene technology similarly surpass the problem-solving ability of the politicians. In a reverse of the ground rule of democracy, the judges feel forced to write law by court decision. Fundamental moral questions prove too unwieldy for political debate and resolution. Abortion, euthanasia, and related questions go to the protection of life guaranteed under the Constitution. Reapportionment of electoral districts, the integration of schools, and discrimination in jobs and in housing are issues of equality under the law. In the debate about citizens' rights as opposed to the power of the government, the issue is the protection of freedom in a democratic state. Surely such questions must be fought out and dealt with in the legislature rather than in the courts.

By shirking their duties as lawmakers to develop a pragmatic consensus on public affairs, politicians enflame the passions of the ignorant and uninformed. Resorting to the courts merely heightens this passion and undermines the integrity of the legal system. The authority of the Supreme Court is diminished by partisan political bickering. Moreover, the change from political discussion to a war of beliefs widens the rift within society and makes it increasingly difficult to find a solution for problems that are fundamentally political.

The Trial as an Alternative to the Political Feud of Distribution

In this world of overcharged expectations, litigation became the alternative to political argument. The rush to courts in contemporary society threatens both the quality of justice and its swiftness. Aggressive assertion of individual rights as a citizen is a part of the American tradition and consciousness. Nevertheless, the explosion of litigation reveals a more contentious society destructive of civil order and amity. The entire world anxiously followed the first sensational palimony trial of the life companion of a Hollywood actor over the distribution of property after a break up of a nonmarital relationship. This trial, followed by countless others like it around the world, is a poignant sign of the vulnerability of human affairs to endless litigation. Patients sue their doctors, consumers sue the producers of faulty products, employees sue their employers, creditors sue banks, taxpayers sue their accountants, corporations sue competitors, individuals or citizens' groups sue environmental offenders—not to forget the clients who sue their lawyers. Most cases are not concerned merely with the restoration of former conditions but, rather, seek punitive damages for negligent or willful malpractice that has led to alleged injuries or to encroachments on personal rights.

Social Revalorization of Litigation

As Walter K. Olson has pointed out in his book *The Litigation Explosion,* the rush to litigation began in the seventies, when legal scholars in the great law schools changed their concept of the social value of litigation. In a leading article in a university press magazine in 1968, the prevailing opinion that trials were a necessary evil and litigation was a nuisance was characterized as "distinctly medieval."[9] Litigation must then be a characteristic of the modern human being who knows his rights and demands them. There are parallels to the simultaneous wave of individual self-discovery and self-esteem movements that are so characteristic of our time. Obviously, 500 years after the discovery of the individual during the Renaissance, we are experiencing a gigantic second wave of focusing on individuals, their rights, and their significance.

The Supreme Court has explicitly dealt with this new theory and in 1971 decided by a narrow margin that trials are no longer to be considered an evil.[10] So much for the theory. In practice, this "deregulation of trials" has led to a veritable litigation fury. American society is no longer satisfied with having accomplished a balance, a kind of neutrality in the assessment of the societal value of trials, but has pushed forward and raised its meaning by a philosophy of the trial as a cathartic and healing force for a democratic society. The judicial system is attributed the function of social adjustment as it is supposed to compensate the victims of society and to distribute in some kind of affirmative action to the "short-changed" ones what the market and politics have denied them.

> *"Lawyers pander to the American illusion that all problems have legal solutions, and the result is a society that requires lawyers to do almost anything."*
>
> Robert J. Samuelson, *"Go Ahead, Bash Lawyers"*

A more dangerous theory justifies civil litigation as punishment and deterrent. Litigation serves the same purpose that Thomas Hobbes saw in the market mechanism. It would correct the conduct of the members of society through warning signals. Obstetricians would exercise extra precautions with a delivery when a colleague pays $3 million in damages to the injured woman for malpractice. Businesses would refrain from charging their customers inflated prices or bringing insufficiently tested products to the market when they read that an attorney for a group of injured persons managed to get $50 million in punitive damages. In this new world, trials are no longer about establishing justice in a particular case between opposing parties, they are about reforming the community.

Olson writes:

> Even a suit that probably will lose can be said to deter misconduct and focus useful social scrutiny on doctors, corporate managements, or whomever. And if a claim or add-on happens not to have a factual basis, so what? This opponent or another very similar one has gotten away scot-free on other occasions and has a large overdue account to pay to the class of which this plaintiff is a member.[11]

The American Judicial System Privileges the Plaintiff

The nation of lawyers was fostered by peculiarities of the American legal system. Unlike other Western countries, the United States does not require the losing party to pay the court costs of the winning party. This reduces the financial risk to the plaintiff of losing the suit. The risk is further reduced by the practice of contingency fees by which lawyers collect their compensation as a percentage of the court award if their client wins the case. The percentage fee is high as a reward for the risk by the law firm. Even the expert witnesses who appear are paid by the litigating parties and are not called up independently by the courts. In addition, the verdict is rendered not by professional judges but by a jury selected at random from the rolls of ordinary citizens.

The Flood of Trials Washes Away the Mainstay of the Constitutional State

All of these "reforms" of the litigation system find approval in the American society because they originate in the moral rigor that is so typical for America and that justifies the elimination of all evil at any cost. Ironically, the result is that not more but less justice is served and that even the greatest achievement of modern times, the constitutional state, is in danger of being hollowed out from the inside. The decisive element of the constitutional state is the security of the law. One is liable to be punished if one participates in an unjust act, but one can be sure that if one does not, one can live in peace and security. Precisely this security has been destroyed by the litiginous search for wrongdoing: an obstetrician who fails to successfully deliver a child is sued, a psychiatrist is taken to court because a patient who has jumped out of a window may have refrained from doing so if he had been given a higher dose of sedatives, an employer who allows an alcoholic employee to continue working in highly sensitive or dangerous conditions is sued for his irresponsible conduct toward his worker's safety, and if he fires the worker, he can count on a lawsuit for unwarranted termination. The attempt to combine all of life's crises into the one and only category of guilt and responsibility (naturally, of the opposing side) and in doing so to make it "judiciable," leads to the disintegration of society.

The disastrous aspect to all of this is that, of course, no one wants to completely exonerate himself or herself from guilt because nobody can feel absolutely innocent—and this is particularly true for responsibly minded people. The aforementioned psychiatrist will naturally ask himself or herself the question whether he or she should not have tried sedatives instead of relying on counseling. Yet this type of soul-searching is definitely not a case for the courts.

The decisive leverage for this development is the monetarization of suffering. By calculating all the troubles of this world into monetary units, suffering became legally manageable. Above all, it became possible, through this increase in quantity of cases, to schematically categorize, specialize, and industrialize the cases. Many attorneys promote themselves as specialists for gynecological/obstetrical malpractice. Like an assembly line procedure, they finish off one trial after another by routine. Others have limited their practice to the defective products of industries, and even others specialize in trials against one particular company.

Although the pretext of acting in the name of the client or even for the general public is unanimously supported, in reality an independent trial industry has been developed that only obeys its own laws and pays notice to its own interests. It is one of the most lucrative industries of the American economy. Young attorneys in Washington, fresh out of law school, earn a starting salary that is sometimes higher than what lawmakers earn. Yet, that is "peanuts" in comparison to what a lawyer can earn after working for some years as an experienced upper-level attorney for a law firm made up of hundreds of attorneys.

Lawyers as Lobbyists

Political representation in Washington of the interests of companies, organizations, and increasingly also of foreign governments has created a vast industry for lawyers in the daily business of lawmaking. This is also true in state capitals and big cities. The words *lobbyist* and *lawyer* are often used synonymously in Washington. Although not every lobbyist is also a lawyer, the most prosperous lawyers in the capital city are registered as lobbyists.

In the end, the lucrative fees charged by lawyers, in exchange for the advice and influence they offer their political clients, are paid for by society. The representatives of interests of big companies in Washington serve to gain special favors of sometimes gigantic proportions for their clients by shaping laws and regulations as well as securing large government contracts. On economic legislation, especially tax legislation, a simple amendment of inclusion or exception can inflate benefits by millions of dollars.

As a result of the so-called "revolving door" government service and private law practice, access to Congress and government is abundantly available. William Greider has pointed out that nearly the entire Democratic party leadership is made up of top-level attorneys whose client lists read like the Forbes 500 list of the largest American companies. The same is true for the Republican Party, when control of the presidency or Congress changes.

In recent years attorneys have discovered a new gold mine: the bankruptcy proceedings in a declining American economy.[12] After lawyers served as willing and highly paid accomplices in the eighties mergers and buyouts that contradicted all economic reason and the partitions and unions of giant conglomerates, they are once again in a position to benefit from the collapse of these grand constructions.

The recently liberalized American bankruptcy laws guarantee failing companies generous protection from their creditors. This was meant to encourage efforts to reconsolidate under the supervision of the courts: It is practically an invitation to the lawyers to exploit the remaining company assets and goodwill through exorbitant fees that hasten the collapse.

The attorneys bill their five-hour flights (first class, of course), for example, from Los Angeles, where they live, to New York, where they work, at hourly rates of $250 to $500; they charge hourly rates for packing their briefcases in the office and unpacking them in the hotel room; they even charge for the time it takes to calculate the bill.[13]

Attorneys believe themselves to be truly a ruling class in the United States. It is certainly no coincidence that despite a recent decline more half of the members of Congress are attorneys, just as in Germany almost half of the Bundestag (Lower House) delegates are civil servants. The United States has, in point of fact, developed from a state of law to a state of lawyers. In no other nation in the world do lawyers have so much influence; no place else have they tried so unscrupulously to expand the dimensions of justice until no public or private business can be done without retaining a lawyer.

The lawyers are the new Mandarins. They live off the expenses that they originally brought about. Meanwhile, as a customary procedure, insurance against trial risks is calculated into the budget of all companies. The insurance costs are added onto the price calculations just like the advertising costs. The same holds true for the premiums for malpractice insurance, which for some physicians reach levels higher than $100,000 per year.[14] These insurance costs surely also augment the doctors' fees and, with that, contribute to the fact that the American health care system is the most expensive in the world. Thus, it is not the "bad guys" who pay the price; just as often, only a fraction of the compensation remains for the actual victims. It is the society as a whole that carries the costs of livelihood for this new social class, which, in its parasitic state of being, enjoys a life of the utmost luxury.

Notes

1. Alexis de Tocqueville, *Democracy in America I*, p. 98.
2. Ibid., p. 99.
3. Ibid., p. 100.
4. Ibid., p. 101, Article VI: "This Constitution . . . shall be the Supreme Law of the Land; and the Judges in every State be bound thereby."
5. Ibid., pp. 102–3.
6. The rules for amendments are determined by Article V.
7. This principle was established with the guiding court decision *Marbury v. Madison* in 1803. The competence of the Supreme Court was not defined precisely in the Constitution. It was the Supreme Court that created its outstanding position in the political system by interpreting extensively Article VI of the Constitution: "The Constitution is the Supreme Law of the Land."
8. Tocqueville, *Democracy in America I*, p. 151.
9. Walter K. Olson, *The Litigation Explosion*, p. 4.
10. From the U.S. Supreme Court decision in *Bates v. State Bar of Arizona* (quoted in Walter K. Olson, *The Litigation Explosion*, p. 29; see also p. 5). The text description of American litigation follows mainly Olson's book.
11. Olson, *The Litigation Explosion*, pp. 269–70.
12. Donald L. Barlett and James B. Steele, *America: What Went Wrong?* chapter 4—"The Lucrative Business of Bankruptcy," p. 66.
13. Ibid., p. 69.
14. Olson, *The Litigation Explosion*, p. 6.

The

Media

In May of 1991, an editorial in the *Tampa Tribune* apologized for reporting a police investigation at the home of the publisher a full nine days after the incident. On April 26, a young woman and several men whom she had met dancing—among them the publisher's son—went to his home, where she allegedly fell asleep and upon waking discovered that she had been sexually assaulted. Jim Urbanski, the publisher, was out of town on that day.

The following notable sentences were among those stating the position of the editors:

> Certainly, Jim Urbanski, our friend and colleague, should have alerted Tribune editors as soon as he got the word. . . . This newspaper's credibility took a hard shot under the heart.[1]

The editorial went on to elaborate that an attempt had been made to sweep the entire incident under the rug, perhaps because the young people were "members of prominent families."

The Self-Perception of the American Journalist

This episode is unusual even by American standards, but it nevertheless dramatically reveals the self-perception of the press as the untiring guardian of the public interest. Anything that the public might find interesting is considered "news." News is public property and should not be withheld. The journalists of the *Tampa Tribune* justified their actions by the fact that they "want to clarify to their readers that this newspaper as an institution doesn't retain news on a supposed rape." The owner of the paper justified his attitude by maintaining that the events that occurred in his house were not actually newsworthy; therefore, he saw no reason to inform the newspaper.

The independence of the American press is not merely a theoretical notion but also a reality vigorously defended by journalists and by publishers and owners as well. Of course, this independence is often stifled in many ways—without the knowledge of the public and sometimes even without the knowledge of those directly involved. However, just as this example and many other cases clearly demonstrate, the ideal of a free and independent press is taken seriously in the American political system. The press—including the telecommunications media—is an "institution," just as the journalists of the *Tampa Tribune* proudly and justly explain; it is the watchdog of democracy that prevents those in power from infringing on the freedom of others and from unjustly spreading their influence. The press is a crucial player in the democratic game.

Tocqueville's Disparaging Judgment of American Journalism

> *"Journalists are notoriously easy to kid. All you have to do is speak to a journalist in a very serious tone of voice, and he will be certain that you are either telling the truth or a big, important lie. It has never occurred to any journalist that he was having his leg pulled."*
>
> P.J. O'Rourke, Parliament of Whores

Alexis de Tocqueville did not think very highly of American journalists. He considered them uneducated and tasteless and accused them of a lack of reservation when reporting on the private lives of politicians:

The characteristics of the American journalist consist in an open and coarse appeal to the passions of his readers; he abandons principles to assail the characters of individuals, to track them into private life and disclose all their weakness and vices.[2]

And in his *Journey to America* he writes:

It is a shame to see what coarse insults, what petty slanders and what impudent calumnies fill the papers that serve as their mouthpieces, and with what disregard of all the social decencies they daily arraign before the tribunal of public opinion the honour of families and the secrets of the domestic hearth.[3]

Here Tocqueville clearly illustrates one characteristic of American journalism, even if he sees it in a purely negative light: the pitilessness and stubbornness with which the curiosity of the public is placed above all other values, such as the right to privacy. In the understanding of American journalism, public figures give journalists the right to examine and investigate them by the very fact that they are public figures. Thus, public figures are, in a sense, public property.

This seems self-explanatory to Americans; after all, the public must know with whom they are dealing. The lack of restraint and the thoroughness with which American journalists examine the private lives of politicians may seem brutal and shameless to Europeans. However, this very attitude, this vocational ethos, enables journalists to pursue every suspicion of illegal behavior on the part of politicians as well as to constantly observe their actions.

American Journalism as the Protector of Political Morality

> *"We journalists don't have to step on roaches. All we have to do is turn on the kitchen light and watch the critters scurry."*
>
> P. J. O'Rourke, Parliament of Whores

The inquisitorial nature of journalism in America has a certain justification. The ideal of politicians as servants of society and of government officials as dutiful and loyal representatives of the state, an ideal that developed over hundreds of years among European officials, is rarely present in the United States. In the early years, the positions in the federal administration of the republic were awarded according to the "spoils system." In other words, each new president had the privilege of filling all the posts with his own people and readily took advantage of this opportunity. In a certain way, the spoils system still exists. Friends and patrons who served well during the election campaign are rewarded with high administrative positions or diplomatic posts.

American pragmatism also has its effects on political morals. The role of the politician is a job like any other; it is not governed by any special ideals except for those that are common to society as a whole.[4] Politicians work for the voters, but they also work for their own interests. In the United States, the politician's relationship to money is uninhibited and unabashed.

In this atmosphere, the press feels free to scrutinize everything that occurs in politics and to report it to the public. The press itself does not create the rules of political morality—this is the task of the public itself—but in order for the public to judge and condemn, it must be adequately informed.

American journalism has changed in some ways over the course of 200 years, but its understanding of its own function—to report objectionable behavior and to keep the public on its toes—has remained constant. Of course, journalists did not always have it easy when the newspaper owners and the corrupt political and business interests were in cahoots. But on the whole, the history of American journalism is an exemplary chronicle of courageous and successful intervention on behalf of the public.

The so-called muckrakers at the beginning of this century left their mark on the history of American journalism. They were courageous and committed journalists, who, together with writers and historians, undertook to expose the scandalous practices in the creation of business trusts and industrial conglomerates and made the public aware of the constant, sometimes criminal, negligence of safety in the workplace and the health of the consumer.

At first, the expression was meant to be derogatory, but soon after it became an honorable title for those journalists committed to cleaning up society by exposing dirty businesses.

American journalism is proud of this tradition. Important examples include the publication of the secret Pentagon Papers, which played a decisive role in changing the American policy in Vietnam, as well as the especially impressive exposure of the Watergate affair.

This case reveals not only the ethos and ideals of the press, but also the chances for success of a kind of journalism that untiringly pursues the facts in order to present them to the public. Without a doubt, the Watergate affair would not have been exposed without the investigative work of Bob Woodward and Carl Bernstein, both reporters for the *Washington Post*. The extent of the manipulations at the center of power would never have been revealed, and President Richard Nixon would have been able to complete his term in the White House. The fact that such a monumental event as the resignation of the president could be initiated and crucially affected by two young reporters speaks for the self-confidence of American journalism as well as for the influence of the press. It must be recognized, especially in the case of the Watergate scandal, that not only the journalists and editors maintained this ethos, but the newspaper owners did as well. They upheld an ethos that stems from the conviction that the press is only good and free when it commits itself exclusively and without prejudice to the service of the public.

There are, however, also frightening examples of irresponsibility on the part of journalists practicing their occupation. They, too, are a direct result of an inexorable quest for news, the quest for ever more new facts to satisfy the curiosity of the public.

Often this urge for news does not stop with the "facts." As part of the search for a good "story," facts are often distorted, exaggerated, embellished, and sometimes even invented. Ironically, another report appearing in the *Washington Post*, this time in the spring of 1991, told the story of an eight-year-old heroin addict. This story enraged the entire nation, and the author won a Pulitzer Prize, the most prestigious American award in journalism. Shortly after the prize was awarded, other journalists discovered that the child addict was a figment of the author's imagination and that the entire story was pure invention.[5]

The American Press as the Fourth Governmental Branch

"Newsmen believe that news is a tacitly acknowledged fourth branch of the federal system. This is why most news about government sounds as if it were federally mandated—serious, bulky and blandly worthwhile, like a high-fiber diet set in type."

P. J. O'Rourke, Parliament of Whores

We can turn it into an amusement for the public.

The American press often regards itself as the fourth branch of the government, along with the classical legislative, executive, and judicial branches. The press is, in fact, a necessary institution in a democratic mass society, although this is not expressly stated in the U.S. Constitution. One could regard it as the communicative, or mediating, branch.

The press has a communicative function in relaying information primarily from the government to the governed. This can be a purely formal activity, in which the press acts merely as a messenger without actually participating. However, this neutrality is not absolute as the amount of potential news is greater than the space available. Thus, the term *mediating branch* is more appropriate. The news is not merely transmitted; rather, it is influenced by the media at least in the form of selection.

In addition, the press wants to influence the opinions of the people, or rather, the press wants to "transmit" its own opinion on matters to the people. Further, the press sees itself as a "transmitter" of ideas from the general public to the people at the top because it likes to be listened to by the governing powers. Thus, it transmits the people's opinion to those powers—not directly, because nobody is able to pin down the opinion of the people; rather, it is done in the form of commentaries which are presented as a fair gauge of public opinion.

The Function of Freedom of the Press in the Democratic System

Americans are fortunate to have had a free press from the very beginning of the nation. In Europe, the rulers feared the idea of a free press and attempted to stifle it for as long as possible. An echo of this fear is still evident in the hysterical control that European political parties—the autocrats of the republican system—exercise over public radio and television.

Freedom of the press is crucial for the freedom of a system of government. That is why this freedom is guaranteed in all democratic constitutions. The reality of the situation is, however, a different matter. Tocqueville points out the significance of a free press for democracy, although he regards it with critical distance:

> I confess that I do not entertain that firm and complete attachment of the liberty of the press which is wont to be excited by things that are supremely good in their very nature. I approve of it from a consideration more of the evils it prevents than of the advantages it ensures.[6]

Tocqueville offers two reasons for the necessity of a free press in a democracy, one practical reason and one having to do with democratic theory. The practical reason is that only the press is capable of watching over the government and warning the public of breaches of the law. The freedom of the press is therefore a decisive safeguard for the freedom of the people. Public opinion shaped by the media puts politicians on trial and passes judgment on their offenses and guards against possible corruption.[7]

In addition, the freedom of the press in a democracy is crucial in informing the population about the variety of opinions and in helping them make judgments. Even if Tocqueville emphasizes the negative side of a free press, i.e., that it incites the passions of the people, he honors the positive role:

> When the right of every citizen to a share in the government of society is acknowledged, everyone must be presumed to be able to choose between the various opinions of his contemporaries and to appreciate the different facts from which inferences may be drawn. The sovereignty of the people and the liberty of the press may therefore be regarded as correlative, just as the censorship of the press and universal suffrage are two things which are irreconcilably opposed and which cannot long be retained among the institutions of the same people.[8]

Change in the Basic Conditions of the Free Press

The nature of a free press has fundamentally changed in the 200 years since it was introduced into political theory and practice. In the beginning, the problem was to establish this freedom from government interference or even oppression. In many countries, this is still the task at hand today. Establishing a free press meant a battle against the authorities in order to inform the public of all facts and opinions, especially if they were uncomfortable for those in power. This freedom has to be fought for again and again.

There is and there always will be an interest on the side of the government in keeping matters secret, which conflicts with the public's need for information. The press therefore will always have to struggle on behalf of the public to expose matters that politicians would prefer to keep hidden.

The fight for the freedom of the press, however, in our times is not so much against the government as it was in the early stages of democracy. Now the freedom of the press is more subtly threatened on three different but somewhat interconnected fronts.

The first danger is the economic concentration of the media, which limits the variety of opinions because they are no longer represented by an organ of expression.

In addition, the press is increasingly influenced by economic considerations, i.e., the interests of the owners, who run newspapers and television channels not as journalists but as businesses purely for profit and by the hidden and sometimes blatant influence of the advertisers.

The third threat to the free press is the disinterest of readers, listeners, and viewers who prefer entertainment to information.

The Concentration of the Press

> *"The newspaper industry remains diverse in ownership. Forty-four groups own only two newspapers, while 80 groups own five or fewer dailies. Fifty groups have total daily circulations of 50,000 or less."*
> '91 Facts about Newspapers, a statistical summary of the newspaper business published by the American Newspaper Publishers Association

Since 1830, the American press has changed decisively, which means some of Tocqueville's judgments on the role and power of the press are no longer valid. During his time, the press was free but weak. There was a surplus of newspapers with different political alignments, and Tocqueville thought correctly that these papers would neutralize one another and thus have only a limited influence on public opinion. For Tocqueville, one of his greatest concerns was the danger that the press could become too strong, too influential, and too one-sided, and that democracy would be controlled by a dictatorship of a united opinion. He writes:

> Hence the number of periodical and semi-periodical publications in the United States is almost incredibly large. The most enlightened Americans attribute the little influence of the press to this excessive dissemination of its power; and it is an axiom of political science in that country that the only way to neutralize the effect of the public journals is to multiply their number.[9]

Today we are confronted with an enormous concentration of the press. However, there are still surprisingly many regional and local newspapers on the market. According to statistics by the American Newspaper Publishers Association, in 1991 there were 1,611 daily newspapers in the United States, 80 percent of which circulated less than 50,000 copies. However, most American newspapers are no longer independent but owned by large newspaper chains. Out of the total circulation of all the daily newspapers—around 62 million copies—the twenty largest groups produce more than half of them, with a circulation of 36 million. They publish 526, or one-third, of the newspapers. The concentration of the press becomes more obvious when one looks at the figures for the groups with more than twenty papers. These ten groups produce 424 newspapers, in other words, one-fourth of the newspapers. By producing around 25 million copies, they control 40 percent of the total circulation. The top three publishing groups alone have a circulation of 9 million with a total of 263 newspapers. This represents 15 percent of all the newspapers sold in the United States.

The concentration of the press increased dramatically in the eighties. Whereas the number of newspapers from 1946 to 1980 remained quite constant, the number dropped from 1,745 to 1,611 in the last decade. This drop affected mostly the small newspapers. Their ranks dropped from 1,504 in 1975 to 1,329, whereas the number of newspapers with a circulation of more than 25,000 increased from 36 to 49 over the same time period.

Some chains grant local editors a great deal of freedom; whereas others exercise strict control over the content of the papers. Most independent newspapers, however, are largely dependent on news agencies when it comes to national and international news. Besides, they leave the commenting on both domestic and foreign news to syndicated columnists, whose articles appear simultaneously in hundreds of newspapers all over the country.

> *"Television fans can now have their tube and read it too."*
> *Comment on the publishing of the first "national" American*
> *newspaper* USA Today, *quoted by Paul Fussell,* BAD

For more than ten years now, the United States has had an actual national newspaper: a novelty in U.S. history. The paper is called *USA Today*—the critics also refer to it as McPaper. It is distributed both nationally and internationally. If one does not count *USA Today,* it holds true that most U.S. cities are controlled by newspaper monopolies. Competition between daily papers exists only in a few cities. The statistics of the American Newspaper Publishers Association, which clearly attempts to hide the increasing concentration of the press, also indicate that forty-one cities have two or more papers with different owners. However, the Association points out with embarrassment that this number also includes those twenty cities in which the newspapers are produced under a cooperative agreement.

The concentration of the press is not limited to newspapers. Most of the large newspaper publishers straddle radio and television stations, weekly papers, news agencies, magazines, and book publishing houses as well. Although radio and television stations are regulated, unlike the press, by federal authorities, the economic concentration—and with it the dangers of standardization—have reached the same levels here as they have in the press.

The Reduction in the Variety of Opinion as a Threat
to the Free Press

In addition to economic concentration, which undeniably limits diversity, there is another development in the press that has led to a standardization of information and commentaries. This is the syndication of columnists, whose political commentaries are published simultaneously in a firmly established network of daily papers.

Because of their national distribution, these columnists become very famous. This is especially true for those who also participate in one of the many political television programs such as "Meet the Press" or "Face the Nation." Their prominence increases the public's faith in their competence, enhancing their influence on public opinion. They are part of an "astrocracy" that offers personal opinion in such an entertaining and spirited way that the average citizen is spared the task of personally forming an opinion.

If one regards freedom of the press as not only the freedom of newspaper owners to present reports and commentaries to the public unimpeded by government influence, if freedom of the press also means a freedom of access to information on the part of the readers, then this freedom is placed in jeopardy by the economic concentration and the dominance of political gurus in the United States today.

The Influence of Business Interests as a Threat to the Free Press

The economic control of the media is as dangerous to freedom of the press as the suppression of the news by the government. The economy, like the government, is interested in informing the public in a way that does not threaten its own power.

Eugene McCarthy illustrates this new manner of limiting the free press in his book *America Revisited.* He states:

> The right of freedom of speech and of the press exists only as the counterpart of the right of truth. Since truth cannot be defined in advance, the only practical approach is to allow free speaking and writing and the dissemination of what is spoken and written. With concentration of control over the press, there is growing concern, by the press and by the public, about whether the press is publicizing the facts it should publicize and whether it is presenting alternatives in matters where there is difference of opinion.[10]

The members of the establishment rebuke these demands for alternatives with a reference to the objectivity and neutrality of their reporting. McCarthy quotes one especially piquant statement by the former president of CBS:

> Our reporters do not cover stories from their point of view. They are presenting them from nobody's point of view.[11]

That is embarrassingly reminiscent of the famous story of Odysseus and Polyphem. The dumb masses are made to believe that "nobody" has an interest in what news is reported and how. In actuality, "nobody" is very much alive in the form of the economic powers that own the media. They do not influence the presentation of the news directly, but they establish a fairly clear pattern of what should and should not be reported.

As economic units, as parts of huge conglomerates, newspapers and the electronic media are part of "corporate America" and thus of the establishment. It is, therefore, inevitable that there is no room in the established media for alternatives to the existing economic system.[12]

Predemocratic governments introduced two tools for controlling information: monopolies and censorship. Both of these measures are used very subtly in today's control of the media through economic power. There is no monopoly in the sense of one single press organ. However, in addition to the actual concentration of the press and the loss of diversity, the cartel of the economic establishment that controls the distribution of information has essentially the same effect because it restricts alternative views of the existing economic system. Censorship, instead of being imposed from the outside, exists as a form of self-censorship.

Democratic Control for the Fourth Branch of the Government

This sort of threat to the free press could not be predicted at the time the republic was founded. At that time, business people were interested in factories, shipyards, construction, banks, and commerce. Communication, let alone entertainment, was not yet part of the economic system, as Tocqueville's description of the situation around 1830 indicates:

> The facility with which newspapers can be established produces a multitude of them; but as the competition prevents any considerable profit, persons of much capacity are rarely led to engage in these undertakings.[13]

Today, the media is big business, in which only those few can participate who either have inherited media organs or have a lot of capital and/or the ability to free up capital. If the media were a business like any other, this would be merely a question that concerns the economic system. However, because the press is crucial to the functioning of democracy and praises itself for its almost constitutional rank, one cannot ignore the question of how to reconcile the fact that in a democratic country, where each individual can vote and be represented, the instruments of information are limited to a select few.

This new threat to the freedom of opinion could be reconciled within the framework of the capitalist system. The first step is for those who control the information channels to allow other societal groups appropriate time and space to express opinions and give information. At first glance, it seems like an impudence that the owners of press organs should have to relinquish part of the control over what their organs produce. However, a press organ is not just any piece of property. We must get away from the notion that the tools for information can be the property of any one person or group. They should be free according to a new, expanded definition of freedom of the press. In order to protect this kind of freedom and develop it, economic control and the control over information must be kept separate. Such a reform is obviously impossible without a radical change in public awareness of what freedom in modern society means.[14]

Conformity to the Readers' Opinion as a Threat to the Free Press

This leads us to the third modern threat to the free press, that of the uninterested readers and viewers. This is a two-way process by which the supposed beneficiaries of the free press, the democratic citizens, are reduced to media consumers who select only those items that they find fitting and entertaining.

The press makes a silent pact with its readers that they will only receive information that corresponds with their world view. Not that the press manipulates the public; rather, it gives up—or at least greatly limits—its freedom to report the truth in exchange for the freedom to please, i.e., to accommodate through its reporting the needs and preconceived opinions of its readership. The problem with the truth is not so much that it can be unpleasant or painful but rather, that it is often simply uninteresting. Because the media is sustained by its public, this means that it must orient itself to its prejudices and entertainment requirements when it selects its themes.

The Desire for Entertainment Replaces the Need for Information

Information, let alone enlightenment, is not big business for profit. Other wishes and needs of the people have to be addressed if the newspapers and the news media are to be economically successful. The media stimulates the need for entertainment more and more intensely and cleverly until this need entirely replaces all other interests. In effect, it is the same mechanism that successfully seduces consumers into developing more needs that must be satisfied.

When the need for information is replaced by the desire for entertainment, the receivers, i.e., the public, abandon the free press. In the modern democracy, the media are free to report whatever they want, but the readers, listeners, and viewers are no longer free enough to demand something other than amusement. This has a direct effect on the press and media organs.

Even the news programs are bound to amuse. They, too, must attract as many viewers as possible to sell their advertisement slots for a lot of money. News selections correspond rather to the interests of the viewing audience than to the relative importance of the news. News programs are dramatically hyped to entertain as well as inform. A news story without camera footage is no news to television. That is the reason for so many meaningless reports about presidents and other prominent figures getting in and out of limousines, airplanes, and helicopters.

The news announcers themselves are a part of these dramatic happenings. They are more than mere reporters; they are an integral part of the complete film package. They have the weighty title "anchor"; as famous television personalities with star qualities, they are more important in attracting viewers than the news itself.

Messages from sponsors are even more important than the anchors, and they must be shown in dramatically paced rhythm. The news is not free—it is sponsored and paid for by Kellogg's Cornflakes, Toyota, Texaco, Preparation H, Purina, and other trifles and heavyweights of the consumer industry. Regardless of how famous the anchor or important the personality or meaningful the topic, when it is time for a commercial, they rudely interrupt the conversation. The viewers are used to it.

The word *message* for a commercial is a further indication of the importance of this part of the program. The advertisement is the new gospel (*evangelium*, the good message). Information about what products are available for purchase is the good news for people who grow up finding the meaning of life in consumption. Hence, the combination of advertisements with the news does not seem embarrassing or inappropriate for Americans. Advertisement is a central aspect of American life and therefore always fitting.

The blending of advertisements into news programs nevertheless has a devastating effect. It distorts the reality of the news and spreads a false optimism, as Paul Fussell points out in his book *BAD:*

> Despite the horrors that real life now and then obliges it to notice, television news is (like its print counterpart, USA Today) unfailingly optimistic, and its anchormen and women are never far from the convention of obligatory showbiz smiles. The optimism of the commercials is indistinguishable from the optimism of the "reporting," and as Mark Crisp Miller has perceived, "in order for TV's ads to seem 'a bonus—not an intrusion,' the rest of television first had to change in many subtle ways, imperceptibly taking on the quality of the commercials."[15]

The commercial spots are produced to resemble small stories, and the film reports about world events are dramatized in the same way. They cannot be distinguished in form and the difference in content is easily blurred when they switch back and forth without transition or when the television personality introduces them in the same tone. Just after the viewers see a small car lifted from the ground in one commercial, a small monster that cleans dirt from the stove in seconds, and a successful woman who has men at her feet after a single use of a certain shampoo, the viewer is presented with starving children, mass car accidents, and people protesting pollution of the environment. What is real and what is unreal? The difference is blurred, something new is created, a median between reality and irreality, in the truest sense something "medial."

Notes

1. Howard Kurtz, "The Press Boss as Reluctant Source," *Washington Post,* May 20, 1991.
2. Alexis de Tocqueville, *Democracy in America I,* p. 187.
3. Alexis de Tocqueville, *Journey to America,* p. 239.
4. An Ethics in Government law has existed since 1978 to which, indeed, several politicians fell victim during the eighties. Compare Paul Slansky, *The Clothes Have No Emperor,* p. 9.
5. Ibid., p. 23.
6. Tocqueville, *Democracy in America I,* p. 181.
7. Tocqueville compares the press with a law court: "[The eye of the press] is constantly open to detect the secret springs of political designs and to summon the leaders of all parties in turn to the bar of the public opinion." Ibid., p. 187.
8. Ibid., p. 183.
9. Ibid., p. 186.
10. Eugene McCarthy, *America Revisited,* pp. 146–47.
11. Ibid., p. 149.
12. This influences directly the program and the news that are selected for broadcast. Greider illustrates this with the example of the broadcasting company NBC and its owner, the electronics giant General Electric. William Greider, *Who Will Tell The People?* p. 329.
13. Tocqueville, *Democracy in America I,* pp. 186–87.
14. Greider agrees with the American consumer lawyer Ralph Nader, who has proposed an "audience network" in which citizens' groups, depending on their size, could be awarded an hour or so of air time to broadcast their own programming. William Greider, *Who Will Tell The People?* p. 329.
15. Paul Fussell, *BAD,* p. 189.

The Flirtation
with the End
of History

The publication of Francis Fukuyama's essay "The End of History?" in 1989 sparked the fascination of American intellectual and political commentators.[1] The idea of world history having reached its completion by the victory of democracy implied the Americanization of the world. In the popular mind, the "end of history" became "we won"—an American dream come true.

Disillusionment followed very soon. Long before the Gulf crisis, domestic problems, especially the budget deficit, made it clear to any sensible American that neither the world nor American society had reached perfection. The collapse of communism was acclaimed, and every fall of a domino in Eastern Europe was greeted with self-congratulation, but a true sense of triumph was missing.

The removal of communism as a monstrous contrast to democracy created a spirit of ambivalence and uneasiness and the need to justify the democratic alternative in its own right, to identify its roots, its values, its purposes from within.

The values upon which American society is based and for which it fought drew strength from the fight, from the struggle against evil. Values gain luster and appreciation under threat. Who appreciates life as a special value as long as life goes on as usual? But how valuable does it appear in sickness or danger—or liberty, one of the main ingredients of the American political culture? Who cares about it really as long as he or she enjoys it? But how valuable it is for anybody who lacks it or just feels it being threatened!

While America was occupied with global commitments, completely absorbed by the task of defending the Western world, engulfed in the mission to bring democracy to the rest of the world, it would put off looking into the mirror and

searching its democratic soul. Americans realize that the victory over communism is also a challenge to define and establish the values it has been fighting for—liberty, self-determination, equality, prosperity, happiness—by living up to them in reality, to present the American dream not just as a message—in its double meaning of a proclamation and an advertisement—but as a working program. The flirtation with "endism" does not bode well in the face of this challenge.

America = Number One

> *"The United States . . . is the most addicted to self-praise and complacency—even more than France."*
>
> *Paul Fussell,* BAD

Most Americans believe their country is the most advanced of all countries on this globe. This conviction is as firm as it is unreflective and undefined. America is just "number one" in the world; there is nothing better. For Europeans, neither the ingenious self-evidence nor the importance of this claim are comprehensible. Always playing the number-one role in the world without evidence appears pretentious and even with evidence is boastful.

But these are minor irritations. More important are the effects on American society itself. A nation convinced that it is thoroughly superior to all the others in its achievements has difficulty reflecting upon itself, examining its flaws, planning its future. The boast of superiority of America in *everything* was already an annoyance to Alexis de Tocqueville who observed it on his visit to the United States in 1830.

That does not mean, however, that the Americans are uncritical of their mistakes and blunders. The economic success of the Japanese, for example, has inspired a merciless self-examination and a public confession of flaws and failures. But they are mainly attributed to human negligence and laziness. The conviction that the American political system and its economic organization are superior to all other societies both in concept and practice is for most Americans basically unshattered.

There are, however, growing signs of hesitation and doubt. In political columns and in conversations with intelligent open-minded people, there are murmurs of fundamental criticism of the American system and praise for alternative models within the democratic spectrum. But it will be some time before the average American becomes doubtful of the certainty of American superiority.

On the positive side, always being number one inspires enormous energies and ambitions in response to threats. America responded to the Sputnik shock, which occurred during a similar period of extreme complacency, with a giant leap forward in the space program. Remember also the incredible increase in industrial production and military mobilization after the shock of Pearl Harbor. But the challenges, while massive, seem less urgent today. Moreover, the global victory of the American system supports an attitude of "business as usual."

The Unfinished Society

> *"The USA is the world headquarters of moral pretension. The American habit of regarding itself for almost half a century as the Leader of the Free World (and thus superb and a model in all respects for the less fortunate) has made it easy for Americans to ignore certain unpleasant facts."*
>
> *Paul Fussell,* BAD

A look beneath the surface shows that this complacency skates on thin ice. American society is clearly not—even under the American criterion of economic or material well-being—the world's most advanced nation. Indeed, its economy and productivity lag significantly behind some Western European countries. Internal tensions and severe social problems plague not only minorities but the middle class as well. It is a troubled and unfinished society, not a society on the verge of fulfillment at the end of its history.

Thomas Jefferson in the Declaration of Independence explicitly justified the existence of a government by its ability to guarantee its citizens the right to pursue their happiness. The political framework for the pursuit of happiness for the settlers of a thinly inhabited country of seemingly limitless bounty in the year 1776 was markedly different from today when 250 million people live in a very complex political organization and are entwined in a net of interrelations with society and dependent for success, even survival, on governmental action. The form and content of this task of government have changed, but the justification of the state as an instrument of the "pursuit of happiness" of its citizens remains.

Not only have the conditions of happiness within American society changed, but the standard of what constitutes happiness has escalated. This standard is independent of the American value system; it is set by the conscience of the advanced societies of the world.

Class Education

Some of the institutions of the American educational system are unsurpassed in the world. This is the case, for example, in medical studies and is generally true for the great universities, as well as many private high schools and even some public schools. But the failures of the American educational system are conspicuous: a public school system on the brink of collapse at least in the big cities, a very low educational standard at these schools, illiteracy, very low admission standards at many colleges, no systematic vocational education.

But the real scandal is not so much the generally low educational standards (excellent achievements in some private institutions notwithstanding), but the fact that one can have good education and training only if one is willing and able to pay a good price.

If one has to pay for a good education because it is not available in a public institution, it may cost at least $3,000 per year from nursery school age up to $20,000 per year and more through college. To send children to private school in the big cities is almost a necessity for parents who fear for the physical well-being and the educational advancement of their children. There are scholarships (from the schools and colleges) and student loans (from the government), but the financial obstacles are all but insurmountable for lower-class families and force middle-class families to limit themselves to one or two children and/or to bring home two salaries in order to pay for education. The consequences for the children and the problems for single mothers are obvious.

In contradiction to basic democratic principles, Americans accept that education costs money; good education costs a lot of money. This is not merely resigned acceptance, but springs from a naive or cynical belief that good education returns the money invested.

Today it is "evident" among civilized people that a decent education is an "unalienable" condition for the "pursuit of happiness," that is, developing one's potential. If a society denies this prerequisite to a large group of its young members—not by force, as is the case with authoritarian societies, but because it is dependent on the ability and willingness of parents to pay—then this society does not live up to the standard of our time. Higher education was at the beginning of the history of the United States a privileged luxury for the few, rather something aristocratic than part of the democratic value system.[2] Today a decent education is necessary in order to lead a decent life in this society. A society that makes good education a privilege of the well-to-do is on the retreat to aristocracy.

Health Is Priceless

America's health care system is one of the real scandals of the modern world. American medical technology and knowledge are undoubtedly number one in the world, but are fully available only for the wealthy, restricted for the middle class by heavy financial burdens, and shamefully unavailable to the poor. The problems of the American health care system originate in a radically wrong-headed conception of health as a private affair. American society has not come to terms with the fact that the fundamental right to life, proclaimed in the Declaration of Independence, has attained a new quality of meaning.

As long as health was more or less in the hands of God, government had nothing to do with it. With the development of modern medicine, health care became a public problem—the responsibility for health moved from God to the state. This created the question of health care as a fundamental right like liberty or a contingent good like wealth. Americans have so far avoided this question.

The Americans know the problems of their health care system. There are many proposals for reform, and it becomes from time to time the most urgent political priority.[3] The grand reforms of 1965 created public health care programs, especially for senior citizens and welfare recipients. But the system is still patchwork, and the proposed reforms will not lift its quality as long as the discussions circle solely around economic statistics and organizational structures and fail to address health as a fundamental human and civil right.

American Capitalism Has Stalled in Its Development

The role of the work force in a capitalist society with all the ensuing social consequences is another problematic field where Americans hold to positions that have been given up long ago by societies of the enlightened capitalist variety. Some rudimentary legal protection of employment exists, and some unions have gained limited job security for their members through special contracts, but basic rights of labor have seriously diminished in recent years. The conventional wisdom supposes that job and wage protection limits the ability of employers to compete in the national and world market.

It is doubtful that this conception of the relation between workers' protection and potential for economic modernization is valid. A look at Japan shows that excellent economic performance can be combined with high job security. But aside from that, there is the fundamental question of whether a free economy means, on the one side, the unrestricted freedom of the entrepreneur to fire his employees and, on the other side, the liberty of the worker to look for another job. It is the question of how highly a society values the role of work in its relation to capital.

Ironically, the way Americans look at the relation between work and capital is not altogether different from the raw analysis of capitalism by Karl Marx.[4] Marx said that the worker binds himself to the capitalist in exchange for wages; the only relation that exists between work and capital is formed by the absolutely neutral and objective medium of money. Money regulates the process whereby work is transformed into capital that then is split into wages and profit.

Modern capitalist societies have mostly rejected this primitive notion of capitalism. Workers are partners of the owners, with equal rights and equal responsibility for the success of an enterprise. This leads to consequences in the forms of codetermination, profit sharing, and job security. If a worker is part of an enterprise, another part cannot dispose of him or her as it likes. On the other hand, employers can demand from their employees more than just work; they can expect loyalty to the firm and commitment to quality production. Money as an absolutely neutral medium is not able to establish ties of any sort between the worker and the business.[5]

Collapse of the Infrastructure

> *"Five years ago [i.e., 1986] American highway bridges were inspected: over 40 percent were found 'deficient.' "*
>
> Paul Fussell, BAD

The infrastructure of a country, like its educational system, serves the democratic ideal of providing equal opportunities. Telephone, television, and automobiles have enormously enhanced the democratization of all societies, not only American society. Infrastructure is the framework that must be supplied by government in order to enable its citizens to pursue their happiness, that is, to realize their individual potential and to participate in what society offers to its members. In stable societies where everyone has a fixed lifelong social status, there is no need or obligation for the state to provide for an infrastructure because no one has a chance or even a right to move. In complex mass societies, however, where mobility not only drives the economic system but is also the path to individual development and fulfillment, the creation, enlargement, and cultivation of a functioning infrastructure ranks with the maintenance of public order as a duty of the state.

America's infrastructure is in many fields (the telephone system for example) highly developed and unsurpassed in the world. The public sector, however, especially the whole area of transportation, from bridges and roads to the railway system to public transportation in the cities, does not match the achievements common to developed countries.

Restoration Instead of Revolution

Political action in the United States often falls grievously short of political promise. It concentrates more often on symptoms than on causes. Analyses and pro-

posals are singularly focused on the economic aspect of social problems. The nation that has brought to the world the ideals of liberty, equality, self-determi-

nation, and the "pursuit of happiness" seems not to understand that its failures
are as much the result of the departure from democratic principles as they are
economic happenstance.

Haunted by an almost paranoid fear of socialism and the welfare state, Americans tend to deny the benefits of enlightened liberalism as it is practiced in much
of Western Europe, a liberalism encompassing social ideas and ideals to satisfy
human aspirations beyond the accumulation of wealth.

The Western European societies (and though out of a different tradition the
Japanese society) are examples of moderation, of compromise between capitalist
freedom and social constraints that could serve as models for a political reorientation in America. Nothing would be more disastrous than to assume that the
victory over communism validates for all time a static American system.

Some Americans offer a theory that the nation has already restructured its
liberal-capitalist democracy to accommodate the present, that it has already gone
through a revolutionary change of values by rejection of "big government," which
began with the Reagan "revolution" in the eighties. One should not underestimate
the spirit introduced into American society by President Ronald Reagan. He was
not a political featherweight; his politics or non-politics have had far-reaching
effects. His political philosophy, even if not intellectually respectable, was
rounded and consistent, deep-rooted in his personality and in American political
instincts. But the so-called Reagan revolution itself was a sentimental journey
back into good old times, a melodramatic incantation of antiquated clichés, a stale
remake of the twenties with a strong accent of militarism.

Reagan was no Caesar, who at the height of the Roman empire perceived its
structural problems and tried to tackle them. He was—if we may go on with this
comparison—a Sulla who threw himself into the wheel of time in order to restore a
political system that could not be sustained. At that time, too, they called it a
revolution; Sulla was celebrated as a savior when he marched into Rome and replaced the hated reforms of Marius with the old order. This man, too, was venerated
as a demigod after leaving politics; he was given a surname that would very well fit
Ronald Reagan and his presidency: Felix—the felicitous. But the restoration that he
forced upon the political system survived his exit from politics but a few years.

> *"The American people and their leaders and political institutions ap-*
> *peared to be sleepwalking through history."*
>
> Haynes Johnson, Sleepwalking through History:
> America in the Reagan Years

Restoration sometimes at first view cannot be distinguished from revolution.
The turbulences and upheavals in a society can also be very intense in a restoration. The decisive factor is not the magnitude of change within a society, but the
direction into which the society moves. The eight years of the Reagan restoration
and their somewhat diluted sequel under George Bush dramatically changed

American society in its structure and in its value orientation. But it was not an advance, nor the fulfillment of the end of its history. Domestic problems and global competition, almost ignored under Reagan's spell, have grown to dangerous dimensions. A real revolution—in spirit and insight—is called for and awaits the national will.

The Yearning for the Happy Ending

Americans appreciate simple solutions. This is undoubtedly in some respect quite advantageous and has helped them to overtake their hesitant, deliberating competitors. But the problems of modern, complex societies defy simple solutions. The yearning for the happy ending, the enthusiasm for the quick fix, which manifests itself in martially tinted campaigns like "war on poverty" and "war on drugs," endangers the political spirit of the society.

In Europe there is a growing tendency to discard any concern about America. The argument goes that the United States has fulfilled its role in world history with the end of the cold war and that it is of no interest if Americans remain mired in their problems. On the other side, many in the United States question the relevancy of European experience to the solution of American problems. This kind of isolationism on either side is both dangerous and foolhardy. The political future of America is as important to Western Europe and now Eastern Europe, too, as it was fifty years ago, and because Americans first advanced and developed the democratic ideas and forms now beginning to dominate the world, it is sensible to assume they will carry them into the future. If the United States abdicates its role or its responsibilities in the free world and betrays its own history, the consequences would be grave.

Liberal democracy is challenged to redefine democratic values in the face of new and unresolved problems such as the end of economic expansion, the dwindling of resources paralleled by ever increasing waste, and the moral challenge posed by the abject poverty of the Third World. If the militarily, politically, and ideologically strongest democratic power bails out of the competition of ideas to reinvent democracy, it would have disastrous consequences for the world and for America itself.

Once before an Escape from History

Americans must remember the results of their first "escape from history" after the military victory of 1918. The nation then isolated itself from world affairs and concentrated on making money. This led to the great Crash of 1929 and the subsequent Great Depression, from which America only recovered during World War II.

Efforts to ignore the ongoing ideological competition of democracy in the world has a parallel to the economic challenge. As long as the Americans dominated the capitalist world almost alone or were at least far ahead because of their long experience, they were uncontested at the top. But when these ideas and practices were adopted by other nations, it was no longer sufficient to rest on authorship. Japan and Germany have successfully challenged the United States in its special field—the organization of a capitalist economy. The same may apply to the advance of democratic government. Now that these ideas have found global acceptance, the rate and mass of development will not necessarily be controlled by historical precedent. Other nations are ambitious and eager to push ahead; America can only be a partner in this competition or fall behind.

Nothing can be gained by ideological isolationism. Only by staying in touch with and looking for the competition with other democratic, liberal, market-oriented systems will Americans get the stimulation and inspiration to rejuvenate and invigorate the system. The paradox of the nineties is that America must look into itself without regarding itself as the navel of the world.

Notes

1. Francis Fukuyama, "The End of History?" *The National Interest,* Summer 1989.

2. "Primary instruction is within the reach of everybody; superior instruction is scarcely to be obtained by any." Alexis de Tocqueville, *Democracy in America I*, p. 52.

3. Medicare and Medicaid have existed since the extensive reform legislation under President Lyndon Johnson in the mid-sixties. Under the Medicare program, most medical costs for those 65 or older—regardless of their income—is paid for. Medicaid is a subsidized medical program for needy people.

The Medicare program developed into a financial nightmare. Medicaid is continuously reduced and locks out many people, especially from the lower middle class.

Twenty-eight percent of all Americans do not have sufficient health insurance.

4. Obviously, things have not changed much since the times of Tocqueville: "The manufacturer asks nothing of the workman but his labor; the workman expects nothing from him but his wages. The one contracts no obligation to protect nor the other to defend, and they are not permanently connected either by habit or by duty." Tocqueville, *Democracy in America II,* p. 160.

5. "The at will rule—that workers have no rights except those they are able to extract by individual negotiation and agreement—is out of step with the systems of job protection adopted by other industrialized nations, and with international norms." Joseph Gordon quoted by Robert N. Bellah et al., *The Good Society,* p. 327, note 25.

Social Decline,

Poverty, and

Crime

Health insurance, education, and job security are primarily concerns of the middle class, even though they are held out as promises to the hopelessly impoverished. But for the American underclass, these merely secondary social gains are obscured by the day-to-day woes of hunger, homelessness, and crime.

All of these problems have the same root, the pursuit of individualism to the neglect of social responsibility. From an emotional standpoint, there can be no doubt that social acceptance of hunger and homelessness is a greater threat to a civilized nation than deprivation of more peripheral social benefits less vital for human survival. But in political terms the erosion of security within society for the middle class is most dangerous, for it is the middle class that is the strongest, indeed the sole base of any democratic society. This is particularly true for American society.[1]

Although poverty and crime in the United States have reached proportions inconsistent with the country's self-image of the "good society," they are not a threat of revolution. Society supplies the minimum support necessary to keep the underclass from resorting to radical action. Homeless shelters and public kitchens provide the bare necessities for subsistence.

Erosion of Social Gains

In some respects, American society reflects the image of prerevolutionary France with its screaming contrasts of obscene luxury and pitiful poverty, but the American underclass believes it has nothing to lose, nor anything to gain, from a change in political circumstances. And then there always remains the American dream, now reduced to the size of consumer goods; this dream is made affordable by petty crime, looting, or credit cards.

211

The American middle class, on the other hand, feels that its social gains are slowly but steadily deteriorating. The purchasing power of the American worker has steadily declined over the past twenty years.[2] It was the great American middle-class dream that children would be better off than their parents. In the years after World War II it seemed to fulfill itself for a short, happy span, something that contributed to American society's optimism at the time.

For people who grew up with this vision of a better future for themselves and their children and who built their lives upon this dream, the vision is dimming. The optimism, sure of its future, has given way to a somber, insecure, and plaintive mood. Of course the ruling powers in economy and politics spare no efforts to rebuild the American faith in the future. But even Madison Avenue and Ronald Reagan are ultimately helpless in view of the irrefutable facts. Even President George Bush's military triumph was only a passing surge of adrenaline for American self-confidence. America has not only lost its economic world dominance, but every day when he or she opens a newspaper, the American middle-class person discovers that more productive and more efficient economies are in the process of surpassing American industry on its home turf.

Added to this is a feeling that can no longer be suppressed: that the United States lives beyond its means. The debt the country accumulated, especially in the eighties, and is continuing to accumulate has taken on astronomic proportions. New burdens, stemming mostly from the mismanagement of the Reagan government, are constantly added, e.g., the cost following the savings-and-loan debacle. Even the most insensitive people have understood by now that the old dream has been reversed, that there won't be an inheritance left to the children from which to start and to reach new heights; rather, there will be an eternal mortgage that they will probably have to hand on to their children even if they themselves are extremely disciplined.

A similar feeling envelops the area of environmental damage, a phenomenon until now largely ignored in the United States. People know that they live at the expense of future generations, that they are using up their offspring's resources while burdening them with their own garbage. Even if the sensation is not strong enough to compel people to act responsibly, a feeling of wrongdoing and guilt reinforces the sense of general malaise.

The Dream of a House of One's Own Is Threatened

While this phenomenon of social decline ultimately remains in the general realm and hardly causes immediate concern, the erosion of concrete social achievements for the middle class can be felt directly. The dream of one's own house is the American dream per se.[3] It had indeed become reality for the middle class in the golden fifties. While in those days it could be achieved by a family with one breadwinner, by now this dream has evaporated for more and more families altogether. Today it seems the rule that a family has two or sometimes three incomes, with moonlighting for many not merely an option to augment their household budget but a strict necessity. Constantly rising property taxes, for many communities the only tax source, are the cause of alarm for retired persons and people on fixed incomes who fear losing their property and their homes.

Even more threatening are the constantly rising health costs that have forced many people to mortgage or sell their homes.[4] A complicated operation with an extended hospital stay can cost $50,000 or more—and who would have that kind of money stashed away? Of course there are health insurances, but they are all more or less private, and they try by all means to separate themselves from "bad risks." The fact that most middle-class Americans are insured by their employers is especially ominous. If the company goes bankrupt, the insurance ceases as well. The "bad risk" with a past cancer operation can obtain insurance only at obscenely high costs, if at all. Thus, a serious illness or an accident can destroy a well-ordered middle-class existence in one fell swoop. Some have experienced it; for many it is a looming fear.

Social Decline through Loss of Employment

Unemployment can mean a similar calamity, not only bringing in its wake short-term costs and restrictions but also definitively leading to social decline. Americans are subjected to these risks to a much larger degree than employees in other countries; part of the reason for this is that the violent swings of economic development are transmitted directly and without any protective social net to personnel strategies; the other is that unemployment payments are relatively meager and made only for a short period. Because a recession can grip not just one company, but a whole branch of industry, a whole region, sometimes the nation as a whole, chances to secure an adequate new job—especially in the same city—often are dim.

There have admittedly always been recessions and unemployment in the United States—many of them more massive than what we are familiar with in Europe—but two things have changed: First, there is a solid middle class that is threatened with the loss of something essential in these catastrophes, their social gains; second, this class, like all Americans, is deep in debt because it succumbed to the temptations of commercial ads and has been living on credit, and because they were barely able to make ends meet when fully employed, they cannot absorb even a small reduction in income. They are not especially irresponsible wastrels but, rather, completely normal average Americans who do nothing else but what they are being daily advised to do: to mortgage their future.[5]

Expenses for the care and education of children equally deplete the reserves of middle-class families because they have been exceeding salary increases for years.[6] During the eighties, tuition at the large private universities regularly rose by about 10 percent annually. Raising children is a luxury in modern societies that significantly lowers living standards in purely monetary terms. Federal subsidies and tax breaks provide inadequate relief for families with children. The middle class has resigned itself to this fact as the price for intangible values by which their own lives are enriched through their children. But the tolerance level is reached sooner or later. Parents are also enlightened enough not to simply resign themselves to the fact that they cannot offer their children a good education. Their fury and outrage is turning against those social forces that are making raising children and education so expensive that it becomes unaffordable.

At the Door of a New Depression?

> *"[T]here is no one looking after the interests of the middle class. They are forgotten Americans."*
>
> Donald L. Barlett and James B. Steele,
> America: What Went Wrong?

It is always possible that America is headed toward another great depression. This time, however, it won't come as a great "crash" but rather in a creeping, suffocating, grinding manner: via, precisely, rising costs for health, education, and housing. The root causes are the same as in the twenties, namely, a lack of moderation, greed, accumulating money by criminal means, and irresponsible politics by the leading forces of society; the difference lies in the fact that the middle class this time is educated, alert, and ready to fight. It will not accept the decline of its dreams and wishes as a calamity handed out by fate. I believe that the American middle class is simply too strong to be wiped out again. The premise is, however, that the middle class finally manages to dissociate itself from an identification with the upper class.

A terrible legacy of the American dream is the inextinguishable idea held by every successful businessperson and every employee who is climbing the career ladder that he or she is different from the super-rich and the members of the power elite only by degrees, that he or she is actually part of the upper class that has made true the American dream of success, power, and wealth.

The Middle Class Threatened by the Greed of the Wealthy

It is not only the secret identification with the upper class that erodes and weakens the political position of the middle class; equally significant is the hostility toward the poor whom they feel to be a threat to their own social achievements. This fear and defensiveness receives enthusiastic support from an interested propaganda machinery that spreads horror tales about millions and billions of tax dollars poured into the pockets of slackers. What is simply being ignored because it is covert, complicated, and simply incomprehensible in its true dimensions are the huge hidden subsidies in the form of tax freedom (!) from certain interest payments, write-offs for imaginary losses, and government subsidies for all links of investments; added to this is an unusually low tax rate combined with a whole array of bonuses, tax abatements, privileges, and tax loopholes that enable the wealthy to shirk their obligation of adequately participating in the financing of society.[7]

A change in public awareness could possibly be occurring in this area. American economic policies (or rather ideologies) of the past decade and their consequences for the economic and social structure of the nation have been scrutinized and those responsible have been held accountable in books, newspaper series, and television documentaries. This is reminiscent of the great era of the muckrakers who uncovered the sometimes criminal tactics robber barons employed in constructing their economic empires; in doing so, muckrakers contributed to a change in the political climate and to the passing of comprehensive reform legislation.

I have mentioned the book by Barlett and Steele, *America: What Went Wrong?*, which outlines in detail the scandalous political mistakes and their horrendous consequences for American society. It became a best-seller right after its publication and remained on the list for several months, an indication that Americans are obviously intensely interested in the question asked by the book's title.

The topic in this and other books is foremost an outline of the tactics practiced by financial jugglers and the role of politicians as conscious or naive helpers in the wild buying and raiding sprees of American industrial complexes; these raids have resulted in the destruction of hundreds of thousands of jobs, which are the economic foundation of the middle class.

The results of this research can be summarized briefly: In a gigantic process of redistribution, the rich became considerably richer during this decade, the poor even poorer, and the middle class began on a steady decline. It remains to be seen if the efforts of the publicists will awaken the population and have an impact on politics similar to what happened at the beginning of the century. Whatever happens, the following needs to be remembered: The middle class will have to realize that it is not threatened by the poor but that both classes are in danger of being extinguished by the insatiable greed of the rich; only when the middle class has learned to feel solidarity with the fate of the underdogs, instead of feeling fearful and defensive, will it have a chance to translate its numerical majority into political weight.

Poverty Threatens the System of Democracy

The existence of poverty and crime—not as an ineradicable residue that is extant in all societies that are not paradise, but as a visible and typical part of American society—is a threat to democracy in America. It does not represent a latent potential for revolution—preconditions for revolutions in the usual sense are nonexistent in America—the danger for democracy lies in its ability to corrupt, to hollow-out, and to destroy the democratic foundations of society.

The existence of poverty threatens the system of democracy because this is where it differs from aristocratic societies and monarchies with their static image of society. In those systems, poverty, like wealth, is part of the situation ordained by God or nature; man has to accept this fate and will not try to change it for the sake of security and peace.[8] There has always been poverty, and there always will be; of course, monarchs and aristocrats are obliged to do their best to diminish it and make it bearable—but not to erase it. That is the great credo of the democratic societies which is invoked regularly in the United States with solemn rhetoric whenever another "war on poverty" is rung in with great pathos.

"You can't get rid of poverty by giving people money."
P. J. O'Rourke, Parliament of Whores

Poverty is a scandal only for that political system that does not resign itself to the status quo, which strives for changes in line with its ideals. Democrats instinctively feel the threat to the system, because the sheer existence of poverty negates the democratic ideal that all should share in the achievements of society. But they overlook that this also works the other way: that it is only the political system with its validation of wealth that makes poverty a social problem and by that creates a responsibility to end it. Poverty is a foreign body within the democratic system but not, as the term *foreign body* could suggest, something introduced from outside but, rather, a self-produced defect within the system.[9]

Extraordinary Wealth as Similarly Threatening

The same is incidentally true for the other extreme, immeasurable wealth in the hands of a few. Society has not yet been sensitized to this corruption of democracy from the other side of the spectrum as it has to poverty whose reprehensible character is evident within the framework of democratic ideas. One of modern democracy's weak points can be seen in the fact that its basic principles were developed simultaneously with the ideas of bourgeois capitalism, which was just entering its practical phase at the same time around the beginning of the nineteenth century. Democratic and capitalist ideals of the early nineteenth-century era of industrial expansion formed an alliance that can still be felt today. Both are based upon the ideal of freedom, of individual self-realization, of the preeminence of the private over the public sphere. Based on the common roots and the long ties, a sort of identification between democracy and capitalism has evolved that has blurred over the naturally existing differences; these differences are to be found above all in the assessment of equality (vis-à-vis freedom), of justice (vis-à-vis self-realization), of solidarity with the community (vis-à-vis individualism). When the idea of modern democracy was born, no one could foresee the possibilities for accumulating enormous wealth that arrived in the wake of industrialization. An overly unbalanced distribution of wealth in a society cannot be reconciled with the democratic principle because it signals an unsound overemphasis of freedom against equality.

The Majority of Victims of Crime Are the Poor

> *"It says a lot about the nature of American poverty that I went to see it with a group of young men trained in the martial arts and operating under military-style discipline instead of with a social worker."*
> *P. J. O'Rourke,* Parliament of Whores

Besides the social decline of the middle class and the growing poverty of the underclass, the increase in crime is a further sign of societal decay threatening democracy in America. Here, as in other areas, it is difficult to put a precise and concrete face on the danger that imperils the survival of a democratic society. There is no fear that public order might collapse because of crime taking over. That is because the largest part of capital crimes such as homicide, manslaughter, rape, and most robberies are played out within the tight circle of the underclass; they are perpetrated against members of their own group.

If, however, the word *crime* is taken in a broader sense, then it is something that indeed concerns all of American society: a criminal morality which does not admit to being such, is rampant, because it feels legitimized by the value system built on money. And yet white-collar crime (economic crime) is only the most telling manifestation of a general lack of responsibility toward basic moral concerns; this expresses itself in reckless environmental pollution, in subtle exploitation of employees, in fraudulent duping of consumers, in ruthless elimination of competitors, in price-fixing, in distorting commercial advertisements, and swindling packaging methods—all of this in the name of sacred success, which justifies all means.

Crime as Imitation of the Capitalist World in the Ghetto

If we remain, however, within the narrow interpretation of the term *crime*, we will find that its effects are essentially limited to the class of the poor. Apart from single cases and a general sense of irritation, the rest of American society is not (yet!) affected by it.

But the bourgeois world does play a certain part in this. For the crimes are not a desperate revolt against the injustices of the world, they are on the contrary an imitation of the capitalist world played out in the ghetto.[10] It is capitalist immorality taken to its extreme that determines events in the ghetto. Here, like there, the goal is the acquisition of consumer goods as status symbols, one of which—remarkably enough—is sneakers.

On the next level, it is a matter of real status, a matter of power, of women, and "real" luxuries (e.g., expensive restaurants, special series Mercedes, trips to the Caribbean). Thus, the goals are the same, the methods assuredly more brutal, the consideration for human life the only essential difference, but no one can say for sure whether this consideration on the part of the bourgeois is motivated by humanitarian concerns or merely by fear of the law.

The criminal milieu in the poverty-ridden sections of America is defined by the drug trade. Most other crimes contained in the criminal statistics are derived from the drug trade. It is the way underprivileged urban youths, who are also suffering from racial discrimination, respond to capitalism. Instead of swimming along in the mainstream of capitalism without hope of ever reaching the surface, these youths have constructed their own form of capitalism. In his autobiographical report, "Dispatches from a Dying Generation," Nathan McCall quotes a black lawyer:

> The drug trade is one of the few places where young, uneducated blacks can say, "I am the boss. This is my corporation." [11]

McCall continues with a report of his own experiences:

> Contrary to some assumptions, there is no lack of work ethic in drug trade. My best friend in school parlayed $20 into a successful drug operation. By the time we were both 18, he had employed a few people, bought a gold tooth and paid cash for a Buick Elektra 225 (a deuce-and-a-quarter in street parlance). College students couldn't do that.[12]

This is reminiscent—down to the smallest detail and stylistic expressions—of the typical capitalist success stories that Americans love to hear. The only disadvantage is that the business this fellow from the ghetto is involved in—the only one he can pursue—is not tolerated by society; the young stock market genius on the other hand, who sells his client worthless shares and makes millions, becomes the icon of American success.

Of course the drug trade could never assume its role as the core of all criminal activities if there were no demand for this merchandise. But the system plays a part here, too, at least in providing an immediate cause. For the drug opens up an exit from a life without hope within this society—even if it only takes the form of a brief oblivion. At the same time, it is also a response to the continual message to brighten up life by consuming something.

Society's Reaction to Poverty and Crime: Indifference and Suppression

American society, however, rejects the notion of culpability, as is evident from its response to the phenomena of poverty and crime. After a sincere and honest attempt in the sixties (sporadically continued but left without real commitment in the seventies), America has today decided no longer to accept these phenomena as social problems but to either disregard them, as in the case of the increasing poverty rate, or to suppress them with more and more repressive means as in the case of crime.

"Those stories about crack wars and the 'murder capital of America' are nonsense, of course—as long as you stay in the part of Washington that concerns itself with real wars and being the regular capital. This is the part that extends northwest along Connecticut, Massachusetts and Wisconsin avenues from the tourist attractions on the Mall to the Maryland suburbs—the 'white pipeline.' People do occasionally venture outside this zone, people who come in to do your cleaning or mow the lawn."

P. J. O'Rourke, Parliament of Whores

It is obvious that these problems cannot be solved either by averting one's eyes or by suppressing them. But America is by now so well conditioned to illusions that it can easily live with them, especially because that part of society that does not want to be informed is in no way affected. When my family and I decided to move to Washington for a year, word had by then gotten to Germany that this was the "murder capital" of the United States, and our relatives and friends were very worried. But I knew that all I had to do was to rent an apartment in one of the good residential parts of town, at a distance of perhaps two or three miles—but in social terms removed by worlds—from the center of the daily shootings, and I would be as safe as in the lap of Abraham. The key to all this is, as always, money.

Society Is Walling Itself In

But there is no absolute safety in securing oneself, in walling oneself in against the violent and threatening rest of society; an unpredictable coincidence, a small carelessness can lead to the crossing of the borders and to contact with this other world, which can have fatal consequences for the inhabitant of the bunker "middle America."

In the novel *The Bonfire of the Vanities,* which is a brilliant sociogram of today's United States, the hero undergoes precisely this traumatic experience: He misses just one exit on the city freeway and by doing so drifts out of the unassailable security of the fortress Manhattan and into the battle zone of the Bronx. This is a luminously conceived key scene for understanding the American society because it proves that outward tranquility is not a peaceful side-by-side existence but, rather, a truce filled with hate. It further shows that the reason why there is no civil war is merely because both sides—for different reasons—are careful not to invade each other's reservation, and it is a sign that the internal security enjoyed by bourgeois America is only the security within a fortress—a very comfortably furnished fortress to be sure—all of this creating a tense, stressful, and peaceless situation which in turn generates an aggressive bunker mentality.

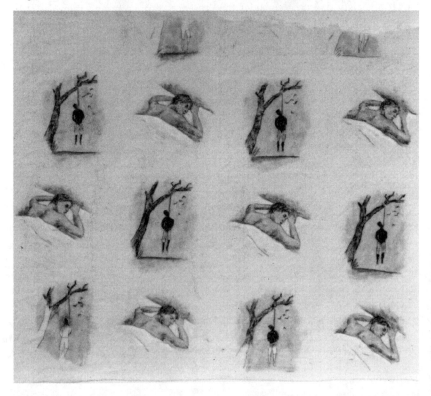

The extent of poverty and crime in the United States is not in harmony with its self-image as an economically developed and civilized nation. I could cite pages and pages of reports, numbers, and statistics to draw up a picture of these shadowy sides of America in greater detail and in its full proportions. I can spare myself this effort for two reasons: For one, everybody who has at least some interest in what is going on in American society has by now become familiar with this social emergency in all its gory details through endless reports in the media, especially in television, but also in books, magazines, newspaper reports and movies. Thus, I refer those who would like a concrete and detailed look at the face of poverty and crime in America to these numerous publications.

The second and decisive reason why I forgo an endless enumeration of facts and data lies in my conviction that quantifying and sensationalizing the problems ultimately do not contribute anything to their understanding or solution. It is a typical American fashion to bring a social phenomenon to the attention of the public by describing a plethora of shocking details. This more journalistic method often has exactly the opposite effect in a society satiated with information; this is because people have developed subtle techniques in rejecting information or in consuming it with lascivious interest but indifference.

If a society does not consider the presence of poverty and crime as its own problem, it won't feel any more affected by a barrage of hair-raising examples. The actual scandal lies in the existence and not the extent of poverty and crime in a rich and democratically civilized nation, and it lies in the refusal of society to recognize the causes of these social ills in its own structure. The real and actual danger for American society does not rest in the revolutionary potential, which could collect in a sediment of poverty and crime, but it rests in the moral corruption that accepts these ills as natural.

Notes

1. "From Aristotle on, republican theorists have stressed the importance of the middle classes for the success of free institutions. . . . The middle classes have been peculiarly central in American society." Robert N. Bellah et al., *Habits of the Heart,* p. viii.
Compare also with Barlett and Steele: "The middle class—one of the underpinnings of democracy in this country," Donald L. Barlett and James B. Steele, *America: What Went Wrong?* p. 2.
This middle class has serious problems due to the developments in the past years. This is the topic of Barlett and Steele's book. Similar observations and conclusions can be found in the books of William Greider and Kevin Phillips.

2. This erosion in purchasing power is not only due to steady inflation, but also to enormous structural changes in the job market. Workers are forced to move from jobs that once paid $15 an hour into jobs that pay $7 due to rationalization or closing of factories. Barlett and Steele, *America: What Went Wrong?* pp. 2, 11.

3. Ibid., p. 3.

4. Barlett and Steele, chapter 7—"Playing Russian Roulette with Health Insurance," *America: What Went Wrong?* p. 124. This chapter is about losing health benefits in bankruptcy, see especially p. 130.

5. There is at the moment a change of attitude due to the shock caused by the recession. American consumers are using remaining money to pay off their debts. According to experts, this is one of the main reasons why America still is in a recession although the

government and the Federal Reserve of the United States made many efforts to strengthen the economy. Compare with Sylvia Nessar, "Why the U.S. Economy Can't Get Going: Excesses of the 1980's Leave a Tough-to-Cure Hangover," *International Herald Tribune,* July 4–5, 1992.

6. Barlett and Steele, *America: What Went Wrong?* p. 3.

7. Compare with Barlett and Steele, Greider, and Phillips. It would fill many pages just to list the most important details. Many tax privileges have been mentioned already in other contexts. The highest tax rate is 31 percent. However, it has to be mentioned that in most states an additional income tax has to be paid. The lowest tax rate is about 15 percent. That makes a difference of 16 percent between the average taxpayer and a billionaire. In reality, the difference is entirely 3 percent. The progressive tax, a milestone in history of social reforms, has been practically eliminated in the United States. Unbelievable as it is, interest on bonds issued by local and state governments is completely exempt from taxation, no matter how high the income from this interest is. This is one of the reasons why many extremely rich people do not pay any taxes in a perfectly legal way. For example, 800,000 people picked up $20.1 billion from their exempt-bond holdings, thereby escaping payment of $5.6 billion in federal income taxes. This lost revenue was made up by 26.5 million people who paid about $7.1 billion in federal income taxes on savings account interest. Compare with Barlett and Steele, *America: What Went Wrong?* p. 9.

8. "Among a nation where aristocracy predominates in society and keeps it stationary, the people in the end get as much accustomed to poverty as the rich to their opulence. The latter bestow no anxiety on their physical comforts because they enjoy them without an effort; the former do not think of things which they despair of obtaining and which they hardly know enough of to desire." Tocqueville, *Democracy in America II,* p. 129.

9. "In prosperous democracies, the problem of poverty has been transformed from one of natural need, into one of recognition. The real injury that is done to poor or homeless people is less to their physical well-being than to their dignity. Because they have no wealth or property, they are not taken seriously by the rest of society." Francis Fukuyama, *The End of History and the Last Man,* p. 292.

10. Wolf von Lojewski also shows parallels between the ethics of the ghetto and the general morals of American society: "Brutality can be necessary in the neighborhood where drugs are dealt as it can be of importance for the businessmen in the legal part of the economy to prove their toughness and forcefulness." Wolf von Lojewski, *Amerika,* p. 171 (German edition).

11. Nathan McCall, "Dispatches from a Dying Generation," *Washington Post,* January 13, 1991, p. C4.

12. Ibid.

Reality

and

Fiction

Two hundred years ago, when Immanuel Kant expounded on his revolutionary concept of human understanding of the world, it seemed as though a steadfast path had been found to differentiate between reality and fiction.[1] In his system, Kant had clearly separated the realm of reality from the world of our imagination and conceptualized both areas. Reality, the "thing as such," exists outside of our world of ideas. The reality with which we operate is that of our imagination and comprehension in which the actual reality is inevitably formed through the means of categories of understanding that we have created for this purpose. How a "thing" actually looks we do not know and cannot experience because we approach all "reality" with our categories of understanding. But it is not ultimately important for us to recognize the "thing as such" because, according to Kant's comforting message, our thought categories are innate and are the same for all humans. Thus, although reality itself does not appear in our minds, the same image of it appears in the minds of all people. Human relations in the world do not require absolute reality. It is sufficient that all humans have the same deduced, secondary experiences of reality on the basis of the homogeneity of our categories of understanding.

Instead of having solved the problem of reality and fiction as Kant believed, he opened a Pandora's box: Mankind was not satisfied with the fact that, through Kant's philosophy, a reliable basis had been laid for comprehending the world and for the human exchange of ideas. People began investigating and questioning every detail about the detachment of human imagination from reality, the concept of which had been established by Kant. If it is really true that imagination and not reality defines our world, then, so the logic goes, one should try to discover how far one can distance oneself from reality and build up a world of one's own in its place. Pushed to its extreme, it should be possible to live completely in a self-created world if the system is sufficiently secure against influences from the outside. In the increasing dynamic of today's world, we are getting closer to this extreme situation of life in an artificially created world.

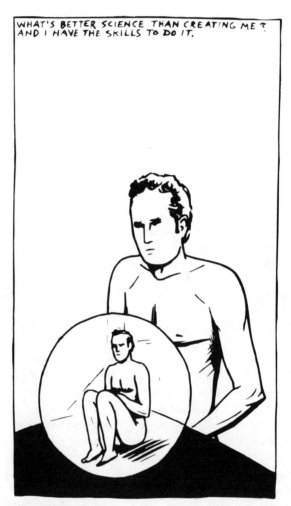

Experience the World in Coexistence—
Disappearance of Causality

As we know now, Kant's basic assumptions of human experience and knowledge are no longer valid in yet another aspect. For Kant, the categories by which humans organize their understanding of the world were innate—they were already present in the structure of human thought before any experience from the outside. We have since learned that these categories, as all other human characteristics, are the result of a slow and complicated learning process and hereditary system from one generation to another in the evolution of mankind. As such, it is not out of the question that humans can also lose these categories in the way that they have developed them, or that they can be suppressed or superimposed by other structures of thinking. This process does not necessarily have to take thousands of years, as did the learning process that has allowed our categories of thought to come into being. Taking into account the immense acceleration of human development that characterizes our epoch, such a reversal could possibly come to pass within several decades.

A harbinger of this process could be the category of causality, which is in danger of separating itself from our thought structures or, at the very least, of losing its significance for world experience and being supplanted by new habits of perception. Our thought system is organized in such a fashion as to allow us to fabricate our causal relationships automatically when events that occur simultaneously or consecutively obviously are not independent from one another.

The habits of perception now are not conducive to this thought system of causality. They are formed as a "survival strategy" in response to the flood of information that can no longer be put in order but that one simply has to take in as simultaneous events or events that follow one after another. In television, which plays an important role in shaping our world view, we have already developed a formal technique for this: channel surfing, zapping, click-click, a new picture, consumed, on to the next one. Our view of events is in the process of transforming from a rational coherence to a sensuous aggregate.

If events are only perceived as aggregate states of occurrences, as television programs on different channels, then reality loses its interdependence and causality. Neil Postman, in the footsteps of Daniel Boorstin examining the connection between media culture and social culture, shows to what degree this "aggregate" way of thinking has already become self-understood in the United States:

> Contradiction, in short, requires that statements and events be perceived as interrelated aspects of a continuous and coherent context. Disappear the context, or fragment it, and contradiction disappears. This point is nowhere made more clear to me than in conferences with my younger students about their writing. "Look here," I say. "In this paragraph you have said one thing. And in that you have said the opposite. Which is to be?" They are polite, and wish to please, but they are as baffled by the question as I am by the response. "I know," they will say, "but that is there and this is here." The difference between us is that I assume "there" and "here," "now" and "then," one paragraph and the next to be connected, to be continuous, to be part of the same coherent world of thought. That is the way of typographic discourse, and typography is the universe I'm "coming from," as they say. But they are coming from a different universe of discourse altogether: the "Now . . . this" world of television. The fundamental assumption of that world is not coherence but discontinuity. And in a world of discontinuities, contradiction is useless as a test of truth or merit, because contradiction does not exist.[2]

Unlike Postman, I believe that we are not in the position to make a value judgment about one worldview or another. Cultural critics often tend to view new developments as symptoms of decline, especially if they can be traced back to such controversial media as television. We should be aware that the time might have come for a different, perhaps a noncausal, worldview and that the media are just the forerunner of this perception paving the way to general acceptance.

American television promotes a worldview of concurrence. Americans have distanced themselves the furthest from the causal worldview. They think and act in a state of coexistence, one after another and beside one another but not interdependent. If one persistently separates oneself from causality, no interdependence remains and the world becomes incredibly simple. Everything has its place; there seems to be no need for choices—one grabs what is suitable and then goes on to something else; you pay attention to one thing and then another.

The worldview of "disconnectedness," which has a striking resemblance to what is now called postmodernism, is deeply rooted in the general thought structure and behavior of the American people.3 This mentality has found its philosophical explanation and foundation in the writings of John Dewey and other philosophers of the so-called American pragmatism. Today's leading representative of this pragmatism, Richard Rorty, has taken up John Dewey's position and further developed his ideas. He characterizes this philosophical way of thinking in the following manner:

> Those who base logic on "truth" are the people who see inquiry as piling up correspondences with the way things are. . . . Pragmatists like Dewey, by con-

trast, do not think that there is a Way the World is. . . . Dewey junked the appearance–reality and subjective-objective distinctions and just talked about more or less successful beliefs, more or less successful rules for guiding action to fulfill one or another want.[4]

A New Definition of Reality and Fiction

It is indisputable that the old concepts of appearance and actuality, fiction and reality, are no longer valid. They are unsuitable for orientation in today's world. To designate appearance as unreal is ridiculous if one takes into consideration what an incredibly influential effect the appearance of things and people have on the real life of people through publicity—it is all in the image. In advertising, the old opposition between appearance and actuality no longer exists. The semblance becomes reality, appearance *is* the reality if one considers reality to be something that gets things realized.

Who could seriously claim that Mickey Mouse is not real? Mickey Mouse is

a part of our reality—he is infinitely more effectual in the world than many humans of flesh and blood. We are replaceable, insignificant, but Mickey Mouse is irreplaceable, ubiquitous and real (in the sense of producing reality) by piling up billions of dollars.

The most famous and most expensive publicity campaigns are those in which the product—reality in the old sense—completely disappears as a result of the newly produced reality of semblance: cigarette ads, perfume ads, alcohol ads. This "unreal" image, not the "real" product, is the motor that keeps the economy going. The image makes the offered goods desirable and creates the impulse to buy. In the fleeting and fictitious appearance, not in the material that can be touched, the consumer finds the satisfaction, the status, and the security that he or she wishes to acquire by buying the product. The advertising experts are the actual stylists of our society. They are continuously shaping and rearranging the artificial world that has been created in place of plain old reality. It is for this reason that people in advertising and public relations are getting the "highest rewards"—at least financially—in a society that lives by image.[5]

Cinema and Television as Creators of Images

Cinema is another conspicuous example for the replacement of reality by appearance. Here, too, image is not pure fiction, but it develops its own actuality. The movies have the function of creating images; they portray roles that become models for society, and they develop new lifestyles and new morals that inevitably mold the society. Hollywood, the so-called dream factory, is more than the center of the entertainment industry; it is a part of the American soul. Americans do not see dreams as much in contrast to reality as Europeans do—the dream world as the world of fiction—for Americans dreams are more likely to be positively charged as a powerful stimulant, as an idea that *still* needs to be realized. It is indicative of the American character that an entire nation can find its identity in a dream, the "American dream."

> *"The best evidence we have of what World War II was like comes from about 300 million movies made during this era, many of them featuring Ronald Reagan."*
>
> Dave Barry, Dave Barry Slept Here

Cinematography is the major cultural achievement of the United States and one that is thoroughly democratic in that movies are not only accessible to all but that they are also purposely oriented toward all social classes. The United States has created a national history through movies. It has spread its national values and built up a national morality, stimulated national emotions, and developed a national humor through its movies. The fictitious world of films has formed reality and is constantly working on changing it.[6]

This is not to say that Hollywood producers create new realities out of nothing. It is a constant reciprocal relationship between society at large and the producers in Hollywood, who study developing trends and behavior of society in everyday life and research the inner life of this society in order to uncover its imaginations, desires, and hopes, which, in turn, often have their roots in images produced in Hollywood. Hollywood's function is to give form to these social impulses and to articulate them and make them comprehensible, thus allowing the audience to imitate them. The self-awareness of the American society develops in large part through the cinematic medium.

Another medium, television, is meanwhile superseding the movies' role of providing models and shaping values because it has an even more direct, frequent, and multifaceted impact on its audience. Many books and studies have been written about television's role in the manipulation of public opinion. It is important, however, to keep the facts—the undeniable influence of television— separate from the evaluation—its supposed manipulative powers.

Because we receive our information about the world around us indirectly through the media, we tend to focus on television as the most attractive and powerful medium because the picture, sound, and motion are combined and give the viewer the sensation of actually experiencing what happens on the screen. But the substitution of reality by mediated events goes back, as Daniel Boorstin has pointed out, to the time when newspapers first began aggressively hunting for news in order to successfully compete for the consumer's interest. Because of this, Boorstin goes on to speak about the "graphic" revolution even when he writes about the effects of television.[7] For him, the graphic revolution is the real fall of man. All other developments in the realm of media are simply variations of it.

Pseudo-Events

Boorstin's culturally pessimistic analysis is based on the assumption that we (he is speaking about modern Americans, but Europeans could easily be included) expect too much from the world around us and have too high expectations of the society in which we live. From this point of view, we create those things for ourselves that the world does not and cannot offer us. For the news field, this means:

> We expect the papers to be full of news. If there is no news visible to the naked eye, or to the average citizen, we still expect it to be there for the enterprising newsman. The successful reporter is one who can find a story.... If he cannot find a story, then he must make one—by the questions he asks of public figures, by the surprising human interest he unfolds from some commonplace event, or by the "news behind the news."...
>
> This change in our attitude toward "news" ... is a symptom of a revolutionary change in our attitude toward what happens in the world.... Toward how life can be enlivened, toward our power and the power of those who inform and educate and guide us, to provide synthetic happenings to make up for the lack of spontaneous events. Demanding more than the world can give us, we require that something be fabricated to make up for the world's deficiency. This is only one example of our demand for illusions.... The new kind of synthetic novelty which has flooded our experience I will call "pseudo-events."[8]

Our search for another reality—in any case a more expanded, multifaceted one than the "real" one—has its reasoning in dissatisfaction and high demands. It is the same attitude that drives the consumers to continually search for new goods to satisfy their artificially created desires. Since fulfillment is never achieved because new wishes are always aroused, it would be wise to take the reverse approach toward goods as well as events and to reduce our expectations and demands. With such an attitude, the imaginary world, created within the media to fulfill our desires for events, would in turn lose its "reality" for our lives.

Outside Determination of One's Own Worldview

The good old days of "objective" reality are past. The world in which we live is always our own creation. However, it is certainly not inconsequential how we view this world. On the contrary, if there are no objective criteria for reality, everything depends on the necessity to see it, at the very least, subjectively correctly. This sounds like a contradiction in itself. How can something subjective be correct at the same time?

For one, if we allow our worldview to be determined as little as possible from outside images, our own self-understood interests must be the criteria in developing our worldview. For this, it is absolutely necessary to drastically reduce our demands on the world.

By having high expectations and high demands, we invite self-deception and encourage the makers of this world, i.e., the news producers, the dream fabricators, the politicians, among others, to offer us their views so that we can assume them as our own. Our worldview becomes the product of extraneous worldviews that are urged upon us, and we become the instrument of the prevailing interests of others. Self-determination and limitless demands cannot be reconciled. The only way to achieve a "sovereignty" of worldview is by renouncing the many prepared "truths" that make themselves so readily available to us.

Perhaps, the artificial world the politicians have created is also a reaction to the exaggerated expectations of and demands on the politicians by their constituencies. The world of politics presents itself to citizens as a completely constructed world, from the language to the substance to the people that appear in it. The politicians allow themselves to be stylized by the advertising and public relations experts. They are presented as artificial products that are streamlined with the presumed taste of the citizen consumers. This is advantageous for the politicians insofar as by presenting themselves as artificial products, they can reach people easily who are already accustomed to artificial products from television commercials and movies.

The Politician as the Mirror Image and Mouthpiece
of the Voters

> "In fact, I wouldn't be surprised if we secretly wanted to be president ourselves. What could be more familiar than that? And who's more like us than we are? It's almost what we got. And it's about what we deserve. 'Hey, the place really is oval. Cool desk. Where do they keep "the button"? Let's send the helicopter out for Chinese.' "
>
> P. J. O'Rourke, Parliament of Whores

This image of his own person that a politician offers to the voters through the media is not merely a touched-up glossy photo of the real person; it is much more a mirror of the wishes and needs of the voters—a projection of their expectations. The formula of modern ads is that they do not present the product itself but successfully express the emotions, wants, needs, and fears of the viewers. Here, political advertising only too gladly follows the tried and true rules of commercial advertising:

> They provide a slogan, a symbol or a focus that creates for viewers a comprehensive and compelling image of themselves.[9]

Postman points out that the basic instincts of human beings evidently show up here in a modern form and are exploited by politicians and their handlers. He makes reference to Xenophanes who, 2,500 years ago, inveighed against the bad habit of creating the gods after people's own images:

> But to this, television politics has added a new wrinkle: Those who would be gods refashion themselves into images the viewers would have them be.[10]

But wait! Are these not the ideal preconditions for a democratic society? Is it not the perfection of democracy that the politicians articulate the moods and feelings that they perceive in their constituents so that they are in the real sense of the word the voice of the people? And in the form of opinion polls—an American invention characteristically—are not highly developed means used to convert the wishes of the voters into political images?

"A new age demands new political techniques," writes George Gallup, the pioneer of opinion polls, in his work descriptively called *The Pulse of Democracy*, which was published in 1940 and opened up the new field of polling in America.[11] In his view, opinion polls are the new instruments to implement democracy in a modern mass society. They make it possible for democracy to be translated into reality in the emphatic sense of Thomas Jefferson's words: "government by public opinion."[12] Gallup is not blind to the dangerous aspects of the new technique. He writes, the opinion polls are:

> undoubtedly "instruments of power," but, in the last analysis, it is not those who administer them, but the public itself, which sets the limit within which they can operate. The limitations and shortcomings of the polls are the limitations and shortcomings of public opinion itself.[13]

Opinion research has undoubtedly brought a new element to the democratic process. Formerly participation of the citizens was limited to voting in elections, but they now intervene in the political process because the conduct of politicians is strongly influenced by published opinion polls on the various issues at hand. Meanwhile, this "participation" of the populace by means of opinion polls in the political decision-making process carries such weight that one can absolutely speak of a new type of "direct democracy." The flipside of the politics of opinion polls, however, has also become clearly evident. Not only do they promote the natural tendency of politicians to adapt their programs to the presumed opinions of the voters, but the inflation of opinion polls on ever more detailed problems, and in ever shorter intervals, ultimately also devalues them.

Politicians as Manipulators

> *"Facts are stupid things."*
> *A slip of the tongue by President Ronald Reagan in his last speech before Congress in 1988 (instead of "facts are stubborn things")*

Politicians do not act merely as antennae that pick up signals from the populace and augment them; they also send signals through their messages on wavelengths that are sure to reach the voters. They aim them at the basest and, thus, strongest instincts: fear, greed, hate, indolence—and of great importance for Americans—the desire for the quick fix and instant gratification. If politicians want to manipulate the citizens, there is no need to ask for their opinions, needs, or wishes; they simply present issues (along with simple solutions) with which they know they can call forth the necessary emotions: crime, taxes, and welfare with the predictable reactions of fear, rage, envy. If the voters are enraged and occupied with their emotions, they are practically eliminated from participating in politics. So, by voluntary incapacity, the citizens of a democracy surrender to politicians as much power as dictators of totalitarian states acquire through brutal oppression.

The long-term effects are even more devastating. Because the voters become accustomed to receiving political "information" in the form of television "messages," they become less and less capable of taking in political information in any other way. This development has gone a long way in the United States, where the voter/consumer through commercial advertising is more or less conditioned to this mode of "information." Postman describes this phenomenon:

> For example, a person who has seen one million television commercials might well believe that all political problems have fast solutions through simple measures—or ought to. Or that complex language is not to be trusted, and that all problems lend themselves to theatrical expression. Or that argument is in bad taste, and leads only to an intolerable uncertainty.[14]

The modes of perception influence the modes of thinking. The techniques of "spots" and "sound bites" have already had a profound effect on the world of politics, far beyond campaign advertisement. There no longer seems to be any reason to deal with complicated reality when the false reality of advertising is so clear and simple. People no longer make the effort to weigh decisions and uncover cloudy issues because the fictitious world so clearly separates wrong from right, good from evil, positive from negative. It is no longer necessary for the citizens to think and form their own opinions because all they have to do is reach in and consume what they are offered.

Politicians as Educators

But even if this danger of becoming manipulators of opinion did not exist, politicians could not be content with a role as mere articulators of public opinion. Politicians are not just empty containers into which the citizens can pour their wishes; they have highly active duties to help the citizens to forge a picture of the world and to learn to effectively deal with the society in which they live.

The political images, wishes, and needs that form a person's view are formed, on the one hand, on the basis of biographically and socially conditioned interests that are themselves the product of experiences and developments. On the other hand, they are formed by the continuous flood of often contradictory information, which comprise fragments of each person's image of the society he or she lives in. Within such a context, it is unrealistic to try to mold politicians into pure receivers of political opinions. Their duty is, quite to the contrary, to become actively engaged in this confusion of messages that storms in on the citizens and to try to help them put together a sensible agenda and convert it into a voiced opinion of the world.

What is the foundation, however, on which politicians base their arguments? Is it their views of things that they offer their constituents as a model of orientation? Or should they try to place themselves in a neutral position toward the interests of the citizens and to form and publicize a point of view from this?

I believe that both models, as different as they appear, contain the potential for arriving at a solution to this problem. It seems reasonable, therefore, to combine them to create a prototype of the politician as educator. The concept of leadership is embodied in the word *educator* or, better yet, in its Latin origin *educare,* to lead out of something. Yet it is not an authoritative leadership that the masses blindly follow to enhance the power of the leaders. The point of departure for all educators is and remains the person who is to be educated. His or her social position, physical and mental constitution, abilities, and needs form the basis for educating. But a good educator is not neutral; he or she cannot and should not hide his or her own person. What is a leader without a goal or, at least, a direction?

Education or training of political awareness must take its direction from the inner convictions of the educator–politician. But this educative effort does not function, it does not result in mature, politically independent citizens, if it is based on personal interests. Unfortunately, in politics the exact opposite is pervasive. Even when personal enrichment and high-flying self-advancement are not involved, politicians make their own interest, or rather the interests of their group, the basis of their political convictions.

The Foundation of a New Political Morality

American political theory of today justifies this practice in that it defines the democratic process as a battle leading to an eventual compromise between various special interests that are represented within society. It is, however, too short-sighted, to see the role of a politician as the representative of one or the other of these respective interests. These interests are, for their part, not the basis but the result of the political process. They evolve, define themselves, and are realized as a result of the many-voiced choir of opinions. In a highly developed society, interests do not originate from nothing. They are themselves the product of information and pressures. This is all the more true the more complex and ramified the interests become.

It is apparent that the citizens do not only need help with the *representation* of their interests, but they also actually need help one step before that, namely, with the *screening* and *weighing* of their interests. Who else, other than politicians, can take responsibility for this task? This is the true function of politicians in a democratic society: to prepare their constituents to make reasonable decisions about their own situations.

Thus, politicians cannot do without a political morality. But how are they supposed to find the basis of a morality in a world in which there is no longer any unchallenged truth? There is no ready answer to this problem; at the most, there is a starting point: The political morality must evolve out of the only apparent secure and reliable fact—that there is no security of judgment. From this, the cornerstones of political *minima moralia* will develop on their own as points of orientation and measures of conduct in a society that is no longer bound together by certain absolute truths.

If nothing is certain, then one of the most important qualities in politics is tolerance; if no one can claim the truth based on higher insights, moderation is the appropriate behavior; if there is no absolute right, compromise is the highest political virtue. Consensus of opinion instead of overpowerment of minority views, politics as never ending endeavor rather than as unbending commitment to rigid principles, readiness for constant reform in deference to the inadequacy of all political programs, willingness to dialogue with the citizens as the basis of political decisions—these are the qualities of a political morality that befits a society deprived of the security of traditions and moral values but firm in refusing the tempting offer of a prefabricated "ersatz" world.

Not surprisingly, this is by no means a new morality; these are the old virtues of the founding fathers of American democracy who understood the inadequacy of all ideologies and the necessity of consensus and tolerance as the basis for any society. These political morals of moderation and tolerance are still alive and robust in American society, but under the onslaught of pretentious and reckless pseudo-truths, there is a precarious position.

The Takeover of Political Power by the World of Appearances

The eighties certainly brought about the high point, to date, of a development in which unreal worlds are produced and presented with the claim of being the actual reality. These artificial worlds can "real"ize this claim as long and as far as they draw attention to themselves by means of advertising and media techniques. What is perceived becomes real—if only until something bigger draws attention to itself and takes over the role of reality in its place. Andy Warhol pointed to this phenomenon with his as yet unsurpassed formula of "everybody's fifteen minutes of fame."

> *"You ain't seen nothin' yet."*
> *Election slogan for President Reagan's reelection*

The final takeover of political power by the world of appearances was symbolized in many aspects by the election of Ronald Reagan as president of the United States. Remarkable is not so much the fact that a former actor could become president of the superpower America, but that Ronald Reagan brought Hollywood with him to Washington and implanted it in the White House.

The satirist Paul Slansky hits the nail on the head when he writes in his chronicle of the Reagan years, *The Clothes Have No Emperor,* that not a former actor became president, but an actor was playing president. In dozens of quotes, Slansky documented that for Reagan, the separation between a fictional and a real world did not exist and that he viewed politics, of which he was the chief administrator, as a type of supershow, which followed the rules of movie production:

> Politics is just like show-business. You have a hell of an opening, coast for a while, and then have a hell of a close.[15]

It is too easy to make fun of the phenomenon of an actor in the White House, who made no secret of viewing the office as a role. It is too easy to comment on it with disgust and indignation or even to speak of Reagan as a senile clown who was pushed around by his directors. These assessments are certainly factual, but they still do not grasp the phenomenon of Reagan.

Reagan's election and reelection by an overwhelming majority, the immense approval with which his presidency is still met by Americans today, the emotional affection that hardly any other American politician has ever received in this century, the major changes that took place in society and politics under his leadership, the influence of his worldview on the perception Americans have of politics and society—all of this suggests that we have witnessed the appearance of a historical personality on the scene. Historical figures do not necessarily have to be intellectually or even politically bright. They come into being when a politician in his personage can internalize and identify the longings and desires of a society in a period of radical change.

The Desire for Easy Solutions

> "So there was much disillusionment among the voting public. The stage was set for yet another dramatic change in the nation's political direction, a shift away from the soul-searching, the uncertainty, the intellectual complexity, and the multisyllabic words of the Carter era; a shift toward a new kind of leader, a man with a gift for communicating the kind of clear, direct, uncomplicated message that had previously been associated only with Tide commercials. It was time for the Reagan revolution."
>
> Dave Barry, Dave Barry Slept Here

Reagan's simplicity hit the nerve of a society that simply no longer felt like keeping up with an increasingly complicated world, because, first, it began to sense that it could not win this race and second, because it had been worn out by enough advertisment to accept the fact that everything is actually very simple. Reagan's belief in his own rhetoric—a matter of course for an actor who plays a role—became the electrifying model in a society that had been mired in uneasiness and self-doubt as a fallout from Vietnam and Watergate.

Reagan's personal credibility made him irresistible to a society that had become accustomed to believe in nothing, least of all in politics. It would be a terrible mistake to equate the fact that Ronald Reagan was acting with him being fake. He was precisely the opposite of the artificial product that is usually concocted and presented to the voters by the politicians. He played only himself and was—in the literal sense—true to his role. That is one of the reasons for the immense emotional esteem that Reagan drew even from those with dissenting political views.

Reagan was no intellectual heavyweight—and, indeed, he had presumably already paid tribute to his age—but he was by no means politically unqualified. He was undoubtedly naive in his belief in easy solutions, in his trust in the old American virtues, in his undifferentiated black/white thinking, but naive also in a positive sense—as the bumbling innocent Parsifal or his American equivalent Forrest Gump. With his unembarrassed worldview, his unconventional political attitude, and sometimes shockingly naive approaches, he was surprisingly suc-cessful and made the conventional wisdom of the political establishment look foolish and empty.

One remarkable example is Reagan's speech in Berlin where he, to the all-around amusement of the political gurus of all hues, publicly challenged Gorbachev to tear down the wall, to open the Brandenburg Gate. *Quel dégoût!* (What bad taste!) This public outbreak of emotions was all right in the first years after the wall was built, but not now that everything had arranged itself nicely and comfortably for every-body. Some years later the wall disappeared and Germany was reunited.

Even if one does not agree with the generally accepted thesis in the United States, namely that President Reagan's politics of military mobilization was the decisive factor in the collapse of communism, in the end he was right in his belief that the communist position, which he saw symbolized in the Berlin Wall, was untenable. He was right, and practically everybody else had been wrong.

In his own way, President Reagan also unmasked the inflated importance of the office of the president in that he showed that the country could function under the leadership of an administratively incompetent and not exactly hard-working chief executive. Reagan's conduct was completely in tune with his role. After all, in the movies it is not the actors who call the shots but the director. Reagan reacted in compliance with instructions from his advisers, and when these failed to appear, he relaxed and distanced himself from his role as presi-dent. Unfortunately, this obvious proof of the relative insignificance of the of-ficeholder for the general functioning of the presidency has not led to a more detached view of the role of the president in the life of the nation and at the same time to stronger congressional control of the handlers of the president and the string-pullers in the White House. But this, of course, is not Reagan's fault.

A Longing for a "Good Feeling"

In the late seventies, American society was in a condition that required a "sim-ple" man like Reagan. The United States enjoyed the Reagan years. It was a period of discharge after all the tension that had built up during the difficult

sixties and seventies within society but especially in the minds of the .
was an inebriating relief, a rush, a period of oblivion. It was "feeling &
was for Middle America the outbreak from the straight jacket of ordinary ι
and the oblivious immersion into a consciousness-raising dream world, actι.
the same experience that the rambunctious youth had made with drugs soιιe
thirty years ago—though in a different form and with a certain time lag. With
Reagan's retirement, the United States sobered up again. As reason slowly set in,
the devastation that was caused under the spell of the intoxication became clear,
but emotionally the nation continued to blissfully dream on about past high
spirits and to long for a repeat performance.

Which mood will keep the upper hand in the United States can hardly be
foreseen. For a while it seemed as though Americans were quite happy, after the
overwhelming show of the Reagan years, that the movie was over and the lights
had been turned on again. President George Bush, a dry, wooden figure, did not
offer himself up, whether due to good sense and better insight or to lack of
passion, as impresario for an intoxicating reimmersion in a surge of "good feeling." But like sex, alcohol, and drugs, any intoxicating agent can become an
addiction. For eight years, Americans were exposed to a regular dose of "good
feeling" brought to them through messages from the safe and intact world that
pep you up and enhance your mood.

The Gulf War could not have come at a more convenient time and could not
have had a better outcome as this practically painless demonstration of American
superiority. The immense, almost hysterical enthusiasm for this victory can be
seen as a revival of the intoxicating "good feeling." Perhaps, the sobering up
after Reagan, if indeed it took place, was too brief and the longing for a reimmersion into the unreal world of appearances has been sparked again. Like some
forms of alcoholism, drug addiction, or sex dependency, this can end in cata-
strophic addiction. Hopefully, this infatuation with a world of false reality will
gradually dwindle, as most things in the United States do, mainly because they
become boring. After all, even the drug culture, which was eagerly lived out by
middle-class youth in the sixties and was considered by many as the ultimate
downfall of America, has been reduced from its position as a central social
phenomenon to a hardly noticeable existence on the outer fringes of society.

Today, the drug problem has mainly shifted to the lower stratums of society
and has taken on a new expression and a new relevance. Presumably, this time
the experiment with drugs will not be overcome with so few problems as last
time. The new drug problem will also disappear some day, but not because one
has had enough of a nice game or because the United States has surpassed itself
and come to grips with the social consequences with a spurt of energy. The
problem with crack, the most-used drug in the ghettos, will be over in ten years
because as Dr. Galanter, director of a drug-therapy center in New York, surmises
"for the people who use 'crack' will . . . then be dead."

Such a consequence is also imaginable for the nosedive of the American body

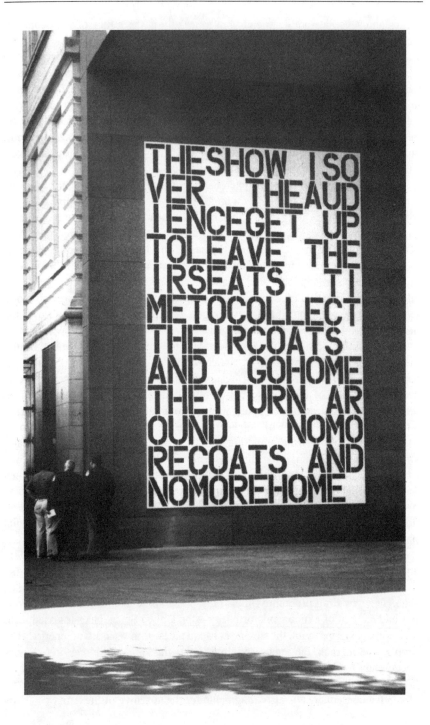

politic into the world of pleasant appearances. The middle-class youth of the sixties had enough reservations about the drug culture and sufficient distance from the drug culture to free itself when the situation became too serious or just was no longer any fun. The lower classes of American society do not have this power of resistance for reasons for which they themselves are not responsible.

Which of the two consequences of the dropout into the world of false promises American democracy will experience depends completely on whether the democratic substance of society has survived the Reagan years unharmed. In any case, the revival of the democratic culture will not come on its own. A great effort is required to bring the democratic spirit out of the exile to which it was expelled by the politics of false beauty.

Notes

1. "About two hundred years ago, the idea that truth was made rather than found began to take hold of the imagination of Europe." Richard Rorty, *Contingency, Irony and Solidarity,* p. 3.

2. Neil Postman, *Amusing Ourselves to Death,* pp. 109–10.

3. A passage in Ralph Waldo Emerson's essays could be the program for postmodern thinking: "A foolish consistency is the hobgoblin of little minds, adored by little statesmen and philosophers and divines. With consistency a great soul has simply nothing to do. . . . Speak what you think now in hard words, and to-morrow speak what to-morrow thinks in hard words again, though it contradict every thing you said to-day." Ralph Waldo Emerson, "Self-Reliance," *Essays II,* p. 33.

4. Richard Rorty, "Just One More Species Doing Its Best," *London Review of Books,* 13, no. 14, July 25, 1991, p. 315.

5. An enormous part of social energy in developed democracies is invested in the creation of dream worlds: advertisements, movies, artworks, media. A great part of social activities consists in consuming these dream worlds.

This is possibly a sign for democratization of society because the creation and the enjoyment of such spectacles was of great interest for the ruling class of predemocratic societies, the nobles.

Each culture is indeed something fictitious, something fabricated, the contrary of "natural reality." This means that life in a dream world is at the same time life in a certain culture. The main problem is not the contrast between reality and fiction. The main point is the quality of the fictitious reality produced by society itself.

6. "The novel, the movie, and the TV program have, gradually but steadily, replaced the sermon and the treatise as the principal vehicles of moral change and progress." Rorty, *Contingency, Irony, and Solidarity,* p. xvi.

7. Daniel J. Boorstin, *The Image,* pp. 8–9.

8. Ibid.

9. Postman, *Amusing Ourselves to Death,* p. 135.

10. Ibid.

11. George Gallup and Saul Forbes Rae, *The Pulse of Democracy,* p. 272.

12. Ibid., p. 283.

13. Ibid., p. 282.

14. Postman, *Amusing Ourselves to Death,* p. 162.

15. Ronald Reagan to aide Stuart Spencer quoted by Paul Slansky, *The Clothes Have No Emperor,* p. 9.

Wild

at

Heart

Nowhere in the civilized world is there as much murder and manslaughter as in the United States. One of the causes for this is the fact that it is very easy for Americans to arm themselves to the teeth. We do not know how the crime statistics of the United States would compare internationally if citizens of other nations had such easy access to weapons.[1] One of the most remarkable aspects of the problem is that it is not even politically possible to require that people register their weapons, let alone have them relinquish their right to buy and keep the most deadly weapons.

Government responds to this by arming its police force to the teeth. In no other civilized country does the police force have such a martial air. Even the traffic police and the guards at government buildings are heavily armed. It creates an atmosphere of imminent war and violence just around every corner in this peaceful world. The appearance strongly influences attitudes; American policemen take their role as the embodiment of state force very literally.

American police brutality is well documented and confirmed from time to time by shocking new occurrences. Although vigorously protested by civil rights activists, this abuse is silently tolerated by a majority as an acceptable means of crime control.

The United States is the only nation in the Western world in which the death penalty continues to be a widespread practice. After it was rejected as unconstitutional in the seventies, it was reinstated by conservative courts. In recent years, politicians have exploited their strong support of the death penalty. During the 1990 primary election for governor in Texas, one of the candidates used a campaign ad to illustrate his point: a series of photos of convicted criminals was shown, all of whom the candidate proudly claimed to have led to their executions during his career as attorney general. The plague of violence is even more prevalent than is reflected in the statistics. Americans themselves complain that "America is a violent society," which points to the fact that the phenomenon of violence cannot be grasped by focusing on violent acts; it is rather an attitude. The discussion of violence in America should, therefore, be based on a wide-ranging and open definition of the term, such as is encompassed by words like *vehemence, fierceness, intensity, severity, impetuosity, hot temper*. In defining violence as intensity, one gets a better picture of the many aspects of violence that are not acted out but are a state of temper. It also becomes clear that in the view of the majority of Americans, there is a distinction between criminal violence and other forms of violent attitudes and activities that are viewed positively and even claimed as national virtues.

A Disposition for Violence as a Sign of a Still Young Nation

The main reasons for the "intensity" by which America distinguishes itself so much from the other civilized nations is the relative youthfulness of the nation. On the surface, the process of civilization in America is at the same level as other nations, or perhaps even more advanced. However, the internal development that all societies had to undergo from the hunter and gatherer stage to tribal organization and the founding of cities and states has been under way for only a few centuries in America.

That is not to say that the process of nation-building in America started at the hunter and gatherer status, but one important stage in this process—the claiming of territory accompanied by the violent expulsion of the indigenous population—only came to a close 100 years ago. The story of the creation of the United States is a story of violence. This is true, after all, for every nation—but for most Western peoples the acts of this kind of violence are far, far beyond memory.

Yet, it is not so much the violent past itself that is of consequence but the effects these events have on the society and how artistic expression reflects these effects. Homer's *Iliad* quite unmistakably makes reference to the Doric land rush and to the expansion of the Greeks to Asia Minor, and it glorifies this period and the virtues that characterized it. For the Greeks, the *Iliad* was the standard ethical work, the bible by which the youth was raised. Values embodied in this work were accepted without question as the foundation of society and passed from generation to generation.

The Portrayal of Violence in American Folklore

In a certain sense one can compare the *Iliad* with American folklore most strongly manifested in Westerns. For Europeans, the Western is a thrilling story; for Americans, it is their history. The birth of the nation out of the conquest of the continent is part of the American national consciousness that has been decisively influenced by the Western. Westerns do not merely tell American history; they mythologize it and give criteria for evaluation. A national morality is developed through them: an American world of virtues and values—perseverance, courage, loyalty, and justice, but also toughness, relentlessness, and violence in protecting one's rights.

Europeans have dealt with and put aside 2,000 years of coming of age from the turbulent mass migration to the tournaments, the civil wars, the duels of honor, the slaughter of two world wars. They should not judge Americans from a detached moral standpoint and should not perceive the American "violent nature" and fascination with violence as a national vice. It is rather something innocent, a youthful vehemence, a naive wildness of the heart.

It is not that long ago that personal weapons were given up in Europe in favor of a state monopoly on the use of force. Only in this century have violence in the family and spousal abuse become matters of concern in civilized societies. Brutality against the weakest members of society, the children, has always been and is still considered a legitimate method of discipline.

Precisely this aspect clearly points to the ambivalent nature of violence. There is a sadistic aspect of violence—taking pleasure in hurting other human beings— and a cynical view—preempting the violence of others. But there is also a more benign nature of violence that fights for a good cause. It was this type of violence that found expression in Western movies.

Violence and Freedom

Many portrayals of violence in the United States suffer because their authors are puzzled by the shock caused by a view into everyday American life. They indulge in endless crime statistics and limit their creativity to stringing together real-life horror stories. But America is not one-dimensional. In America, one encounters violence and benevolence side by side, often within the same person. The spontaneous friendliness of the American people, their natural openness, overwhelming hospitality, immense willingness to help strangers—all this is the flipside of the unleashed "vehemence" with which Americans contact and confront others. Both types of behavior are the result of a youthful and unexperienced state of mind that "makes no bones about it." Americans are wild at heart, both good and evil.

Another aspect that plays into these attitudes is the fascination with freedom that Americans experience not only through their minds but also through their emotions. Americans are who they are, violent and benevolent. Just as they despise any force or any limitation on their freedom, they resist any forces that put pressure on their emotions. It is said that these expressions of friendliness, openness, and helpfulness are merely superficial. Some European observers even go so far as to dispute whether Americans have the ability to feel deep emotions.

Without going into this dispute, it may be said that the so-called American superficiality extends to the violent aspect of American society as well. In any case, American violence, as awful as the consequences may be, is fundamentally superficial, an affectation, a spontaneous expression, not a systematic act of evil.

Uncovering Hidden Violence in the Modern Society

Often underestimated in reports about violence in the United States are the serious efforts undertaken by American society to critically analyze and deal with this phenomenon. Americans have by no means resigned themselves to the violence in their own country, neither the consequences nor the underlying causes.

While the values formed by Westerns were unquestionably accepted until the sixties, the exposure to violence in society and the resulting repugnance has developed into a dynamic force that is slowly making its way into the national consciousness. Despite strong reactionary movements for the preservation of old values, one can already speak of a revolutionary situation in that the long accepted foundation of a pattern of behavior in the United States is being questioned for the first time on a large scale.

Just as the values of Homer's world were challenged by the Greek philosophers of the fifth century B.C., a struggle between a tradition long held and a new view of life is coming into being in the United States. It is not concerned, as in Europe, solely with seeking out the despised violence in hidden corners of society and exposing it; in the United States the main concern is to devalue violence as a social attitude.

Precisely because the condemnation of violence in the United States is not universal, its critics search it out in all the structures of society—violence at the workplace, in the family, against nature, in advertising, and in the superficially peaceful political process.

The Glorification of Violence in Action Movies

There are, however, strong countermovements that can delay or even reverse this process. Action movies, which are slowly taking the place of Westerns, are one of these dangerous forces. In Westerns, violence was a part of the national history; it had its inner logic, its entitlement in the context of the whole story; it was an aspect of the entire world of values that, as an accepted ethic, gave additional legitimacy to each individual value. Action movies are a presentation of violence solely for the sake of entertainment. They have taken on the external structural elements of Westerns, but they are, as the name indicates, only interested in violent action.

Action movies, like pornos, string together generic scenes; the plot, if there is one, is perceived as a tiresome distraction. Just as a porno movie stimulates the sexual appetite by pictures, here the sensations of fear and excitement are stimulated by scenes of violence and its consequences.

> *"Movie blockbusters are as empty of grown-up content as that other typical and expressive American invention, light beer. The only thing they offer more of than TV dramas, perforce censored for family viewing, is violence, with chain-saw massacres and kickings in the crotch constituting what you can see nowhere else and exactly what you go to movies to see."*
>
> *Paul Fussell,* BAD

Unlike porno movies, action movies are socially accepted and may be indulged in without social reservations. On the contrary, it can be combined with patriotism or general moral goodwill. After all, thin threads of plots are developed just far enough to legitimate violence under the purpose of fighting off the "bad guys" by the "good guys." The "good guys" are usually Americans forced to "commit violence" against internal or foreign enemies.

Competition and Supersession

Aside from legitimacy conferred by morality—good must guard against and overcome evil with violence—there is still another justification for violence that is the law of nature in the American reasoning. In this context one does not speak of violence but, rather, calls it competition. Yet the ideology behind competition, in which the stronger prevails over the weaker through repression and annihilation, regards violence to be not only inevitable but also desirable. Violence is undoubtedly a law of nature that can be observed in thousands of phenomena: suppression and destruction of the weak to make room for the stronger and more viable ones, competition and the fight for survival. Yet nature also offers other forms of life without aggression or at the cost of other living beings: blooming, maturing, developing, a reciprocal give-and-take for collective survival, the symbiotic relationship of animals and plants for mutual protection and usage, forms of altruism in the animal kingdom, and the widespread phenomenon of the instinct to play.

The diversity of life is larger than a simple "survival of the fittest," a formula attributed to Darwin as the basic law of nature. Darwin's discoveries are much more subtle and diversified and cannot be pressed into such a handy formula of "survival of the fittest" (at which end humankind is unquestionably the fittest of all of the fit). Millions of beings have survived that are in no way especially fit; rather, they found niches in which to hide and so escaped the competition. Moreover, the destructiveness of nature, launched by the human race, has led to the awareness that even the fittest cannot survive when it has destroyed all others. Survival is a delicate balance of give and take, and annihilation of others is self-destructive.

"The growth of a large business is merely a survival of the fittest."
John D. Rockefeller, My Memories of Eighty Years

But Darwin's formula caught the spirit of his time. It not only influenced the natural sciences, but it also found its way into philosophy and sociology. Americans may not have invented Social Darwinism—it was developed by an Englishman, Herbert Spencer—but Spencer's transfer of Darwin's principle of "survival of the fittest" onto human society and especially onto economic life was greeted in the United States as a revelation. At the end of the nineteenth century, Spencer was *the* American national philosopher.[2] His thesis brought the justification for both the birth of the nation in the spirit of violence, a phase that was just ending at that time, as well as for the principles of social and economic exploitive and repressive competition, a concept the society was at that time embracing wholeheartedly. Enormous acts of violence upon which the nation had been founded were viewed as simple fulfillment of natural laws; the repressed, exploited, suppressed, and destroyed could be seen as victims of nature not of human viciousness, the perpetrators in their brutality and insensibility simply as the executioners of the inner law of nature.

Social Darwinism as Apology for the Violent Spirit in the Rise of the Nation

In interpreting American history, the religiously based belief in a certain mission assigned to the Americans is complemented by pseudo-scientific Social Darwinism. Together they created a formidable ideology: the extinction of the Native Americans was necessary and justified because they were not capable of developing the country to its fullest potential, to answer nature's calling. The extinction of the Native Americans not only made progress possible, it was progress.

Even the second great national act of violence, the enslavement of blacks, is given meaning in the view of Social Darwinism. People who allow themselves to become enslaved are not victims of violence, they are just not "fit" enough to survive in the tough competition of life.

Racism, still prevalent in American society, especially toward the black population, has its strongest roots in contempt for these victims of a social selection process.[3] It is registered as a form of inferiority complex on the side of the victims as well. Although racism all over the world is based upon the belief in the superiority of one's own race, the extent and persistence of racism in the United States can only be attributed to the conviction that these superstitions are scientifically provable by Social Darwinism.

The Civil War, in which the disloyal Southern states were brought back into the fold of the Union, is the apotheosis of violence as the savior of the nation. Civil wars are considered tragedies in the history of nations. In the United States, the Civil War went into history as a heroic event, even with all the lamenting over the victims. It is permanently anchored in the national consciousness as a necessary rite of passage on the way to nationhood.

With this war the formerly voluntary alliance of the states was forcibly made indissoluble. In 1835, Alexis de Tocqueville still claimed that the United States was a federation on the basis of mutual benefit and that the federation would not stop any state from seceding if the state no longer saw the relationship as beneficial.[4] Indeed, in 1860, this was an alternative that only became unthinkable after the fact. Social Darwinism justifies the preservation of the Union as the one and only legitimate goal because the strong side, i.e., according to the natural law of society the better side, has succeeded. The goal is legitimized by the result.

> *"This epitomized the feeling of despair that was widespread in the Confederacy as the war ended, and it left a vast reservoir of bitterness toward the North. But as the old saying goes, 'Time heals all wounds,' and in the more than 120 years that have passed since the Civil War ended, most of this bitterness gradually gave way to subdued loathing, which is where we stand today."*
>
> Dave Barry, Dave Barry Slept Here

The destruction that the North inflicted on the South, not just militarily, but also politically, culturally, and economically is justified by the struggle for survival in nature in which the weak side, in this case the identity of the Southern states, disappears. The view of events from the other side is indirectly confirmed once again. The Southerners for a long time after the Civil War did not consider themselves the victims, just the losers. Geoffrey Gorer in his book about the Americans has stressed that the hostility of the inhabitants of the Southern states toward those of the North stemmed from self-doubt and lack of self-confidence of the apparent weaker side towards the stronger side.[5]

Colonization as the Rape of Nature

We now recognize territorial expansion and the consequent exploitation of resources as acts of violence. This "rape" of nature took place, no doubt, at the
same time as the expulsion and annihilation of the Native Americans, yet it is a
separate, independent act with its own ideology. Even nature is a type of opponent that must be overpowered by the American people, the representatives of
progress. Territorial expansion is stamped in the memory of the national consciousness as a heroic act by which nature submitted to the will of man so that
America could be created out of the raw state in which it was found.

"There was nothing but land: not a country at all, but the material out of
which countries are made,"[6] writes Willa Cather, one of the many great American authors who paid literary homage to the heroic act of territorial expansion
and settlement of the continent.

Antagonism toward nature is the given attitude of all colonizers. It remains the
dominant position of most Americans toward nature. This is not because the days
of hardship and the struggle are relatively recent in history. The spirit of trailblaz-
ing is enhanced under Social Darwinism. If nature yields to progress, this is in
itself a law of nature. Practice confirms the superiority of man's creation over
natural conditions: It is better to dam up the Colorado River and produce electric
power for farms and cities in California than to let this treasure flow to the Gulf of
Mexico. Progress can be clearly distinguished from the natural condition when
gardens and golf courses appear on desert sand, rivers are tamed, swamps are
dried, and jungles torn out to make room for agriculture and cattle breeding. It is
obviously more clever to pull the oil from the earth so that its energy can stimulate
the economy and raise the level of prosperity than to leave it at the bottom of the
sea or closed in the Arctic tundra as nature has done for millenniums.

The American realtors and developers thrive on this type of glorification of
the pioneering spirit. Nowhere else in the Western world do developers enjoy
such high esteem. By transforming fallow land to valuable real estate, developers
contribute to progress in a similar fashion as companies who dig up the hidden
treasures of oil, coal, metals, and minerals for human usage. In the eyes of a
large majority of Americans, these developers are the legitimate heirs to the
pioneers. They have claimed America's nature, and they are designing its future.

Now there is growing awareness of the damage unconstrained abuse of nature
has added to the long list of man's evils. There is a diverse and politically
influential movement for the protection of the environment. It fights not only
powerful economic interests, but also against an ideology that claims unlimited
and unquestioned progress as an absolute good.

Social Darwinism as the Legitimating Theory of Capitalism

While the theories of Social Darwinism indirectly legitimized the violent genesis
of the United States, in retrospect Spencer's philosophy in its time was direct and

obvious support for the prevailing economic and social ethics. The brutal competition, the exploitation of the weak by the strong at the economic level, the social squalor of a large portion of society, all of this was part of an inexorable law of nature that only functioned for the well-being of humankind. To express it in Spencer's words:

> The poverty of the incapable, the idle, and those shoulderings aside of the weak by the strong, which leave so many "in shallows and in miseries," are the decrees of a large, far-seeing benevolence. . . . Under the natural order of things, society is constantly excreting its unhealthy, imbecile, slow, vacillating, faithless members.[7]

The essence of Spencer's philosophy still finds acceptance among a great many Americans who see poverty and other social nuisances as the failures of individuals. They believe that society should separate itself from these parasites. They admire all those who have succeeded in attaining their goals and reaching the top, no matter the means. I previously addressed the indifference toward poverty and its demoralizing effect on the democratic spirit. In this section I will examine the glorification of competition as a factor contributing to social formation and its relationship to democracy.

Power and Competition in the Democratic System

Americans fundamentally understand democracy to mean competition. According to James Madison (*The Federalist Papers,* No. 51), the American governmental system is organized in such fashion that "ambition must be made to counteract ambition." The entire political process is a rivalry of interests and a clashing of powers. Democracy does not resolve this conflict; it merely regulates it.

But even a quick look at Madison's argument exposes a fundamental contrast to a Social Darwinist theory of society and political life. Madison does not see competition as a means of displacement but as a struggle to achieve a balance; it is not the right of the stronger power to enforce itself that guarantees the continuation of society; it is the fact that this right has its limits. Force is recognized as an energizing factor of society, but it is precisely the need to control force that is declared as the basic principle.

Popular American democratic ideology overlooks Madison's crucial point that society as a self-regulating system is a human construction and therefore is vulnerable. Competition does not create a balance of powers when the powers within society are distributed unevenly. Dominance of one power turns a contest into overwhelming defeat for the other. But Americans carry their naive trust in the power of the market over to the functioning mechanism of the democratic conflict of interests.

Excessive reliance on competition as the basic principle of the democratic system is a dangerous narrowing of the democratic idea. The institutional mechanism of pressure and counter pressure cannot work its positive power without a common value system. In *Habits of the Heart,* Robert Bellah et al. write:

> Yet all [founding fathers of the nation] were agreed that a republic needed a government that was more than an arena within which various interests could compete, protected by a set of procedural rules. Republican government, they insisted, could survive only if animated by a spirit of virtue and concern for the public good.[8]

Power and Competition in the Economy

Characteristically, the word *aggressive* does not have the negative connotation in the American language as the term with the same root in German. It is often used in a positive sense to describe concentrated effort that results in success in the economic and in the political world, in sports, and even in private endeavors.

An "aggressive salesman" is by no means an "aggressor" but, rather, one who takes his career seriously and makes an earnest effort to sell his goods. Americans have no scruples about overwhelming the client or customer. In the fight for survival, the more competent people simply win out. As a consequence, it is not considered reprehensible to deceive a client or business partner. Taken freely from Spencer, the idiot has only himself to blame.

In such a context there is little room for a critical perspective of advertisement and its underlying abuse of the consumer through manipulative information and constant exaggeration. The dominant opinion still assumes a level playing field between the producer and the buyer, just as it is naively believed that competing television commercials of different brands balance each other out.

Advertising is a constitutional right—it falls under the terms of freedom of speech. It is part of the democratic mechanism that is seen as a contest between opposing forces. Like "pressure groups" in politics, the power of money in advertising carries such weight in the economy it has become overpowering. Americans have recognized this in individual cases and dealt with it correspondingly. For example, cigarette advertisements are obligated to bear a label warning against the dangers of smoking, and nicotine advertising is completely banned on television.

In his examination of the dominating role of competition in American society, Gorer also takes the relationship between producers and consumers and the role of advertising into consideration. He clearly elaborates the latent violence on the part of producers and advertisers:

> The public falls more into the category of things, of raw material, than into human beings. Continuing the mineral analogy, the purchasing power has to be extracted from the consuming public, as though it were silver being extracted from the baser ore. . . . The devices of advertising . . . demonstrate a consistent and profound contempt for the public on the part of the advertisers and their employers. . . . For the producer the consumer is never an equal or near-equal; fooling the public, "putting one over" on the consumer, is an act of which nobody need be ashamed; indeed it is a proper subject for boasting.[9]

Latent Violence as the Source of Horror

Advertising is just one example in a whole array of forms of hidden violence in American society: Discrimination by race and social class and particularly against women are others. Tocqueville also described public opinion as a hidden power and spoke of the tyranny of public opinion in the United States that forces the individual to conform.

If Jefferson were to see the United States of today, he would certainly denounce a hidden power in political structures and institutions that erodes the energy of democracy. The basic element of life in democracy is the participation of the citizens. There is no open violence against this participation, as in authoritarian systems. But the interest in political participation capitulates or diminishes in the face of benevolent powers of bureaucratic organizations and the dynamics of political structures that are rendering themselves independent. Established institutions develop their own political field of power in which initiative is swallowed up like in a black hole. Frustration is followed by resignation and finally capitulates to the overpowering energy of the black hole.

The relationship between money and violence is multifaceted and complex. It is accepted that the money mania is a motivating force behind violence. It is evident in an economic morality that sees the exploitation of others for self-enrichment as a source of general progress in society. The monetarization of society afflicting the United States continues to destroy traditional values. Just as all absolute rulers, money is not satisfied with its status and must constantly expand its area of rule until everything is subjected to the value system of money.

Latent violence, however elusive, creates an unconscious but oppressive atmosphere of terror that is compressed and eventually explodes in horror. The American culture of horror finds expression in novels, movies, and art but also in cartoons, slapstick comedies, and satires, which demonstrates a cultural awareness of this tension and the readiness to confront it. Although much of the material produced by Hollywood and the book market is cheap mass goods that only imitate the form, the way modern American society deals with horror is innovative, daring, diverse, and exemplary for other nations.

The masterworks of American horror art show the safe and sound world of middle class normalcy in an inimitable way. Under this thin facade, hidden violence suddenly explodes. The American productions of horror art come in waves and reflect the various intensities of shock and the ever present underlying threats. Even the themes and symbols of horror change according to the atmosphere of shock in the American society at any given time. An often repeated theme is nature breaking into the secure American world, sometimes in the form of natural catastrophes, usually in the form of gigantic, enlarged insects and monstrous beasts. Perhaps this reflects the fear of the revenge of nature against the settlers and against the modern crimes of pollution, poisoning, and radiation of nature.

Laughing as Protection against Horror

Another protection against horror in the modern world is laughter. Laughter finds its artistic expression in satire, comedy, and caricature. Americans possess a natural talent for the art of covering the craziness of everyday life in laughter. Slapstick comedies, which were produced en masse in the early years of Hollywood, were refined to masterworks of observation and clarification of latent horror by the great actors Charlie Chaplin, the Marx Brothers, Buster Keaton, and others. No other artwork has expressed the latent violence of the Industrial Age as well as Charlie Chaplin's *Modern Times*. Woody Allen's work is in the same tradition, using different techniques and other themes. Moving always in a chaotic state beneath the well-ordered surface of modern life, Allen lets us overcome our panic through laughter. The television series "The Simpsons" is a remarkable series of artistic efforts to cloak the latent violence in the modern mass society with laughter.

American cartoons and caricatures are used to dealing with the horror hidden behind the facade of middle class decency and political rhetoric. Through ridicule, they take much of the fear out of reality. However, cartoons of this type that take issue with the false security of middle class America and the arrogant deceitfulness of politicians are only a small segment of the strips that are published daily in newspapers; unfortunately, most of the comics are a glorification of the peaceful world.

The massive presence of violence in televised programs, in the cinema, in magazines, and in books reflects its ubiquitous presence in American society. It is also an indication that this society has recognized the problem and is coming to terms with it. The infinite forms that violence takes are made visible.

But this also has undesirable consequences in that the preoccupation with violence and the portrayal of its horrid forms and terrible results does more than shock, disillusion, and enlighten reason; it also gives a thrill, provides fascination, and inspires more violence.

In part, the violent nature of American society stems from its relative youth, which has not yet passed through the common stages of detachment, disenchantment, and moderation. In this respect older European nations have reached a more mature stage in moderating and controlling violence that could be the model for American society.

More probable, however, is the reverse effect of the cultural dominance by the United States through its various media productions—television series, movies, pop music, brutal sports, and wild recreational activities. The ubiquitous messages of violence are changing attitudes and creating a dangerous new atmosphere. The cultural lead that the Europeans have gained through their sorrowful experiences with violence throughout history can very easily be undermined by a steady flow of violence as a media experience. The American reality manifested in these media productions gives violence a place in our worldview, first in our minds and emotions and then in reality.

Notes

1. "The homicide rate among young men in the United States is 4 to 73 times the rate in other industrialized nations. Firearms were used in three-fourths of the killings in this country and in only one-fourth of those overseas." Report in the *New York Times,* June 27, 1990, quoted by Paul Fussell, *BAD,* pp. 193–94.

2. Richard Hofstadter writes: "Herbert Spencer was idolized in the United States as has been no other philosopher before or since." Richard Hofstadter, *The American Political Tradition,* p. 168.

However, the Americans, too, had a very important and influential representative of Social Darwinism, William Graham Sumner.

3. Andrew Hacker referred in his book *Two Nations, Black and White, Separate, Hostile, Unequal* to the deeper reasons for the race problems in America: "But as much as anything, being "black" in America bears the mark of slavery. Even after emancipation . . . the ideology that had provided the rationale for slavery by no means disappeared. Blacks continued to be seen as an inferior species, not only unsuited for equality but not even meriting a chance to show their worth. Immigrants only hours off the boat, while subjected to scorn, were allowed to assert their superiority to black Americans.

"And in our time, must it be admitted . . . that residues of slavery continue to exist? The answer is obviously yes." Andrew Hacker, *Two Nations, Black and White, Separate, Hostile, Unequal,* p. 14. Compare also with chapter 2—"Race and Racism: Inferiority vs. Equality," p. 17, especially pp. 30, 60.

4. Alexis de Tocqueville, *Democracy in America I,* p. 389.

5. Geoffrey Gorer, *The Americans,* p. 201. Gorer made this observation in the late forties. Later on, the antagonism between the North and South over the civil rights movement was vehemently set aflame again because the Southern states again felt they were being kept in tutelage by the rest of the nation. Since then, tensions have subsided considerably, due mainly to the economic improvement of the South. The South is finally able to be self-confident.

6. Willa Cather, *My Ántonia,* p. 7.

7. Herbert Spencer, "Poor Laws," in *Social Statics,* p. 289. Spencer's philosophy is not dead in America. His books are republished by a foundation and can be bought at

absurdly low prices. It is similar to the practice of the Gideon Bible Association, which provides hotels worldwide with free Bibles.

The "philosophical" heritage of Herbert Spencer has been taken over by the so-called objectivist movement founded by Ayn Rand (see notes to the chapter "Pursuit of Happiness").

8. Bellah et al. point out that it was Madison—the founding father who, in contrast to the idealists and democratic firebrands Thomas Jefferson and Thomas Paine, is traditionally painted as the cold advocate of the mechanism of "checks and balances"—who passionately stressed the idea of a "citizen's virtue" and the necessity for orientation to the public good as inalienable for the success of the democratic experiment. They refer to *The Federalist Papers,* No. 45, and quote Madison: "The public good, the real welfare of the body of the people, is the supreme object to be pursued." Robert N. Bellah et al., *Habits of the Heart,* p. 253.

9. Gorer, *The Americans,* pp. 131–32.

Life Is Fun
Part I

The Pathology
of Happiness

The reproach I address to the principle of equality is not that it leads men away in the pursuit of forbidden enjoyments, but that it absorbs them wholly in quest of those which are allowed. By these means a kind of virtuous materialism may ultimately be established in the world, which would not corrupt, but enervate, the soul and noiselessly unbend its spring of action.[1]

In no part of American society is the transformation of values and self-understanding as apparent as in its attitude toward pleasure. From the Puritans, who had little to laugh about, it has run to the other extreme, where the entertainment industry supplies the public with computerized canned laughter. A preoccupation with "fun" dominates every area of life. In Alexis de Tocqueville's times, judging from his observations, the "pursuit of happiness" in America was congruent with the search for personal wealth. It is certainly a positive development that fun—entertainment and amusement—now has joined the list of attractive goals of life. Europeans tend to discount American high esteem of entertainment as cultural decay, which is a rather one-sided view. This attitude can also be interpreted as a determined acceptance of world's secular nature that modern man has to confront after experiencing the collapse of metaphysics and the futility of transcendental religious promises. Society's recognition of the secular concept that life should bring joy is the further advancement of the revolutionary claim of the founding fathers, that happiness is to be pursued here on earth. As a thoroughly worldly philosophy of life, this claim is in addition an important bulwark against fundamentalist ideology.

Life Is Fun—A Radically Democratic Concept

If it is an aspect of life to have fun, then this principle must apply to everyone. As such, "life is fun" is an essentially democratic expression. It would not fit into a society in which many must suffer to provide pleasure for the few, an accepted idea in classical antiquity and the Middle Ages. The American artist and art theorist David Robbins characterizes the relation between entertainment and democratic culture in the following manner:

> The United States is an entertainment culture, not an art culture. . . . Entertainment includes the idea that pleasure cannot itself be hierarchized; its symbols may be hierarchized—champagne versus beer, for example—but pleasure itself as a human experience may not. And this is a radical cultural idea, radically democratic.[2]

The motto "life is fun" seems to be a suitable response to the irrational aspect of the world and of life in general. This is expressed clearly in the dual meaning of the word "fun" in the American language. It is defined as "pleasure, mirth, amusement." At the same time, "funny" is also "strange, odd," or "confusing" and "unexpected." "Life is fun" is recognition that the world is not as it should be. It is the healthy alternative to depression and despair in the face of the imperfection, injustice, and unpredictability of the world.

It is an entirely wholesome attitude, not just for the individual but for society. It contributes to the unveiling of the pompousness, the relativizing of demands, the undermining of positions, and with that to the weakening of power. The search for "fun" in everything explains a surprising irreverence so important to the preservation of the democratic spirit in America.

All in all, the expression "life is fun" is another aspect of the struggle of the individual against the demands of mega-institutions such as the church, the state, the company. It bears witness to the priority given to individual self-realization in American society.

> *"In order to really get people to respond to your story, you have to couch it in a kind of entertainment."*
> *Ernest Dickerson, director and coauthor of* Juice,
> *a film about juvenile delinquency*

Fun and entertainment are not reserved for leisure time but are a continuous aspect of life. One of the consequences is the strenuous efforts in the American

educational system to make learning a pleasant and entertaining experience for
children. Certainly, the competition with the entertainment industry for the attention of the youth plays a role, but, in essence, the theory is that schoolchildren
are entitled to have fun during their schooldays.

Most working class Americans regard work as a necessary evil to earn a
living. Thus a pseudo-science of "human relations" has been developed in America—and has spread all over the world—to promote personal satisfaction in the
workplace by enhancing the work environment with artificial or psychological
gimmicks. It is based on the theory that workers who are happy with what they
are doing produce better work and are more successful salespeople. The promotion of "human relations" has been cynically characterized by its critics as "raising self-esteem instead of wages."

> *"How about a nation in which tens of millions are so culturally and
> spiritually empty that their main way of defining themselves and
> achieving self-respect is to 'go shopping'?"*
>
> *Paul Fussell,* BAD

The desire for entertainment displays itself at the fullest in the realm of leisure
and pastime, part of which in modern society is "going shopping." Shopping is

not a troublesome task—it is a pleasurable activity, probably the chief entertainment in many people's lives. American merchants do everything to satisfy this demand, from the convenient hours to an enticingly overwhelming environment. Many American shopping malls are architectural masterpieces. Not only consumer-oriented people are captivated by their aesthetic sophistication. American shopping malls are the cathedrals of consumerism in which the festival of shopping is celebrated. Shopping reflects some of the characteristics of a religious experience: excitement, enthusiasm, devotion, and satisfaction.

This is no cause for cultural pessimism. After all, shopping—under a different name—was the most elegant leisure activity of the idle aristocracy in feudal societies. What we witness today is simply the democratization of a desire that is apparently a basic human urge. It should be remembered that in centuries past people enjoyed country wakes and church fairs, not only to shop for the most basic goods but certainly also for the sheer pleasure of looking and buying.

Politics as Entertainment

Americans require their political leaders to be entertaining—they do not necessarily have to be humorous or comical. Voters and politicians alike want to have fun.

What makes American politics so refreshingly lively is that the participants really enjoy the political business. They enjoy the rituals of debate and dealing. Hubert Humphrey, vice president under former President Lyndon Johnson, preached a politics of joy and was called the "happy warrior." Anyone can see just how much fun the Americans have with political events by watching televised national conventions for the nomination of the presidential candidates.

Publicity Is Entertainment

In the media, entertainment is a vehicle for commercial advertisement.[3] The ads are a part of the entertainment, not only in form—most ads are, at least at first glance, "more fun" than many programs—but especially in their messages that purchasing or consuming products is fun, brings joy, and makes life entertaining.

Many television shows are structured in such a way that the advertising messages actually become part of the program itself. The so-called sitcoms are not one continuous story line but, rather, a series of comic situations or remarks held together by a weak plot. In such a series of "spots," an amusing commercial is hardly considered an interruption or an alien element.

The entertainment industry has capitalized on the discontinuous character of modern American society in which life is experienced as an aggregate of disconnected happenings. It has no beginning or end, no goal, no cause. Its center is constant change, the need for something new even if it is a repetition of something old.

The Incompatibility of Entertainment and Happiness

It becomes clear that entertainment cannot be increased indefinitely, at least not qualitatively. Yet, it is not only physical exhaustion that dooms the dream of finding endless happiness in continuous entertainment. Entertainment and happiness are incompatible in their structures. Happiness is an ultimate goal; entertainment, on the other hand, is a continuous happening. Similarly, happiness cannot be equated with possession. Entertainment and possession indisputably contribute to happiness. It is difficult to imagine a happy life without a certain material state of well-being and without fun and entertainment.

But they themselves are not happiness. When they are enjoyed in excess or overvalued, their potential to bring about happiness has the opposite effect. They can destroy any chance for a happy life.

Entertainment has taken on pathological dimensions in American society. The perceived need for entertainment has become an addiction, and the expression "life is fun" has taken on abnormal significance. Perhaps America's traditional puritanism has created a pent-up demand for life's pleasures. One could also presume that Americans, who in their early years could not fathom doing anything that did not bring gain, are irresistibly drawn to this newly discovered temptation. But the search for pleasure is not any different from the search for monetary gain. It is the same driving force with a different goal. Both tendencies carry everything to the extreme, to the limit and beyond. It is this common drive that is predominant and not the difference between the two.

As such, the most outstanding quality of this pathological form of the "pursuit of happiness" is that it defies moderation. The constant urge to lose oneself in a new diversion results in a hectic dissatisfaction that misses the goal, namely

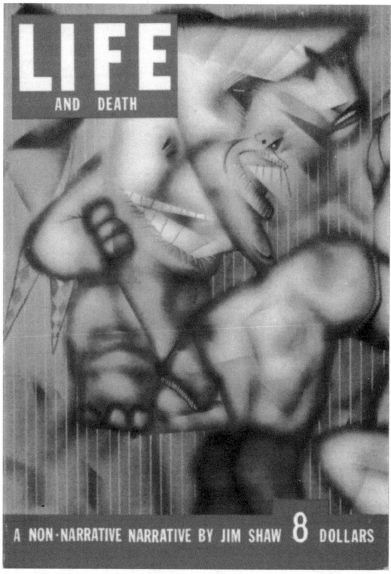

LIFE

AND DEATH

A NON-NARRATIVE NARRATIVE BY JIM SHAW 8 DOLLARS

"Life goes to a party"

happiness and satisfaction. It is hard to say whether this excess is an inherent or socialized behavior. In any case, it exquisitely serves the interests that rule this society because it is not satisfaction but dissatisfaction that keeps the wheels of the American economy in motion. Dissatisfaction is actually a necessary principle because it contributes to continued ambition, to new endeavors, and, with that, to progress in society. The entertainment industry on the one hand or consumerism on the other—it is the same never-ending spiral, an endless desire for more and more fed by endless advertising.

Another aspect of this pathology is the inflation of happiness. One no longer searches for happiness in depth but rather in breadth. Happiness as the most valuable good is rare and elusive. If it is made an everyday feature, easily available everywhere, it becomes trivial. Witness a book that appeared in the United States some years ago: *The Happy Book: 14,000 Things to be Happy About*.[4] The author lists, among other things: "shiny hair; Raquel Welch, actress; getting a back scratch; fake glitter; the Nixon transcripts; an off-the-cuff compliment; mischievousness; a Calvin Klein jean skirt worn with a gold snake belt; coffee, tea or milk; 'keep on truckin'; unusual toilet seats; getting a job" and so on 13,988 more times. This bizarre catalog of things that have made the author happy over the past twenty years can be viewed as a parody of Thomas Jefferson's democratization of happiness. The book *The Happy Book: 14,000 Things to be Happy About* was on the best-seller list for a long time. Of course, the always alert American humor industry immediately responded with a book, *1,401 Things that P*ss Me Off*.[5]

Instant Satisfaction

In the end, however, the trivializing of happiness is a relatively harmless pastime; the real danger is the passion for instant gratification. The American language has meanwhile developed a term for this attitude: "now-ism." People not only have the right to their happiness but they deserve to get it now. Starting at the moment a toddler is able to stare at the television screen, commercials offer the fulfillment of their every desire and need. For every problem and every wish there is a fast, convenient solution—you just have to grab it, you just have to buy a certain product. Not even a shortage of money can come between you and the fulfillment of your wishes: "Buy now—pay later."

The American belief in the quick fix extends to happiness. The entire fast-food industry is based on instant satisfaction. An abundant selection of pain relievers and antidepressants is offered with the same promise: immediate relief two or three times more effectively than the competitive product.

> *"It is one more measure of our lack of seriousness that we won't dispassionately investigate or rationally debate which drugs do what damage and whether or how much of that damage is the result of criminalization. We'd rather work ourselves into a screaming fit of puritanism and then go home and take a pill."*
>
> P.J. O'Rourke, Parliament of Whores

Happiness can be bought with a pill in the United States, at least in advertisements. This is what Aldous Huxley foresaw with his wonderdrug "Soma" in his utopian work *Brave New World*. From watching the ads of the pain relievers, one gets the impression that the borders to the so-called illegal drug culture are already open. The difference in the effects of the legal and illegal drugs is not absolutely clear-cut. The prohibition of the one kind and the tolerance of others is arbitrary. It is inevitable that a society oriented to instant satisfaction is conditioned to drug use. It is an irony of language that in English, contrary to most languages, the word "drug" is used to describe both legal and illegal substances.

The addiction to pills and drugs is another pathological aspect of the American search for happiness: escapism. Happiness is pursued as an escape from oneself and as a retreat from society. Happiness is equated with total freedom, with escape from all responsibilities. Escapism is related to the growing monetarization of society. Money itself is—as Georg Simmel pointed out—the most extreme embodiment of freedom. As long as wealth was tied to landed property, this possession imposed certain obligations. With the "liquefaction" of property by monetarization, obligations to the employees, the family, and the society are diminished. The sociologist Robert Nisbet coined the term "loose individual" for the type of person who answers only to himself. The loose individual is the postmodern human for whom essence of life is entertainment. It is an attitude of being without obligations, "in between," open to all sides. Nisbet impressively demonstrated how the loose individual[6] prevails in all areas of American life and undermines the foundations on which the society is built. For this pathological aspect of the "pursuit of happiness," a suitable term has been coined: "me-ism."

Inability to Enjoy Happiness for Fear of Loss

Beyond "now-ism" or "me-ism," happiness is threatened by the inability to enjoy it out of fear of being deprived of it by outside forces. Instead of being happy, one spends all of one's time and energy in protecting it against imaginary intruders into one's happiness. This human experience is well known as a topic in fairy tales and similar literature: the sad rich man who is so worried about all of his belongings that he cannot find pleasure in any of it.

> *"The point is not whether people want to kill us. . . . We're interested in whether they can. The Soviets can. So can the Chinese. And the French, for that matter. Then there are those countries, some run by complete lunatics, that have a bomb or two or could make one or will be able to make one soon: Israel, South Africa, India, Pakistan, Iraq, Iran, Egypt, Libya, Argentina, Brazil, both Koreas. . . . The need for technologically advanced defense programs does not end with Russia throwing in the towel."*
>
> P.J. O'Rourke, Parliament of Whores

The American nation may enjoy all of the benefits of an essentially well-organized, well-functioning democratic system and take advantage of its natural resources and hardworking inhabitants. Yet, the society lives in a constant panic that someone will threaten or destroy this well-being. Until recently, it was the "Reds," then various Arab dictators, perhaps tomorrow it will be trans-Caucasian anarchists.

To protect itself from this threat, the United States maintains gigantic military power that ruins the state and impoverishes the society. Epicurus, the prophet of an enlightened hedonism, recognized that the greatest hindrance to a joyful life is fear, and he strongly encouraged people to free themselves both of groundless fear and the fear of things that are unavoidable.

In effect, happiness requires an ability to stay calm and composed. This means letting things come close to you and accepting them. The American philosophy of happiness is, however, thoroughly activist. One does not wait for happiness to happen; one pursues it. Happiness is a goal as all others that one can come to grips with, with the tried and proved American "know-how." As such it is perfectly natural that a great part of the huge "how-to" literature is devoted to achieving happiness. These how-to books inevitably miss the essence of happiness because happiness is coincidence—in the literal sense, something that happens by chance. Language gives a strong indication: Happiness stems from the root *hap* (coincidence), to happen. There are similar relations in other European languages: *eudaimonia, fortuna, bonheur, Glück*, they all imply that happiness "happens" and is not created by human effort.

Yet, in the United States happiness is not left to chance. Even leisure time, which is, after all, supposed to satisfy life's pleasures, is essentially not distinguishable from the world of work. Even during leisure time the categories and values of work are dominant: purpose, efficiency, cost-benefit calculations, progress, competition, officiousness, conformity, and monotony. Leisure time is taken much too seriously to be gambled away without a plan. One look at the aerobics studios and body-building salons demonstrates the concentration and effort needed to make leisure work. Even sex—a leisure activity with high potential for pleasure—is put under performance pressure and becomes a ritual of self-confirmation.

Workaholism as a Perverted Form of the Pleasure of Life

The absolute perversion of the concept of the joy of life is workaholism, an addiction to work as pleasure. Workaholism is the American solution to saving humanity from the threat of increased leisure time. It is the fortunate combination of duty and attraction—a self-imposed duty to enjoy life and the true love of work.

It is so integrated into the general success-oriented attitude toward life that having fun, being happy, entertaining oneself, have become duties. It is a reversal of Kant's ethic of duty: Amuse yourself and be happy because otherwise you are a loser. Happiness becomes an aspect of success in life. By enjoying life one can prove to others that one has made it.

The unavoidable consequence of such a philosophy of happiness leaves the determination of the essence of happiness to an outside force. But happiness can only be experienced at the individual level. There is no national model of happiness, no happiness thermometer, no happiness catalog from which one can order things according to need and financial state. Therefore, neither consumerism nor entertainment fits Jefferson's concept of the pursuit of happiness. Actually, they are diametrically opposed to it. One cannot buy happiness because it does not come from the outside but from within. Consumerism and entertainment make promises that they cannot keep.

Notes

1. Alexis de Tocqueville, *Democracy in America II*, p. 133.
2. David Robbins, *The Camera Believes Everything*, p. 101.
3. The final completion of the symbiosis between entertainment and advertising is the program structure of MTV. The rock and pop videos that last three to five minutes are more or less commercials for records and compact discs.
4. Barbara Ann Kipfer, *The Happy Book*.
5. I.M. Peeved, *1,401 Things that P*ss Me Off*.
6. Robert Nisbet, *The Present Age*, chapter III—"The Loose Individual," p. 84.

Life Is Fun, Part II

Outlook

Americans are certainly not blind to the dangers of a national obsession with entertainment. A heated debate continues about measures to curb the excessive need for entertainment as escapism. Paradoxically, the discussion itself invites a mistaken return to the American habit of constructing pat solutions.

Happiness Is Not Manageable

A search for a genial plan, a panacea based on the old quick fix, the how-to strategy, the can-do attitude will not succeed. It requires instead a momentous change in worldview, a whole new philosophy of life, a readiness to scrutinize and modify some of the most cherished American attitudes. It requires a willingness to reexamine traditional American virtues of two centuries in the light of new realities and values. Attitudes deeply ingrained over decades and centuries can only be changed over a long period of time. America would have to be patient—not exactly one of its stronger virtues.

> *"They'll say: 'we never complained, no, we were happy, because we had **values** in those days, and if you had values you didn't need a lot of money or food or toilet paper, which was a luxury in those days to the point where we'd get through a whole year—this was a family of eleven—on just **six squares** of toilet paper, because we had this system where if you had to . . . HEY! Come back here!' "*
>
> Dave Barry, Dave Barry Slept Here

It is philosophically and politically popular to regularly call for a return to the values that made America great. The prophets of the good old America urge community spirit in place of the greedy and self-fulfilling me-ism. They preach frugality and voluntary self-denial in place of instant gratification. They caution that, under the intoxicating influence of now-ism, one may weaken the pillars of prosperity that many Americans enjoy. They push for a return to tried and tested discipline (preferably self-discipline) in school, at work, and in the family, instead of the "permissiveness" undermining America's social fiber. They call for a new (the old) morality in politics, economics, and all other areas of society.

These values are undeniably positive in their results but challenged by new realities. For example, can the old work ethic play the supporting role to society that many wish for, considering the fact that work is currently in the process of losing its thousands-of-years-old primary significance to humanity?[1] It is, at the very least, questionable to look to this work ethic as a cure-all for the ills of modern society with its radically changing set of values and international relations. Proven success in the past alone is not convincing enough as a remedy for the future.

Aristocratizing Happiness Is a Regressive Tactic

Another nostalgic trend is to harness progress because its consequences are not foreseen and no longer controllable. But progress itself is not the problem, rather it is the people's attitudes toward it. Because progress cannot be curbed artificially, the only sane approach is to convince society not to expect improvement in everything that is new and not to constantly and everywhere demand something new. Progress will slow when society is prepared to modify its demands, exercise moderation, and lower its expectations.

Another danger is the notion of happiness as the province of the elite. This is the route to noble despair. The "happy few" would leave society to its fate because they feel that nothing can be saved. This is the typical attitude of classical philosophers who considered the *hoi polloi* (the masses) incapable of true happiness and, therefore, reserved this option for the elite.

The idea of reserving happiness for a chosen few may seem attractive, but it is politically outdated. One of American democracy's greatest and longest enduring achievements is that it has freed itself from the bonds of this ancient philosophy and made the pursuit of happiness accessible to all of its citizens. It is worth every effort not to surrender this achievement.

Hoping for Changes in Attitude

Neither is happiness achieved by pursuing the utopia of an ideal society. This again would be a betrayal of the standards set by the American founding fathers who, with their democratic concept, laid the groundwork for a "utopia in existence," which is a dynamic social system designed by its inherent tensions and opportunities to develop to perfection.

This belief in development that constitutes the base of the "American dream" should not be abandoned in resignation that changes in behavioral attitudes are more or less hopeless. As experience has convincingly shown, people are capable of learning, and they do react to changes in their surroundings. How should they not? After all, this is the basic law of evolution that has controlled and continues to influence all development, including that of the human race.

This can be demonstrated by the progress in the handling of environmental issues. In recent years, a dramatic change has taken place in the understanding, the attitudes, and the conduct of environmental affairs, chiefly because the effects of the unrestrained growth and irresponsible exploitation could no longer be overlooked. Humans as individuals and as a society react to these experiences with a slow but clear and irreversible change in lifestyles and habits.

Alternatives to the Western Concept of Happiness

> *"It's time we in the industrialized nations admitted what safe, comfortable and fun-filled lives we lead. If we keep sniveling and whining, we may cause irreparable harm to the poor people of the world—they may laugh themselves to death listening to us."*
>
> P.J. O'Rourke, Parliament of Whores

Half a millenium after the beginning of modern times, a belief pervades the Western world that "modernism," in spite of its undeniable successes, has come to a dead end. We see with dismay that the Copernican mobilization[2] of humanity, the achievements modern man is proud of—rationality, science, and technology— have also created the means with which to destroy ourselves. We have arrived at the point at which the Promethian virtues that set our development into motion and continued to stimulate it over the years—discovery, conquest, invention, and organization—now appear questionable and dangerous. We feel that it is no longer feasible to come to grips with the problems that we have brought upon ourselves. Our values are burned out and cannot be revived by themselves. Therefore, it is understandable and absolutely useful to look to other cultures and former value systems to find new impetus for thought and judgment.

On the American continent there once existed an alternative culture dominated by a very different value system. Five hundred years after the discovery of America, which signified the beginning of the end for the Native American social order, a rediscovery of their value system and social concepts could motivate the search for an alternative model for the "good life" of the individual in society. This idea is not as far-fetched and bizarre as it may appear at first glance. Although the prevailing point of view of historical writings portrayed the Native Americans as wild and primitive, backward, and culturally inferior to the immigrants, there were always voices in the United States that understood and recognized the value of the Native American lifestyle and social system.

Thomas Jefferson repeatedly referred to the Native Americans as proof of his thesis that organized human existence can persist even without a formal governing power. For Jefferson, the Native Americans had, in their own way, a civilized society with a developed and intact value system and political organization, loose and unwritten though it may have been. Jefferson's design of a four-level state structure for the United States—from the "ward republics" to the federal level—was actually inspired by the Native American tribal organization.

To Jefferson, the social ideas of the Native Americans seemed to be an important corrective element for Western political ideology.

> It made a question, whether no law, as among the savage Americans, or too much law, as among the civilized Europeans, submits man to the greatest evil, one who has seen both conditions of existence would pronounce it to be the last: and that the sheep are happier of themselves, than under care of the wolves. It will be said, that great societies cannot exist without government. The savages therefore break them into small pieces.[3]

Alexis de Tocqueville likewise recognized that the individual and social characteristics of the Native Americans were by no means culturally or morally primitive—though they were hopelessly inferior in their practical realization within the dynamic and "developed" moral system of the white man. Tocqueville points out some characteristic traits of the Native American culture: an indifference to possessions, a disdain toward work, an independence from material values, and a highly developed community spirit. These all are values that could potentially be regarded as corrective elements for our own extremely outwardly motivated, materially oriented, and disintegrating society.

It is perhaps no coincidence that a genuine interest in the cultural heritage of the original inhabitants of the North American continent is becoming apparent in recent years in the United States. Kevin Costner's movie *Dances with Wolves* carries far more significance than a fashionable phase of enthusiasm for Native American folklore or a moral campaign to show the other side of the Native American battles. It may also be an aspect of America's search for alternatives to its prevailing value system.

Correcting Modern Extremism

In order to avoid any misunderstandings: Nothing would be gained by replacing the prevailing Western concepts with a "Native American" value system in this current stage of disorientation. The issue is rather one of a necessary corrective element.

The achievements of modern times—personal freedom, individual self-realization, an elected political system of government, security before the law and by the law, civil rights, prosperity—are fundamentally unquestionable. Yet they are precisely at risk of destroying themselves in their own excesses. The search for alternatives is not a criticism of these achievements but of the excesses to which they have been carried.

Change in thought and behavior is subject to a genuine willingness to move away from self-righteousness and fundamental certainty and to open one's own values in relativity. American philosophy has already laid groundwork for such a new view of the world. Richard Rorty introduced the term "contingency" into the moral value system of a society; in his view, for people of a society based on a "contingent" value system, a compulsion to an ironic attitude, to a Socratic ignorance, and to a restraint in value judgment comes naturally because there is no security of value judgment anymore in the world. This "insecurity," on the other hand, is an opportunity to overcome the isolating barriers of fundamentalistic self-assurance and to quantitatively and qualitatively expand the feeling of "togetherness" into an attitude of "solidarity," which in Rorty's opinion all human beings are already basically disposed to.

Most of the problems threatening democracy in modern mass society can be traced back to the excessive realization of the democratic principles: excess of freedom, excess of individualism, excess in money orientation. Modification as a fundamental principle of all reasonable human behavior can bring the democratic society out of the self-imposed impasse created by its own extremism. Although it is impossible to force a morality of moderation upon a society, there are ways that lead to this result by their own means. This is the hour of politicians who live up to their vocation. They must lead and educate their constituencies. Once the audience has been disabused of the idea that "the sky is the limit," expectations are lowered. Moderation does not mean passive behavior but, rather, a renouncement of insubstantial activism, of activity for its own sake. It also signifies an end to absolute competition, which, as a self-driven principle, ends in ruinous violence and senseless repression.

Moderation Also in Politics

This desired trend toward moderation would also have a meliorating influence on American foreign policy as an end to imperial politics. Whatever the reasons may be for this type of politics—whether it is a pathological fear of an unreal threat, a misled interpretation of a destiny or the desire for order and reliability in the world, the plain and simple intention of self-enrichment, or a combination of all the above—the self-imposed compulsion to control the rest of the world with an overpowering military might causes the nation to practically bleed itself materially dry and to structurally disintegrate.

The danger to the democratic spirit is self-evident. "We cannot build an empire in the East and keep America a republic," Mark Twain warned at the beginning of American imperialism. Coming from a humorist, this warning was presumably taken as a joke—and, until this day, it is not taken seriously. Militarism is like a cancerous growth that is eating at the material and moral substance of American democracy.

Freedom from the Fixation on Money and Possessions

Aside from the imperial impulse, the greatest threat to democracy is greed and the identification of happiness with material possessions.

A return to a society without private ownership is neither possible nor worthy. The failure of the communist promise is evident. As has been previously stated, the monetary economy has had an enormous influence on the freeing of the individual and on democratizing society. The growth in prosperity has freed the people from the gnawing worry about security for their subsistence. Yet, this freedom is endangered by the temptation of money. They are incapable of freeing themselves from its inner energy that is focused on constant growth. By putting everything under the law of money, they conduct themselves like the legendary King Midas for whom everything that he touched turned to gold, with the result that he would have starved if the god had not retracted the fulfillment of this senseless wish.

The people of modern society cannot call upon a god to help them; they must themselves control the power of money in democracy.

A democratic society is not helplessly at the mercy of the power of money. Society can break money's overpowering grip with sensible laws that will, in time, also change people's attitudes toward it. We have already considered a "public philosophy" of money that might include the limitation of the inheritance of fortunes, a social assessment of the relative values of capital and work, and, finally, an effective enforcement of the social responsibility of ownership. Fortunately, there are hopeful signs of a change of attitudes in Western societies. Within the predominantly materialistic atmosphere, there is a palpable search for spiritual and transcendental needs in recent years that may over time diminish the significance of material values.

Change in the Attitude toward Work

The American word *satisfaction*, which has its origin in the Latin word *satis* (enough), has unfortunately lost its original meaning. The only way to attain freedom is to let something be enough instead of always demanding more. Continual dissatisfaction permits exploitation of the immoderate by the even more immoderate. There are always nations that are even more fanatic than those Western Protestant nations that honor work for its own sake. The very spirit created by American enterprise is returning to challenge it. The Japanese advance in the American market with means of irresistible supplies of ever new consumer goods is nothing else than a major exploitation of an insatiable nation by a society even more obsessed with money and work. The United States has the alternative to compete either by attempting to produce less expensively and more efficiently with a work ethic ever more dogged and grim or by exercising restraint amidst superabundance and satisfaction with what is sufficient. The attitude of the "wild Indians" toward work was not as primitive as it may have seemed to the American settlers and to us today. In essence, their attitude reflected the culture of the Greek and Roman classical period where leisure was valued as the true fulfillment of life. Leisure was not defined as freedom from work, but work was seen as a distraction from leisure. This is expressed in both cultures in the language with the positive term for leisure (*scholä and otium*), and the negative term for work (*ascholia-negotium*).

Greek and Roman society relied almost entirely on the work of slaves. Contempt for work was the privilege of the elite. A large portion of the populace was actually exploited by the elite, too. Modern society has not only abolished slavery but has also raised the living standard for workers to a level even beyond that of earlier privileged classes. Modern society offers conditions for a true culture of leisure—quality instead of quantity, reflection instead of consumption, pastime instead of "time is money." Economic interests that profit from the circulation of "earning money–spending money" hinder such a change in values and also our concept of freedom, which is governed by a deep misunderstanding of the term.[4] Modern man forgot that freedom itself is an empty shell and can only be filled by "freedom for something." The completely free human, the "loose individual" is again subjected, knowingly or unknowingly, to the corrupting influences of consumerism and empty entertainment.

No Private Happiness without Public Happiness

Real freedom and self-determination are not achievements enjoyed for life. Self-determination must be achieved and guarded through ceaseless vigilance against threats both personal and public.

Jefferson once said "private happiness" is not possible without "public happiness." This means a life that is politically constrained fails the test of self-determination. Surely it is not possible to determine one's life as a citizen in complete autarchy. But this is the case in private life as well, which is subject to many limitations. In essence, the issue is whether the citizen is satisfied to be a passive consumer of politics or wants to take on responsibility in the political process. The political participation of citizens, as insignificant as it may be in the overall scope of society, is essential to the survival of democracy as an idea and as an institution. All efforts for reform must be focused on increasing opportunities for citizen participation in the political process and on actively encouraging citizens to seize upon these opportunities and become politically active.[5]

> *"So when can we quit passing laws and raising taxes? When can we say of our political system, 'Stick a fork in it, it's done?' When will our officers, officials and magistrates realize their jobs are finished and return, like Cincinnatus, to the plow or, as it were, to the law practice or the car dealership? The mystery of government is not how Washington works but how to make it stop."*
>
> P.J. O'Rourke, Parliament of Whores

In spite of the indisputable decline of the republican spirit in the United States, the rest of the world can still learn much from its example. Nowhere else in the world is there such a wide variety of opportunity to participate in affairs, and nowhere else is the willingness of the citizens to try their hand in politics as strong as in the United States. Tocqueville's observation 160 years ago about the difference of political participation of citizens in the United States and in Europe still holds true in today's world. Yet even in the United States the willingness to participate is declining, and the inclination to view politics as a consumer good is increasing. More and more, government assumes control over social and economic activities without personal involvement of the citizenry. The overwhelming mass of complex problems clearly demands more and not less participation on the part of citizens.

Political Participation as a Way to Promote Tolerance

The more that citizens take their own affairs in hand, the less arrogant the political system becomes, the more the role of the politician diminishes. Politicians are no longer expected to find solutions to all of society's problems, and they are no longer viewed as the medicine men of primitive tribal societies. They are human like other people, and they make mistakes; they are by no means superior beings and can easily be replaced.

The other important consequence of political participation is the cultivation of tolerance and compromise that comes naturally when different members of society are tackling problems together. They are confronted with differing opinions and learn that their own problems can look completely different from another perspective. Above all, they learn about the needs and problems of other people and set aside egotism for the sake of cooperation in pursuing a common goal.

Beyond that, confrontation with other opinions and the need for tolerance and compromise are strong barriers against ideological and fundamentalist tendencies and can promote a healthy pragmatic outlook that keeps democracy, the most delicate of all forms of government, from drifting into totalitarian patterns. It is not by coincidence that the political philosophy of pragmatism has developed in the United States where democratic participation is still the most intensive and most developed of anywhere in the world. Even the United States, however, is not immune to the lure of political fundamentalism.

American pragmatism is a legacy of the founding fathers of the republic, and it is, like their entire political philosophy, the product of the Enlightenment, which questioned all ideologies. It replaced belief and so-called revelation with skepticism and critical reasoning. "Enlightenment is the exit of mankind out of its self-inflicted immaturity," Immanuel Kant wrote. Immaturity, according to

Kant, is not a temporary stage in the development of human history, once over-come forever a thing of the past. It is self-induced and voluntary and can there-fore reemerge at any time. The Enlightenment was not a permanent achievement. It must be constantly renewed.

For this reason, the founding fathers, especially Jefferson, placed primary stress on the education of the nation's citizens. The serious decline of the Ameri-can educational system is the subject of more speeches than action, a condition extremely dangerous for the development of the society. Not only because it leaves a severe shortage of trained workers but also because it threatens democ-racy at its core. Democracy, unlike other forms of government, requires the support of an educated, skeptical, and pragmatic people.

Television Is Displacing School

Perhaps the most consequential decision for the success of democracy in the United States was the establishment of general education from the very begin-ning of the founding of the nation. The government was responsible for the maintenance of schools throughout the colonization of the country. Through the schools, the government was able to teach each new generation of young Ameri-cans the values of democracy. The schools were the medium by which the government was able to communicate with its citizens.

The crisis in the American educational system goes deeper than the decline of the public school system. The collapse of the educational system began when new forms of communication—i.e., radio and television—began undermining the influence of the schools on the transmission of knowledge, the building of character and people's attitudes toward life in general and when government formally allowed these powers of mass influence to develop and grow on their own without any social restraint.

> *"American culture has been privatized, atomized, and perhaps irre-versibly idiotized by the combination of television and Epcot-style education."*
>
> *Barbara Ehrenreich quoted by Paul Fussell,* BAD

The decision of the American government to hand over television, a most powerful instrument of influence, almost completely to commercial interests, will presumably have serious consequences. It is a fatal mistake to believe that this instrument would be handled in a neutral, disinterested, or inconsequential way just because the government refrains from becoming involved in it. Televi-sion gives those who know how to use its manipulative powers an irresistible tool by which to reach people, to penetrate their thoughts, to influence them. By letting the commercial entertainment industry control television, the education of the American people has been transferred to those who are interested in main-taining their immaturity.

The new value system of television dismisses responsibility and effort in favor of uninhibited and immediate pleasure. It glorifies a new kind of happiness in which there is no room for the freedom of self-determination; it offers a ready-made guide to happiness.

A population uneducated, lazy, and indifferent to the concerns of society is not new to the history of the world. On the contrary, that was the rule. The populace was always considered stupid and was kept stupid by those who took it upon themselves to be in charge. As such, the development toward stupidity and apathy in the United States is "nothing new under the sun."

The decidedly different aspect to this problem is that earlier societies were directly built on the ignorance of people. Completely contrary to this, democracy was founded on and depends on the political comprehension and the participation of the population.

Democracy is in gravest danger when a society is no longer in motion. The greatest mistake of the people of an established democracy is to equate democracy with mere freedom from government. It is the opportunity but also the duty to become involved in the organization of the larger community. When the political involvement of a democratic people declines because the members of the society are fully and wholly consumed with their private interests, the difference between democratic and "administrated" societies ceases to exist.

Tocqueville hits the nail on the head concerning the essence of democracy when he says:

> Agitation amd mutability are inherent in the nature of democratic republics, just as stagnation and sleepiness are the law of absolute monarchies.[6]

He does not mean senseless activity but, rather, political mobility and attentiveness. He sees, however, democracy in danger when the characteristic mobility of a democratic society no longer focuses on politics but concentrates solely on private affairs. Such a society can proclaim immense outward mobility, yet politically it is dead. Tocqueville pointedly warns that the increase in activity in the private sector as a result of fear for one's possessions and the search for entertainment will lead to political stagnation. He fears that this type of society—completely obsessed with private affairs—increasingly turns away from all innovation, social progress, and intellectual challenges and wastes away in political immobility:

> If men continue to shut themselves more closely within the narrow circle of domestic interests and to live on that kind of excitement, it is to be apprehended that they may ultimately become inaccessible to those great and powerful public emotions which perturb nations, but which develop them and recruit them. When property becomes so fluctuating and the love of property so restless and so ardent, I cannot but fear that men may arrive at such a state as to regard every new theory as a peril, every innovation as an irksome toil,

every social improvement as a stepping-stone to revolution, and so refuse to move altogether for fear of being moved too far. I dread, and I confess it, lest they should at last so entirely give way to a cowardly love of present enjoyment as to lose sight of the interests of their future selves and those of their descendants and prefer to glide along the easy current of life rather than to make, when it is necessary, a strong and sudden effort to a higher purpose.[7]

It is as though Tocqueville has given a description of the current situation in the United States and other developed democracies. Democratic societies are in the process of giving up their real essence, in spite of all outward mobility, which is apparent in the continuous accumulation of prosperity and the never-ending search for new forms of pleasure in private life. They are going nowhere, content with their achievements, unaware or uninterested in the important issues and questions of their time.

The middle class—both creator and creature of democracy—is confronted with the same problems as the feudal society at the end of the eighteenth century. The latter perceived its prosperity and luxurious life as a self-evident fact and certainly as a deserved reward. The demands of the masses for a share in this prosperity were ignored much as the world today ignores the idea that other nations have a moral right to share in the collective prosperity of the developed nations.

We react in the same way as the aristocracy of the eighteenth century, which insisted upon the legitimacy of its property for no reason other than that it had always been that way. In the realm of democratic ideas, such inherited rights do not exist. Either the democratic society takes up this new challenge and broadens its worldview or it will be blown away as was the aristocracy in its time.

The important assignment then, of the developed democracies, is the globalization of the concepts of democracy but not as a propagation of formal political structures in other countries but as quantitative and qualitative expansion of the principles on which democracy is founded. The democratic societies must begin to think in greater dimensions, spatially as well as temporally. They must come to terms with the fact that they must include future generations as well as the other nations on this earth. In concrete terms, this requires a policy of trusteeship instead of exploitation with respect to the natural resources of this earth and a transformation of foreign policy into a domestic policy for a global society.

"We are obviously in dire need of a revolution of ideas right now in America," says Robert Nisbet at the end of his book *The Present Age*.[8] "But it seems not to be the privilege of man to will his own revolution when he wants it. Time and circumstances are sovereign."[9] Like most Americans, Nisbet believes that the story of the founding of America is a source of hope. "It was an intellectual revolution in the Colonies that led to the United States."[10] The American Revolution was not about the overthrow of a class system. Yet, it is no coincidence that it took place precisely at the time when in Europe the ruling classes were being overthrown. The prerevolutionary period was characterized by a growing rigidity of political structures, ironically coincidental with the highest intellectual flexibility that promoted the emergence of the great ideas of the future. Perhaps we are at a similar turning point. It seems likely that the criteria set by Tocqueville for periods of great change, are emerging now:

> But between these two extremes of the history of nations is an intermediate period, a period of glory as well as of ferment, when the conditions of men are not sufficiently settled for the mind to be lulled in torpor, when they are sufficiently unequal for men to exercise a vast power on the minds of one another, and when some few may modify the convictions of all. It is at such times that great reformers arise and new ideas suddenly change the face of the world.[11]

The intellectual foundations of this reformation are already being laid around the world. However, a political impetus will be necessary for it to be realized. Without or in conflict with the United States it will not happen. On the contrary, the only chance for its realization lies in the hope that one nation will make this cause its own, the nation that is to this day the most open and mobile of all nations in the world: America.

Notes

1. Bernd Guggenberger, *Wenn uns die Arbeit ausgeht,* especially pp. 94 and 106.

2. A term coined by Peter Sloterdijk for the spirit that formed the modern Western society but also caused its problems. Peter Sloterdijk, *Kopernikanische Mobilmachung und Ptolemäische Abrüstung.*

3. Notes on the State of Virginia, Query XI, Aborigines, *The Portable Jefferson,* p. 134. Compare also with Jefferson to Edward Carrington, January 16, 1787, *The Portable Jefferson,* p. 415: "I am convinced that those societies (as the Indians) which live without government enjoy in their general mass an infinitely greater degree of happiness than those who live under European governments. Among the former, public opinion is in the place of law, and restrains morals as powerfully as laws ever did any where."

4. Henry David Thoreau wrote about these phenomena and developed an alternative way of living out of his understanding of work. He remarked that due to his modesty he only had to work six weeks a year to have enough money to live for the rest of the year. In his opinion, the fact that people work more than they need for a living has two dangerous consequences: 1) People lose the true meaning of life, the self-discovery, the development of an own indentity and personality, and 2) work itself is also depreciated because people do not work for the work but for a different goal—the money (David L. Norton, "The Moral Individualism of H.D. Thoreau," p. 251). Money distorts the nature of work and thus work corrupts the nature of human beings.

5. Bellah et al. described this idea as the main problem of American society: "The key to the survival of free institutions is the relationship between private and public life." Robert N. Bellah et al., *Habits of the Heart,* p. vii. They refer to Tocqueville and the importance he gives to this aspect of American society.

6. Alexis de Tocqueville, *Democracy in America I,* p. 311.

7. Tocqueville, *Democracy in America II,* pp. 262–63.

8. Robert Nisbet, *The Present Age,* p. 135.

9. Ibid.

10. Ibid.

11. Tocqueville, *Democracy in America II,* pp. 259–60, fn. 1.

Bibliography

Arendt, Hannah. *On Revolution.* London: Penguin Books, 1988.

Barlett, Donald L., and Steele, James B. *America: What Went Wrong?* Kansas City: Andrew McMeel, Universal Press Syndicate, 1992.

Barry, Dave. *Dave Barry Slept Here: A Sort of History of the United States.* New York: Random House, Fawcett Columbine, 1989.

Baudrillard, Jean. *America.* London and New York: Verso, 1988.

Bellah, Robert N. *The Broken Covenant: American Civil Religion in Time of Trial.* New York: Seabury Press, Crossroad, 1975.

Bellah, Robert N; Madsen, Richard; Sullivan, William M.; Swidler, Ann; and Tipton, Steven M. *The Good Society.* New York: Alfred A. Knopf, 1991.

————. *Habits of the Heart.* New York: Harper & Row, 1991 (original hardcover edition: University of California Press, 1985).

Bloom, Allan. *The Closing of the American Mind.* New York: Simon and Schuster, 1987.

Boorstin, Daniel J. *The Image.* New York: Atheneum, 1962.

Boyte, Harry C. *Common Wealth: A Return to Citizen Politics.* New York: Macmillan, Free Press, 1989.

Burrough, Bryan, and Helyar, John. *Barbarians at the Gate: The Fall of RJR Nabisco.* New York: Harper Perennial, 1990.

"Campaign Financing in Federal Elections: A Guide to the Law and Its Operations." Congressional Research Service, Library of Congress, August 8, 1986, with Supplement from July 31, 1989.

Cather, Willa. *My Ántonia.* Boston: Houghton Mifflin, 1988.

Cockburn, Alexander. "The Perot Program." *The Nation,* June 15, 1992.

Commager, Henry Steele. *Jefferson: Nationalism and the Enlightenment.* New York: George Braziller, 1975.

Dahl, Robert A. *Democracy and Its Critics.* New Haven and London: Yale University Press, 1989.

Dahms, Helmut Günther. *Grundzüge der Geschichte der Vereinigten Staaten.* Darmstadt: Wissenschaftliche Buchgesellschaft, 1991 (German edition).

Dionne, E.J., Jr. *Why Americans Hate Politics.* New York: Simon & Schuster, 1991.

Eco, Umberto. *Über Gott und die Welt: Essays und Glossen.* Munich: dtv, 1988 (German edition).

Ellerbee, Linda. *Move On: Adventures in the Real World.* New York: G.P. Putnam's Sons, 1991.

The Essays of Ralph Waldo Emerson. Edited by Alfred R. Ferguson and Jean Ferguson Carr. Cambridge, London: Belknap Press, 1987.

The Federalist Papers. Essays by Alexander Hamilton, James Madison, and John Jay. Edited by Clinton Rossiter. New York: Penguin, 1961.

Fukuyama, Francis. "The End of History?" *The National Interest,* Summer 1989.

————. *The End of History and the Last Man.* New York: Free Press, 1992.

Fulbright, J. William. *The Arrogance of Power.* New York: Random House, Vintage Books, 1966.

Fussell, Paul. *BAD, or The Dumbing of America.* New York: Simon & Schuster, Summit Books, 1991.

———. *Class.* New York: Ballantine Books, 1983.

Galbraith, John Kenneth. *The Affluent Society.* Boston: Mentor Books, 1958.

———. *The Anatomy of Power.* Boston: Houghton Mifflin, 1983.

———. *The Culture of Contentment.* Boston: Houghton Mifflin, 1992.

Gallup, George, and Forbes Rae, Saul. *The Pulse of Democracy.* New York: Simon & Schuster, 1940.

Garreau, Joel. *Edge City: Life on the New Frontier.* New York: Doubleday, 1991.

Gorer, Geoffrey. *The Americans.* London: Cresset Press, 1949.

Greider, William. *Who Will Tell the People? The Betrayal of American Democracy.* New York: Simon & Schuster, 1992.

Griffin, Kelley. *More Action for a Change* (introduction by Ralph Nader). New York: Dembner Books, 1987.

Guggenberger, Bernd. *Wenn uns die Arbeit ausgeht.* Munich: Verlag Hanser, 1988 (German edition).

Hacker, Andrew. *Two Nations, Black and White, Separate, Hostile, Unequal.* New York: Charles Scribner's Sons, 1992.

Hamilton, Alexander. *The Reports of Alexander Hamilton.* Edited by Jacob E. Cooke. New York: Harper & Row, 1964.

Herberg, Will. "America's Civil Religion: What It Is and Whence It Comes." In *From Marxism to Judaism: The Collected Essays of Will Herberg,* ed. David G. Dalin. New York: Marcus Wiener, 1989.

Hofstadter, Richard. *The American Political Tradition.* New York: Random House, Vintage Books, 1948.

———. *The Paranoid Style in American Politics and Other Essays.* Chicago: University of Chicago Press, 1975 (first edition 1952).

———. *Social Darwinism in American Thought.* Boston: Beacon Press, 1955 (first edition 1944).

Jefferson, Thomas. *The Papers of Thomas Jefferson* (Volume 12). Edited by Julian P. Boyd. Princeton, N.J.: Princeton University Press, 1955.

———. *The Papers of Thomas Jefferson* (Volume 23). Edited by Charles T. Callen. Princeton, N.J.: Princeton University Press, 1990.

———. *The Portable Thomas Jefferson.* Edited by Merrill D. Peterson. New York: Penguin Books, 1975.

———. *The Republic of Letters* (Volume 1). Edited by James Morton Smith. New York, London: W.W. Norton, 1995.

———. *Writings.* New York: Library of America, 1984.

Johnson, Haynes. *Sleepwalking through History: America in the Reagan Years.* New York: Doubleday, Anchor Books, 1991.

Jungk, Robert. *Die Zukunft hat schon begonnen.* Munich: Wilhelm Heyne Verlag, 1990 (German edition).

Kennedy, Paul. *The Rise and Fall of the Great Powers.* New York: Random House, Vintage Books, 1989.

King, Alexander, and Schneider, Bertrand. *The First Global Revolution: A Report by the Council of the Club of Rome.* New York: Pantheon Books, 1991.

Kipfer, Barbara Ann. *The Happy Book: 14,000 Things to Be Happy About.* New York: Workman, 1990.

Kodalle, Klaus-M., ed. *Gott und Politik in U.S.A.: Über den Einfluß des Religiösen.* Frankfurt: Athenäum Verlag, 1988.

Kozol, Jonathan. *Savage Inequalities: Children in America's Schools.* New York: Crown, 1991.

Krugman, Paul. *The Age of Diminished Expectations: U.S. Economic Policy in the 1990s.* Cambridge, Mass. and London: MIT Press, 1992.

Kuttner, Robert. *The End of Laissez-Faire. National Purpose and the Global Economy after the Cold War.* Philadelphia: University of Philadelphia Press, 1991.

Lewis, Michael. *Liar's Poker: Rising through the Wreckage on Wall Street.* New York: Penguin Books, 1990.

————. *The Money Culture.* New York and London: W.W. Norton, 1991.

Lippmann, Walter. *Public Opinion.* New York: Free Press, 1965.

The Essential Lippmann: A Public Philosophy for Liberal Democracy. Edited by Clinton Rossiter and James Lare. Cambridge, Mass.: Harvard University Press, 1982.

Locke, John. *Second Treatise of Government.* Indianapolis and Cambridge, Mass.: Hackett, 1980.

Lojewski, Wolf von. *Amerika: Ein Traum vom neuen Leben.* Hamburg: Hoffmann und Campe, 1991 (German edition).

Lösche, Peter. *Amerika in Perspektive: Politik und Gesellschaft der Vereinigten Staaten.* Darmstadt: Wissenschaftliche Buchgesellschaft, 1989 (German edition).

McCarthy, Eugene J. *America Revisited: 150 Years after Tocqueville.* New York: Doubleday, 1978.

McCoy, Drew R. *The Last of the Fathers: James Madison and the Republican Legacy.* New York: Cambridge University Press, 1989.

Marcuse, Ludwig. *Amerikanisches Philosohieren.* Hamburg: Rowohlt, 1959 (German edition).

Marx, Leo. *The Machine in the Garden. Technology and the Pastoral Ideal in America.* New York: Oxford University Press, 1967.

Matthews, Richard K. *The Radical Politics of Thomas Jefferson: A Revisionist View.* Lawrence, Kans.: University Press of Kansas, 1984.

Mayer, Jane, and McManus, Doyle. *Landslide: The Unmaking of the President, 1984–1988.* Boston: Houghton Mifflin, 1989.

Miller, Donald L., ed. *The Lewis Mumford Reader.* New York: Pantheon, 1986.

Mills, C. Wright. *The Power Elite.* New York: Oxford University Press, 1959.

Murray, Charles. *In Pursuit: Of Happiness and Good Government.* New York: Simon & Schuster, 1988.

————. *Losing Ground: American Policy 1950–1980.* New York: Harper Collins, Basic Books, 1984.

Neustadt, Richard E. *Presidential Power: The Politics of Leadership.* New York: John Wiley & Sons, 1967 (first edition 1960).

Nisbet, Robert. *The Present Age: Progress and Anarchy in Modern America.* New York: Perennial Library, 1988.

Noonan, Peggy. *What I Saw at the Revolution: A Political Life in the Reagan Era.* New York: Random House, 1990.

Norton, David L. "The Moral Individualism of H. D. Thoreau." In *American Philosophy,* ed. Marcus G. Singer. London: Cambridge University Press, 1985.

Olson, Walter K. *The Litigation Explosion: What Happened When America Unleashed the Lawsuit.* New York: Truman Talley Books, 1991.

O'Rourke, P.J. *Parliament of Whores: A Lone Humorist Attempts to Explain the Entire U.S. Government.* New York: Atlantic Monthly Press, Morton Entrekin Book, 1991.

Peeved, I. M. *1,401 Things that P*ss Me Off.* New York: Putnam, 1991.

Paine, Thomas. *The Thomas Paine Reader.* Edited by Michael Foot and Isaac Kramnick. New York: Penguin Books, 1987.

Pfaff, William. *Barbarian Sentiments: How the American Century Ends.* New York: Hill and Wang, 1989.

Phillips, Kevin. *The Politics of Rich and Poor. Wealth and the American Electorate in the Reagan Aftermath.* New York: Random House, 1990.

Postman, Neil. *Amusing Ourselves to Death.* New York: Penguin Books, 1986.

Public Papers of the Presidents of the United States. Dwight D. Eisenhower 1960– 61. Washington, D.C.: Office of the Federal Register, National Archives and Records Service, General Services Administration, 1961.

———. Lyndon B. Johnson 1965. Book I. Washington, D.C., Office of the Federal Register, National Archives and Records Service, General Services Administration, 1961.

Rand, Ayn. *The Virtue of Selfishness.* New York: Penguin Books, New American Library, 1961.

Reedy, George E. *The Twilight of the Presidency.* New York: Penguin Books, Mentor Book, 1988 (first edition 1970).

Reichley, A. James, ed. *Elections American Style.* Washington, D.C.: Brookings Institution, 1987.

Robbins, David. *The Camera Believes Everything.* Stuttgart: Edition Patricia Schwarz, 1988.

Rorty, Richard. *Contingency, Irony, and Solidarity.* New York: Cambridge University Press, 1991.

———. "Just One More Species Doing Its Best." *London Review of Books* 13, no. 14, July 25, 1991, p. 315.

———. "The Priority of Democracy to Philosophy." In *Objectivity, Relativism, and Truth.* Philosophical Papers, vol. 1. Cambridge: Cambridge University Press, 1991.

———. *Contingency, Irony and Solidarity.* Cambridge: Cambridge University Press, 1989.

Samuelson, Robert J. "Go Ahead, Bash Lawyers." *Washington Post*, April 22, 1992, p. A21.

Schlesinger, Arthur M., Jr., *The Cycles of American History.* Boston: Houghton Mifflin, 1986.

———. *The Imperial Presidency.* Boston: Houghton Mifflin, 1973.

Schumpeter, J. A. *Imperialism and Social Classes.* Philadelphia: Orion Editions, 1991.

Simmel, Georg. *The Philosophy of Money.* London and Boston: Routledge and Kegan Paul, 1978.

Singer, Marcus G., ed. *American Philosophy.* New York: Cambridge University Press, 1985.

Slansky, Paul. *The Clothes Have No Emperor.* New York: Simon & Schuster, Fireside, 1989.

Sloterdijk, Peter. *Kopernikanische Mobilmachung und Ptolemäische Abrüstung.* Frankfurt: Verlag Suhrkamp, 1986 (German edition).

Solm, Rudolph. *Institutionen: Geschichte und System des Römischen Privatrechts.* München/Leipzig, 1920 (German edition). Quoted by the German publisher in Alexis de Tocqueville, *Democracy in America I.* Zürich: Manesse Verlag, 1987. (German edition).

Spencer, Herbert. *Social Statics.* New York: Robert Schalkenbach Foundation, 1970 (first published in 1850, reprinted in 1954).

Steinbeck, John. *America and Americans.* New York: Viking Press, 1966.

Thoreau, Henry David. *Walden; or, Life in the Woods.* New York: Dover, 1995 (first published in 1854 by Ticknor and Fields, Boston, Mass.).

Tocqueville, Alexis de. *Democracy in America* (Volumes I and II). New York: Random House, Vintage Classics, 1990 [vol. I first published in 1835; vol. II, 1840].

————. *Journey to America*. New Haven: Yale University Press, 1960.

Vidal, Gore. *At Home: Essays 1982–1988*. New York: Random House, Vintage Books, 1990.

Wattenberg, Martin P. *The Decline of American Political Parties, 1952–1988*. Cambridge: Harvard University Press, 1990.

Winter, Rolf. *Ami Go Home*. Munich: Goldmann Verlag, 1989 (third German edition).

Wood, Gordon S. *The Radicalism of the American Revolution*. New York: Alfred A. Knopf, 1992.

Wolfe, Tom. *The Bonfire of the Vanities*. New York: Bantam Books, 1988.

Dr. Werner Peters, born in 1941, is a native of Germany and lives in Cologne. He studied Greek and Latin literature and philosophy at the University of Bonn, and American studies at Harvard University in 1967-68 on a fellowship from the Harkness Foundation.

In the late sixties, he was a Congressional Fellow on the staffs of Representative Lee Hamilton, D-Ind., and Senator Eugene McCarthy, D-Minn. He later served as Director of the McCarthy Historical Project, a documentation of the 1968 presidential campaign now at Georgetown University.

After his return to Germany in 1970, Dr. Peters worked for two years in the National Headquarters of the Christian Democratic Party (CDU) as assistant to the executive director. He then opened his own political consulting firm.

In recent years, Dr. Peters has shifted his focus from political to philosophical consulting. He is a member of the Gesellschaft fuer philosophische Praxis (Society for Philosophical Practice).

Dr. Peters owns and operates a well-known hotel and restaurant in Cologne, which has developed into a meeting place for people in the international art world and also into an intellectual forum with a philosophy lecture series now into its eighth year.

Dr. Peters has traveled extensively throughout the United States, returning almost every year since 1970. In 1989-90, he lived in Washington while doing research for the German edition of this book, *The Existential Runner: Über die Demokratie in Amerika (On Democracy in America),* which was published in 1992 and favorably reviewed by major newspapers and magazines *(Frankfurter Allgemeine, Süddeutsche Zeitung,* etc.).

In April of 1993, Dr. Peters was invited to give a lecture as part of Georgetown University's Rev. Bunn Memorial Lecture Series.

Dr. Peters continues to write for magazines and to lecture on American political culture and democracy in the contemporary world.